JOHN

God's Word
for the
Biblically-Inept™ SERIES

Lin Johnson

CARTOONS BY
Reverend Fun
(Dennis "Max" Hengeveld)
Dennis is a graphic designer for Gospel Films and the author of *Has Anybody Seen My Locust?* His cartoons can be seen worldwide at www.reverendfun.com.

STARBURST PUBLISHERS®

P. O. Box 4123, Lancaster, Pennsylvania 17604

To schedule author appearances, write:
Author Appearances
Starburst Publishers
P.O. Box 4123
Lancaster, Pennsylvania 17604
(717) 293-0939

www.starburstpublishers.com

CREDITS:
Cover design by David Marty Design
Text design and composition by John Reinhardt Book Design
Illustrations by Mark Ammerman and Melissa A. Burkhart
Cartoons by Dennis "Max" Hengeveld

First Printing, March 2001

ISBN: 1-892016-43-5
Library of Congress Number 00-108570

Printed in the United States of America

READ THIS PAGE BEFORE YOU READ THIS BOOK . . .

Welcome to the *God's Word for the Biblically-Inept*™ series. If you find reading the Bible overwhelming, baffling, and frustrating, then this Revolutionary Commentary™ is for you!

Each page of the series is organized for easy reading with icons, sidebars, and bullets to make the Bible's message easy to understand. *God's Word for the Biblically-Inept*™ series includes opinions and insights from Bible experts of all kinds, so you get various opinions on Bible teachings—not just one!

There are more *God's Word for the Biblically-Inept*™ titles on the way. The following is a list of available books. (See the following page for ordering information.) We have assigned each title an abbreviated **title code**. This code along with page numbers is incorporated in the text **throughout the series**, allowing easy reference from one title to another.

God's Word for the Biblically-Inept™ Series

The Bible by Larry Richards	ISBN 0914984551	**GWBI**	**$16.95**
Daniel by Daymond R. Duck	ISBN 0914984489	**GWDN**	**$16.95**
Genesis by Joyce Gibson	ISBN 1892016125	**GWGN**	**$16.95**
Health & Nutrition by Kathleen O'Bannon Baldinger	ISBN 0914984055	**GWHN**	**$16.95**
John by Lin Johnson	ISBN 1892016435	**GWJN**	**$16.95**
Life of Christ, Volume 1 by Robert C. Girard	ISBN 1892016230	**GWLC**	**$16.95**
Life of Christ, Volume 2 by Robert C. Girard	ISBN 1892016397	**GWLC2**	**$16.95**
Men of the Bible by D. Larry Miller	ISBN 1892016079	**GWMB**	**$16.95**
Prophecies of the Bible by Daymond R. Duck	ISBN 1892016222	**GWPB**	**$16.95**
Revelation by Daymond R. Duck	ISBN 0914984985	**GWRV**	**$16.95**
Romans by Gib Martin	ISBN 1892016273	**GWRM**	**$16.95**
Women of the Bible by Kathy Collard Miller	ISBN 0914984063	**GWWB**	**$16.95**

CHAPTERS AT A GLANCE

CHAPTERS AT A GLANCE

PART TWO: Jesus' Private Ministry

PART THREE: Jesus' Death and Resurrection

CHAPTERS AT A GLANCE

ILLUSTRATIONS

INTRODUCTION

Welcome to *John—God's Word for the Biblically-Inept™*. It's part of a series that makes the Bible easy to understand even for people who know little or nothing about it. This REVOLUTIONARY COMMENTARY™ is different from other commentaries and Bible study books. It won't bore you or put you to sleep or discourage you with a lot of big words and religious terms. My goal is to help you discover that knowing and studying the Bible is enjoyable. And in the process of using this book, you will Learn the Word™.

To Gain Your Confidence

John—God's Word for the Biblically-Inept™ is for people who want an easy-to-read, verse-by-verse study of the most popular book in the Bible. You'll find Bible verses, icons, and brief chunks of information to help you understand the text and how it relates to you today. You'll meet Jesus Christ when he lived here on earth. As you get to know him from John's perspective, I hope you will want to read the <u>other books</u> about his life and teachings.

What Is The Bible?

Although we treat it as one book, the Bible is a collection of sixty-six books. They were written by many different authors over a period of about 1500 years. These books are grouped in two sections: the Old Testament with thirty-nine books and the New Testament with twenty-seven books. The Old Testament was written mostly in Hebrew between 1400 and 400 B.C. It begins with God's creation of the world and tells the history of the Jewish people until they returned to the land of Israel after captivity to other nations. Then four hundred years went by, during which God did not give us any Bible books. This period of silence was followed by the New Testament, written in Greek between A.D. 40 and 100.

CHAPTER HIGHLIGHTS
(Chapter Highlights)

Let's Get Started
(Let's Get Started)

John 1:1 In the beginning was the Word . . .

(Verse of Scripture)

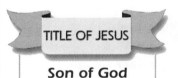

TITLE OF JESUS

Son of God

(Title of Jesus)

☞ **GO TO:**

Matthew, Mark, Luke
(other books)

(Go To)

B.C.: before Christ

A.D.: from the Latin phrase anno domini, "in the year of our Lord"

It tells about Jesus' birth, life, teachings, death, and **resurrection** and about the church, which was started by people who believed Jesus was the Son of God.

Many years after the Bible was written, Bible experts divided the books into chapters and verses. Now it's quick and easy to find a reference. So if someone refers to John 3:16, you can locate the book of John, find the third chapter, and then find verse 16 without having to scan through pages of text.

Why Study The Bible?

One reason to study the Bible is because God gave it to us, so we can know him. It's his primary way of communicating to humans—his letters to us. Even though we can learn some things about him from nature, we can't really know him unless we read the Bible. It tells us what he is like and how he acts.

Another reason to study the Bible is because it gives answers to questions people have asked since the beginning of time. Questions like: How did the world begin? What is my purpose in life? Why do people act the way they do? What will happen to me when I die? Where is the world headed?

A third reason to study the Bible is because it's the best-selling and most influential book in history. Our literature is filled with references to Bible stories and people. Most of our laws are based on the Bible's moral code. An education is not complete without some knowledge of this book.

Still another reason to study the Bible is because it has power to change lives. No one can read it with an open mind and not be changed by the truth it contains. Ultimately, it will lead you to a personal relationship with the God of the universe.

Conversations with Christ

(Conversations with Christ)

Why Study John?

When a person's life generates a lot of interest, multiple biographies appear in bookstores. The person who has caused the most interest through the years is Jesus Christ. In fact, the first four biographies about him, called the **Gospels**, begin the New Testament.

These books are not normal biographies though. Instead, they present the message of eternal life through **faith** in the historic person of Jesus of Nazareth. As John put it, *"Jesus did many other miraculous signs in the presence of his disciples, which are not recorded in this book. But these are written that you may believe that Jesus is the Christ, the Son of God, and that by believing you may have life in his name"* (John 20:30–31).

The first three books—Matthew, Mark, and Luke—are called the **synoptic** Gospels since they are similar in content and approach. John, the fourth book, doesn't cover as many events but includes more of Jesus' teaching.

While the Book of John focuses on Jesus' life, it is not an exhaustive biography. In other words, it doesn't tell everything there is to know about Jesus. It begins *"in the beginning"* with Jesus' relationship with God the Father. Then—unlike the other Gospels—John skips the details of Jesus' birth and goes right to his public ministry. To prove Jesus is the Son of God, John selected a few **miracles** from the many Jesus performed that are related to his main teaching.

synoptic: *tell the story in similar fashion*

miracles: *supernatural acts of God*

Merrill C. Tenney: Although [John] deals with the same broad sequence of events to be found in the pages of the others, it is quite different in structure and in style. It contains no parables and only seven miracles, five of which are not recorded elsewhere. The **discourses** of Jesus in it are concerned chiefly with his person rather than with the ethical teaching of the **kingdom**. Personal interviews are multiplied, and Jesus' relationship to individuals is stressed more than His general contact with the public. The Gospel is strongly **theological**, and it deals particularly with the nature of His person and with the meaning of faith in Him.[1]

What Others are Saying:

discourses: *speeches*

kingdom: *God's future rule on earth*

theological: *dealing with teaching about God*

A Comparison Of The Four Gospels

Gospel	Matthew	Mark	Luke	John
Author	Matthew	John Mark	Luke	John
Author's Job	Tax collector	Companion	Doctor	Fisherman
Author's Nationality	Jew	Jew	Gentile	Jew
Author's Focus	Disciple	Missionary	Missionary	Disciple
Readers	Jewish people	Romans	Greeks	The world
Author's View of Jesus	King	Servant	Son of Man	Son of God

Warren W. Wiersbe: Whereas the first three Gospels major on describing *events* in the life of Christ, John emphasizes the *meaning* of these events. For example, all four Gospels record the feeding of the 5,000 but only John records Jesus' sermon on "The Bread of Life" which followed that miracle when He interpreted it for the people.[2]

What Others are Saying:

(What Others Are Saying)

Who Wrote John?

John, the son of Zebedee and Salome and brother of James, was a fisherman on the Sea of Galilee when Jesus called him as one of his first **disciples**. He was one of the <u>inner circle</u> of three disciples who were privileged to be with Jesus for certain events. Thus he was an eyewitness to the events and teachings he wrote about.

John was called the <u>beloved disciple</u>. He was an intimate friend of Jesus, the one who leaned on Jesus' breast at the last **Passover** dinner just before Jesus' death. He was also the one Jesus asked to take care of his mother after his death.

John apparently had a temper since Jesus called him and his brother <u>sons of thunder</u>. And he was selfish and ambitious. But later he was known as the apostle of love because one of his other books (1 John) focuses on this quality.

John was a thinker who focused on the big picture. He preferred to deal with abstract terms and concepts, rather than with actions like Mark. Throughout this Gospel, John emphasized contrasts like belief and unbelief, light and darkness, and love and hatred. He also highlighted symbols like the time Jesus turned water into wine.

Next to Paul, John wrote more New Testament books than anyone else—Gospel of John, 1 John, 2 John, 3 John, and Revelation. He penned John around A.D. 85–90. The oldest New Testament manuscript we have is a fragment of the Gospel of John copied a few years after it was originally written (see WBFT, page 14). The fragment is written on paper made from papyrus (see illustration, page xv).

What Is John All About?

John is one of four selective biographies of Jesus Christ, God's Son. In it John tells about

- Jesus' existence before he was born here on earth
- Jesus' miracles
- Jesus' teachings
- Jesus' private teaching with his disciples
- Jesus' death and resurrection

disciples: followers

Passover: Jewish holiday that celebrates their ancestors' freedom from slavery in Egypt

☞ **GO TO:**

Mark 5:37; 9:2; 14:33
(inner circle)

John 21:20, 24
(beloved disciple)

Mark 3:17
(sons of thunder)

(Culture Clue)

(Remember This)

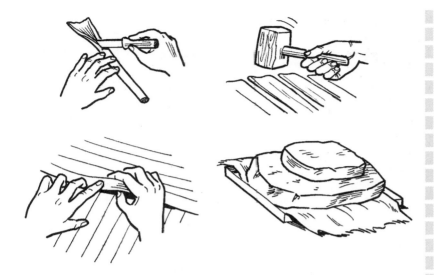

Which Translation Of The Bible Should I Read?

John wrote this book in Greek. Since most of us can't read that language, Bible experts have **translated** it into English. Today we have a number of Bible translations and paraphrases to read. But how do we choose which one to use? Because this series is written for people who may be new to the Bible, we chose the New International Version (NIV). It accurately expresses the original Scriptures in clear and contemporary English and faithfully communicates the thoughts of the writers.

translated: *literature taken from one language and expressed in another language*

How To Use *John—God's Word For The Biblically-Inept™*

Sit down with this book and your Bible.

- Start the book at chapter 1.
- As you work through each chapter, read the Bible verses in your Bible.
- Use the sidebars loaded with icons and helpful information to give you a knowledge boost.
- Answer the Study Questions and review with the Chapter Wrap-Up.
- Then go on to the next chapter. It's simple!

This book contains a variety of special features that will help you learn. They're illustrated in the outside column of this introduction. Here they are, with a brief explanation of each.

Dig Deeper

(Dig Deeper)

Something to Ponder

(Something to Ponder)

Sections and Icons	What's It For?
CHAPTER HIGHLIGHTS	the most prominent points of the chapter
Let's Get Started	a chapter warm-up
Bible Quote	what you came for—the Bible
Commentary	my thoughts on what the verses mean
GO TO:	other Bible verses to help you better understand (underlined in the text)
What?	the meaning of a word (bold in the text)
KEY POINT	major point of the chapter
What Others Are Saying:	if you don't believe me, listen to the experts
Illustrations	a picture is worth ten thousand words
Conversations with Christ	talks Jesus had with people and how his teaching affected them
CULTURE CLUE	understanding the customs in Jesus' day
THE FAITH FACTOR	spotlights the important theme of faith and belief
TITLE OF JESUS	word or phrase that describes Jesus
Something to Ponder	interesting points to get you thinking
Remember This . . .	don't forget this
Dig Deeper	find out more from the Bible
Study Questions	questions to get you discussing, studying, and digging deeper
CHAPTER WRAP-UP	the most prominent points revisited

THE FAITH FACTOR

(The Faith Factor)

Study Questions

(Study Questions)

CHAPTER WRAP-UP

(Chapter Summary)

A Word About Words

You will notice several interchangeable terms: Scripture, Scriptures, Word, Word of God, God's Word. All these mean the same thing and come under the broad heading called the Bible. I use each of these terms at various times. Gospel refers to one of four books that tell about Jesus and his life here on earth.

The word "Lord" in the Old Testament refers to Yahweh, God. In the New Testament, it refers to Jesus Christ, God's Son.

One Final Word

As you read the Bible text and the study helps in this book, you're going to learn a lot. You'll get acquainted with Jesus as he really is—not as people have described him or pictured him. But remember this: God didn't give us the Bible so we can collect a lot of facts to fill our heads. He gave it to us so we can have a personal relationship with him.

As you read and study John, do so prayerfully. When you ask God to speak to you through this book, he will. And when you finish it, you'll be surprised at how much you've learned and changed.

Bible Quote: This is where you'll read a quote from the Bible.

> **James 1:5** If any of you lacks wisdom, he should ask God, who gives generously to all without finding fault, and it will be given to him.

Decisions, Decisions: In Or Out?

James, the brother of Jesus, is writing to the new believers who were scattered about the Roman world (see GWBI, pages 213–214) when they fled from persecution. James knows that godly wisdom is a great gift. He gives a simple plan to get it: if you need wisdom, ask for it. God will give it to us.

Up 'til now we've concentrated on finding the wind for the sails of your drifting marriage and overcoming marital problems. But you may be the reader who is shaking her head, thinking that I just don't understand what you're going through. You can't take the abuse any longer; you've forgiven the **infidelity** time after time; and in order for you and your children to survive, you see no alternative but divorce.

So let me tell you husband get out and abuse sec... ing to you; they are also harmful to your children's physical and emotional state.

When you feel you've depleted all of your options, continue to ask God for wisdom in order to have the knowledge to make the right decisions. Wise women seek God. God is the <u>source</u> of wisdom and wisdom is found in Christ and the Word.

Gary Chapman, Ph.D.: Is there hope for women who suffer physical abuse from their husbands? Does reality living offer any genuine hope? I believe the answer to those questions is yes.[6]

Give It Away

You don't have to be a farmer to understand what the Apostle Paul wrote to the Corinthian church (see illustration, page 143). A picture is worth a thousand words, and Paul is painting a masterpiece. He reminds us of what any smart farmer knows: in order to produce a bountiful harvest, he has to plan for it.

Commentary: This is where you'll read commentary about the biblical quote.

"What?": When you see a word in bold, go to the sidebar for a definition.

infidelity: sexual unfaithfulness of a spouse

Go To: When you see a word or phrase that's underlined, go to the sidebar for a biblical cross-reference.

☞ **GO TO:**

Psalm 111:10 (source)

Remember This . . .

What Others are Saying:

What Others Are Saying: This is where you'll read what an expert has to say about the subject at hand.

Feature with icon in the sidebar: Throughout the book you will see sections of text with corresponding icons in the sidebar. See the chart on page xvi for a description of all the features in this book.

MEN OF POWER: LESSONS IN MIGHT AND MISSTEPS 9

127

Part One

JESUS' PUBLIC MINISTRY

REVEREND FUN

"And a breath mint has never been needed so bad since."

JOHN 1: JESUS THE WORD

CHAPTER HIGHLIGHTS

- Jesus the Creator
- John the Witness
- God Undercover
- John the Voice
- Jesus the Recruiter

Let's Get Started

Imagine you are in a room with no light or sound. You put your hand in front of your eyes and wriggle your fingers, but you see nothing and you hear nothing. Suddenly, someone turns on a light, and you see you are standing in the middle of a room as big as a football stadium. Everywhere you look, there are diamonds, gold coins, jewels, and priceless treasures—covering the floor around you, packed into corners, stacked to the ceiling.

Wouldn't that be wondrous? Well, when God created the world, he did something infinitely more wondrous than filling a stadium with gold and jewels. He filled a void with life. Where once there was chaos, now spinning galaxies swirled into being. Where once there was darkness, now there was light. Where once there was deadness, now there was life—more critters and creatures than you can imagine. And human beings.

But before all that creation, there was just God—God the Father, God the Son (known as Jesus), and God the Holy Spirit.

That's where the apostle John began this book about Jesus—long before Jesus was born. And John wasted no time in introducing his readers to Jesus. He got right to the point and stayed there until the end of the book.

JESUS THE CREATOR

> **John 1:1–2** In the beginning was the Word, and the Word was with God, and the Word was God. He was with God in the beginning.

TITLE OF JESUS

The Word

☞ **GO TO:**

Genesis 1:1
(in the beginning)

John 8:58
(always existed)

with: face-to-face

What Others
are Saying:

*Something
to Ponder*

☞ **GO TO:**

Genesis 1; Colossians
1:16; Hebrews 1:2
(creating)

Jesus Before His Birth

John was a gutsy writer. He began this book with an amazing statement. His early readers, who were familiar with Scripture, would have recognized the opening words. The first book in the Bible, Genesis, begins with the same phrase. That book introduces the creation of the world and man; John introduces the Creator.

"The Word" refers to Jesus, as we'll discover later in this chapter. The Greek word *logos,* translated "Word," means the spoken word that communicates meaning, or a message. So Jesus communicates to us what God is like—his actions, thoughts, feelings, and attitudes. Jesus was *"with God <u>in the beginning</u>."* Unlike us, he <u>always existed</u>; his life didn't begin when he was born as a baby on earth. The word "**with**" indicates a personal relationship between two or more people. In other words, they are both God but not two different Gods.

Lawrence O. Richards: In Greek philosophical thought *logos* was used of the rational principle or Mind that ruled the universe. In Hebrew thought "the word of God" was His active self-expression, that revelation of Himself to humanity through which a person not only receives truth about God, but meets God face-to-face.[1]

Jesus gave up his home in heaven and face-to-face company with God the Father to come to this earth to show us what God is like. He traded a place where everything is perfect for one where sin and suffering are prevalent. That was a *huge* move for him.

> **John 1:3** Through him all things were made; without him nothing was made that has been made.

The Ultimate Creator

Jesus was God's agent in <u>creating</u> everything—light, darkness, sky, water, land, vegetation, sun, moon, stars, animals, fish, birds, people—that is in the world. Even before he was born as a human, he showed us what God is like through creation. From creation, we can see that God is creative, orderly, and powerful.

The Book of Genesis begins by describing God's creation of the world (see GWGN, pages 4–35). But John says here that Jesus made everything. We don't know all the details of how the

Godhead operates. (If we understood it all, we'd be God!) But we do know that John's statement makes Jesus equal with God—a fact that caused a lot of trouble when Jesus was here on earth.

Godhead: three names and natures of God in one word

Manford George Gutzke: John is declaring this amazing truth in all its fulness and glory: Jesus Christ actually existed before the world began. Who then was He? John makes it very clear that He was and is the Son of God, eternal with the Father. John also points out that He was the Creator. . . . This is difficult to understand with our finite minds. We cannot grasp the operation of Almighty God in the creation of the world. . . . One of the ways in which the believer understands God is to separate His person and functions. . . . In his gospel, John is declaring that the Son of God is the Maker of all that was created.[2]

What Others are Saying:

TITLE OF JESUS

Creator

> **John 1:4–5** In him was life, and that life was the light of men. The light shines in the darkness, but the darkness has not understood it.

Life From The Source

Jesus not only showed us God in the creation of the world; he also showed us God in the creation of living creatures and people. Life, both physical and spiritual, originates in Jesus, a living, eternal Being. Through him, God makes his power and purpose known to people.

☞ **GO TO:**

John 5:26 (life)

Light also originates in Jesus. The purpose of light is to banish darkness. When John used the terms "light" and "darkness," he was referring to good and evil, holiness and sin. Thus Jesus, who is morally pure, meaning sinless, became God's light in a spiritually dark world full of sin and evil behavior, thoughts, and attitudes. People in the world resisted the spiritual light Jesus brought partly because they didn't understand it. When they did catch glimpses of understanding, they saw that they had done bad things and they didn't like that feeling. Although sin and darkness are powerful, they can't overcome or conquer Jesus' light. The light and holiness of Jesus is always more powerful than any forces of darkness and evil.

TITLE OF JESUS

Light of Men

J. Dwight Pentecost: Light in John's concept is equated with a knowledge of God. Darkness, as the absence of knowledge, is ignorance of God. Those who had been given light by creation were in darkness. Paul in Romans 1:18–23 carefully traced the pro-

What Others are Saying:

gression of ignorance as man moved from light to darkness. Willful rejection of the light of revelation through creation brought progressive darkness until men were ignorant of God. Jesus Christ came to dispel that ignorance. He who is God came in flesh so that men might see that revelation and come out of ignorance into knowledge.[3]

Themes Of Life And Light

Dig Deeper

John traces the themes of life and light throughout his book. To John, "life" means more than physical well-being. It has a spiritual dimension, enabling a believer to live abundantly in this life and to be sure of resurrection with God after death. When John uses "light," he focuses on spiritual understanding and guidance.

Reference	Theme of Life
John 1:4–5	Jesus is the source of all life.
John 3:15	Jesus gives eternal life to those who believe in him.
John 5:19–23	God the Father and God the Son have control over life and death.
John 5:24	We move from eternal death to eternal life through faith in God.
John 6:68	Only Jesus' words, which we have in the Bible, can produce eternal life.
John 10:10	Jesus came to give us a full, satisfying life now and in eternity.
John 12:23–26	Hanging onto our selfish desires will cost us eternal life.
John 14:5–6	Jesus is the source of life, not death.
John 15:12–13	The greatest demonstration of love for others is sacrificing our lives for them.
John 17:3	Eternal life is personally knowing the one true God and Jesus Christ, his Son.

Reference	Theme of Light
John 1:4–5	Jesus was God's light in a dark, sinful world.
John 3:19	Jesus brought God's light to earth, but people prefer the darkness of evil because they are sinners.
John 5:35	John the Baptist brought God's light to people, pointing them to Jesus.
John 9:5	As the Light of the World, Jesus offers a way out of the darkness of sin.
John 12:35–36	We will not have the opportunity to choose to follow Jesus' light forever.

JOHN THE WITNESS

> **John 1:6–9** There came a man who was sent from God; his name was John. He came as a witness to testify concerning that light, so that through him all men might believe. He himself was not the light; he came only as a witness to the light. The true light that gives light to every man was coming into the world.

To Tell The Truth

The John in these verses is <u>John the Baptist</u>, Jesus' cousin, not the author of this Bible book. God chose him for a specific ministry—to prepare the Jewish people for Jesus' coming and to point to Jesus. His job was to identify Jesus to the people as the "light," to introduce him to the Jewish people, and to get them ready for his ministry. John preached that the time for the long-awaited, promised **Messiah**—who was written about in the **Hebrew Scriptures**—had come. He also called the people to **repentance** from their sin. His goal was to encourage them to **trust** Jesus for salvation from their sin.

The light John testified about was Jesus, who *"gives light to every man."* As the *"true light,"* he reveals people's sin.

Leon Morris: Testimony is a serious matter and it is required to substantiate the truth of a matter. It is clear that our author wants us to take what he writes as reliable. He is insistent that there is good evidence for the things he sets down. Witness establishes the truth.

It does more. It commits a man. If I take my stand in the witness box and testify that such-and-such is the truth of the matter I am no longer neutral. I have committed myself. John lets us see that there are those like John the Baptist who have committed themselves by their witness to Christ.[4]

John drew attention to Jesus, not himself. Isn't that just the opposite of us? We want to be sure people notice us. We want to take the credit, to be the star, to be the center of attention. But not John. Instead, he wanted people to notice Jesus, who is far more important.

☞ **GO TO:**

Malachi 3:1; Mark 1:1–8 (John the Baptist)

Messiah: God's anointed King

Hebrew Scriptures: Old Testament

repentance: turning from sin

trust: commit oneself to

What Others are Saying:

Something to Ponder

GOD UNDERCOVER

> **John 1:10–13** He was in the world, and though the world was made through him, the world did not recognize him. He came to that which was his own, but his own did not receive him. Yet to all who received him, to those who believed in his name, he gave the right to become children of God—children born not of natural descent, nor of human decision or a husband's will, but born of God.

God With Skin On

world: people and society

☞ **GO TO:**

John 12:37
(didn't believe)

Psalm 2:6–9 (his own)

John 3:5–7
(born again)

Gentiles: non-Jewish people

sacrifice: Jesus' death

became: changed their nature

God's children: members of God's kingdom

faith: trust, commitment

Jesus became a man and lived in our **world**. Although he created humans, the people of his day didn't know who he was—didn't know him as a friend or have a relationship with him—because they were blinded by sin. So they <u>didn't believe</u> he was the promised Messiah from God.

Jesus went to <u>his own</u> things or home. He had created this world. It was his. Within the world, Jesus chose to become a Jew. But sadly, leaders of the Jewish nation and many of his own Jewish people—as well as **Gentiles**—rejected him instead of welcoming him. They did not believe he was the Messiah whom God had promised to them (see GWPB, pages 64–66).

Although most of the Jewish people rejected Jesus, some received him. They trusted him as the **sacrifice** for sin and, as a result, **became God's children**. To use a phrase Jesus used later in this book, they were <u>born again</u>. In this passage, John equates believing with receiving. Belief is more than mental assent.

No one automatically or naturally belongs to God. That relationship doesn't result from being born Jewish or Christian or Muslim or Russian or American. We don't become a child of God because of who our parents are. Instead, relationship with God is a supernatural gift from him through **faith** in Jesus. And we need to reach out and accept that gift, demonstrating that we believe it is real.

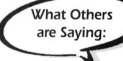

What Others are Saying:

Leon Morris: We might translate the opening words, "he came home." . . . When the Word came to this world He did not come as an alien. He came home. Moreover, He came to Israel. Had He come to some other nation it would have been bad enough, but

Israel was peculiarly God's own people. The Word did not go where He could not have expected to be known. He came home, where the people ought to have known Him.[5]

J. Dwight Pentecost: The Jews . . . considered themselves to be acceptable to God. The fact of physical birth was sufficient to guarantee any Jew, according to Jewish concept, a right to Messiah's kingdom, for God had entered into a covenant with the Jewish nation. In contrast to this thought, John said the only ones who have the right to become the children of God are those who put faith in the person of Jesus Christ.[6]

THE FAITH FACTOR—The word "belief" and its variants, "believed" and "believing," were important to John. He used them over eighty-eight times in this book. John wanted his readers to believe that Jesus was God's Son. When we believe this, we become God's adopted children.

If the doorbell rang today and Jesus was standing there when you opened the door, would you welcome him and invite him in? Or would you close the door and leave him on the doorstep while you continued whatever you were doing?

> **John 1:14** The Word became flesh and made his dwelling among us. We have seen his glory, the glory of the One and Only, who came from the Father, full of grace and truth.

When God Became One Of Us

Jesus, the eternal God, became—at a specific point in time—a human being and lived among humans without losing his deity. He became one of us while remaining God. This action is called the incarnation. In this verse, John equated the Word with Jesus, clearly defining who the Word is.

The author, John, was an eyewitness to Jesus' life and **_glory_**. He **saw** Jesus' awesomeness as the unique Son of God, a Son in a way that humans can't be. He is eternal, of the same **essence** as God the Father. *"Full of **grace** and truth"* means the same as *"abounding in love and faithfulness"* (Exodus 34:6), the description of God's glory as shown to **Moses** (see GWMB, pages 71–90).

What Others are Saying:

Something to Ponder

☞ **GO TO:**

Philippians 2:5–9 (human being)

Colossians 2:9 (glory)

glory: *display of God's nature*

saw: *observed, scrutinized*

essence: *nature*

grace: *something we don't deserve*

Moses: *first leader of Jewish people*

What Others are Saying:

Merrill C. Tenney: He expressed Himself in a human personality that was visible, audible, and tangible. He partook of flesh and blood with its limitations of space and time, and with its physical handicaps of fatigue, hunger, and susceptibility to suffering, so that He belongs to humanity as well as to God.[7]

CULTURE CLUE

For John to say that God became a human being was a radical concept in his day. Jewish people believed humans could not become gods and vice versa. Greek philosophers taught that what is invisible is far more important than what we can see and touch. So to announce that *"the Word became flesh and made his dwelling among us"* was thinking outside the box.

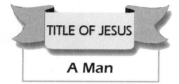

TITLE OF JESUS

A Man

Something to Ponder

Jesus, who is God, became a baby who cried, burped, and messed his diapers. He grew into a child who probably played in the mud, made enemies, and later broke girls' hearts. He worked with his hands, lost his earthly father, and got tired and hungry. He was like us.

Remember This . . .

Jesus is fully God and fully human. He didn't give up being God with all his perfection. And because he became a man, he understands our limitations and temptations. So he can help us get through the tough times if we ask him to.

JOHN THE VOICE

John 1:15–18 John testifies concerning him. He cries out, saying, "This was he of whom I said, 'He who comes after me has surpassed me because he was before me.' " From the fullness of his grace we have all received one blessing after another. For the law was given through Moses; grace and truth came through Jesus Christ. No one has ever seen God, but God the One and Only, who is at the Father's side, has made him known.

KEY POINT

Jesus became a man to communicate to us what God is like.

☞ **GO TO:**

Luke 1:57–80 (John was born)

Out With The Old, In With The New

This verse logically follows verses 7 and 8, since it continues the narrative about John the Baptist. Even though this <u>John was born</u>

six months before Jesus and began his ministry first, Jesus was more important. He existed long before John was conceived and was greater than John because he was God. This statement was radical in Jesus' day since people believed that what or who came first chronologically was superior.

From Jesus we've received lots of **blessings**. God's grace or favor toward us—which we don't deserve and can't earn—can never be exhausted; there is an unlimited supply of it.

God gave the **Law**, the first five books of the Old Testament, to Moses and his people to show them his standards of right behavior and attitudes. If anyone could keep the Law (although that was impossible), doing so wouldn't make that person a child of God. In contrast to the Law, Jesus showed us God's attitude—love and faithfulness.

Although God is invisible and no human can see him, he has **made himself known** to us through Jesus. When Jesus made God known, he told God's story, disclosing who he is and giving a trustworthy account about him. Again John asserted that Jesus is God and that he existed before he was born on earth. So John ended this section by coming full circle to how he began it: writing about *"the Word"* who *"was with God in the beginning."*

Edwin A. Blum: Because of the fullness of His grace . . . one blessing after another (. . . lit., "grace in place of grace") comes to Christians as waves continue to come to the shore. The Christian life is the constant reception of one evidence of God's grace replacing another.[8]

Warren W. Wiersbe: John did not suggest that there was no grace under the Law of Moses, because there was. Each sacrifice [for sins] was an expression of the grace of God. The Law also revealed God's truth. But in Jesus Christ, grace and truth reach their fullness; and this fullness is available to us. . . . John hinted that a whole new order had come in, replacing the **Mosaic system**.[9]

Merrill C. Tenney: The being and nature of God, which cannot be perceived directly by ordinary senses, have been adequately presented to us by the **Incarnation**. The life and words of Jesus are more than an announcement; they are an explanation of God's attitude toward humans and of his purpose for them.[10]

blessings: *God's good gifts to us*

☞ **GO TO:**

Ephesians 2:8–9 (can't earn)

James 4:6 (unlimited supply)

Exodus 20 (gave the Law)

Law: *Ten Commandments plus other laws*

made himself known: *explained or interpreted*

What Others are Saying:

TITLE OF JESUS

God the One and Only

Mosaic system: *God's commandments through Moses for pleasing him*

incarnation: *God in human form*

Something to Ponder

John could have had a big ego since he was older than Jesus and because God chose him to introduce Jesus to the Jewish people. But he didn't. Instead, he humbly did his job of telling people to repent and of introducing people to Jesus.

> **John 1:19–23** Now this was John's testimony when the Jews of Jerusalem sent priests and Levites to ask him who he was. He did not fail to confess, but confessed freely, "I am not the Christ."
>
> They asked him, "Then who are you? Are you Elijah?"
>
> He said, "I am not."
>
> "Are you the Prophet?"
>
> He answered, "No."
>
> Finally they said, "Who are you? Give us an answer to take back to those who sent us. What do you say about yourself?"
>
> John replied in the words of Isaiah the prophet, "I am the voice of one calling in the desert, 'Make straight the way for the Lord.' "

Radical Preacher

TITLE OF JESUS

The Lord

John the Baptist was not your run-of-the-mill preacher. He lived in the desert, ate locusts and wild honey, wore a camel-hair robe, and told people to get their acts together. His lifestyle and message attracted a lot of attention. That's why a committee of religious leaders—**priests** and **Levites**—from Jerusalem went out to the desert of Judea (see appendix A) to investigate him. They **plied** John with questions, which he clearly answered.

Of course, since John wasn't acting normally, they wanted to know who he was. Keep in mind that Messiah-fever was hot back then (see GWLC, page 5). Everyone was looking for the Messiah who would free the Jewish people from Roman rule. First, John denied he was that expected Messiah. Second, he denied he was Elijah, an Old Testament prophet who the people thought would come back to announce the Messiah. Then, he denied he was the Prophet, another name for the expected Messiah. When the leaders ran out of true-false questions, they finally asked, "Who are you?" John answered by calling himself a voice in the desert.

priests: *supervised worship and offered sacrifices*

Levites: *priests' assistants*

plied: *kept supplying*

 GO TO:

Malachi 4:5 (Elijah)

Deuteronomy 18:15–18; Acts 3:22–23 (the Prophet)

Isaiah 40:3 (voice)

> **John 1:24–28** Now some Pharisees who had been sent questioned him, "Why then do you baptize if you are not the Christ, nor Elijah, nor the Prophet?"
>
> "I baptize with water," John replied, "but among you stands one you do not know. He is the one who comes after me, the thongs of whose sandals I am not worthy to untie."
>
> This all happened at Bethany on the other side of the Jordan, where John was baptizing.

"I'm A Nobody"

These big shots didn't go find John the Baptist so they could be preached at. Once they found out who he was, they wanted to know what he was doing—why he was baptizing. It was customary for religious leaders to **baptize** Gentiles who converted to Judaism. But they didn't baptize Jewish people, like John did. In doing so, John treated Jewish people like pagans, which was unheard of and offensive.

So in answer to the **Pharisees**' question, John pointed his **inquisitors** to Jesus, whose ministry would follow his and who was a much greater person. In fact, John said he was a nobody in comparison to Jesus. Untying sandals was a job that belonged to the least important household servant (see illustration below).

John ended this section by identifying the location as Bethany, which was on the east bank of the Jordan River (see appendix A). It is also called Bethabara. This is not the same Bethany that is mentioned later in the book, a suburb of Jerusalem.

baptize: *perform water ritual of initiation in the faith*

Pharisees: *exclusive teachers of religious law and tradition*

inquisitors: *questioners*

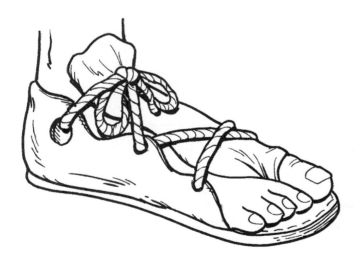

Roman Sandal

People in Jesus' day wore open sandals with ties. Sandals of the wealthy had heel caps or sides that came up over their arches as shown here.

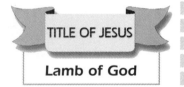
James Montgomery Boice: The delegation from Jerusalem could think of three things that John might claim to be, and the first of these quite obviously was "the Messiah." Was he the Messiah? We must remember as we read these words that the Jews were a people living under the dominion of Rome and that they were looking with great expectation for their deliverer, as any captive people do. . . . Moreover, there had been many messianic pretenders. . . . It would have been easy for John, who by this time had received quite an impressive following, to have announced that he was the Messiah. But not only did he reject the temptation, he even rejected it with the hint that the One who actually was the Messiah was present.[11]

> **John 1:29–31** The next day John saw Jesus coming toward him and said, "Look, the Lamb of God, who takes away the sin of the world! This is the one I meant when I said, 'A man who comes after me has surpassed me because he was before me.' I myself did not know him, but the reason I came baptizing with water was that he might be revealed to Israel."

Lamb Confession

The day after the religious leaders questioned John, Jesus showed up while John was preaching and baptizing. So John introduced him as the Lamb of God—not The Great God of the Universe who created everyone and everything in it. The Jewish people, to whom he was preaching, would have recognized the title Lamb of God, although many didn't get the true meaning of it. They were used to <u>sacrificing lambs</u> as a means to gain forgiveness for their sins. But they weren't expecting this human Lamb.

John clearly identified Jesus as the person to whom he referred earlier—the one who was greater even though he came later than John.

TITLE OF JESUS

Lamb of God

☞ **GO TO:**

Exodus 12–13;
Numbers 28:4
(sacrificing lambs)

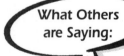
Warren W. Wiersbe: The people of Israel were familiar with lambs for the sacrifices. At Passover, each family had to have a lamb; and during the year, two lambs a day were sacrificed at the temple altar, plus all the other lambs brought for personal sacrifices. Those lambs were brought by men to men, but here is God's Lamb, given by God to men! Those lambs could not take away sin, but the Lamb of God can take away sin. Those lambs were for Israel alone, but this Lamb would shed His blood for the whole world![12]

The people of Jesus' day, especially the religious leaders, had certain expectations about the Messiah that God had promised to send. Because of their political situation, they were looking for a political leader and didn't recognize him as a lamb who would die for their sins. Have your religious expectations kept you from seeing the real Jesus?

Something to Ponder

> **John 1:32–34** Then John gave this testimony: "I saw the Spirit come down from heaven as a dove and remain on him. I would not have known him, except that the one who sent me to baptize with water told me, 'The man on whom you see the Spirit come down and remain is he who will baptize with the Holy Spirit.' I have seen and I testify that this is the Son of God."

TITLE OF JESUS

Son of God

Look For The Dove

Jesus was John's <u>cousin</u>, and they probably spent a lot of time together as children and teens. When they were children, John didn't know Jesus was God's Son. He didn't discover that truth until Jesus came to him for baptism. God's sign that Jesus was the Son of God, the Lamb, was the **Holy Spirit** in the form of a dove who <u>alighted</u> on Jesus when John baptized him. And just in case John missed the sign, the dove was accompanied by God's voice saying, *"This is my Son, whom I love; with him I am well pleased"* (Matthew 3:17).

Can you imagine witnessing *that* scene? And hearing God's voice out loud? Many of us might have been tempted to keep it to ourselves so people wouldn't think we're crazy. But not John. Once he knew who Jesus really was, John told everyone who would listen—and did so with confidence.

☞ **GO TO:**

Luke 1 (cousin)

Matthew 3:13–17; Mark 1:9–10; Luke 3:21–22 (alighted)

Holy Spirit: *person of the Godhead*

JESUS THE RECRUITER

> **John 1:35–39** The next day John was there again with two of his disciples. When he saw Jesus passing by, he said, "Look, the Lamb of God!"
>
> When the two disciples heard him say this, they followed Jesus. Turning around, Jesus saw them following and asked, "What do you want?"

> They said, "Rabbi" (which means Teacher), "where are you staying?"
>
> "Come," he replied, "and you will see."
>
> So they went and saw where he was staying, and spent that day with him. It was about the tenth hour.

"Hey, Look!"

On the third day that John recorded of this week, John the Baptist again pointed people to Jesus as the Lamb of God. John said, "Hey, look! Here's Jesus. Don't miss him!"

disciples: followers

John, who wrote this book, and Andrew were two of John the Baptist's **disciples** who were with him at this time. They immediately left John and followed Jesus, an action that pleased John instead of making him mad.

To be sure Andrew and John followed him for the right reasons, Jesus asked them what they were after. Instead of answering, they asked him where he was staying, implying that they would come see him later if he was too busy to talk right then. But Jesus invited them

tenth hour: 4:00 P.M.

to spend the evening with him, since it was the **tenth hour**. No doubt he answered their questions and told them about his ministry.

What Others are Saying:

William Barclay: "Come and see!" The Jewish Rabbis had a way of using that phrase in their teaching. They would say: "Do you want to know the answer to this question? Do you want to know the solution to this problem? Come and see, and we will think about it together." When Jesus said: "Come and see!" he was inviting them, not only to come and talk, but to come and find the things that he alone could open out to them.[13]

Something to Ponder

John didn't mind taking second place after he had enjoyed first place for a while. Instead of holding on to first, he *encouraged* his disciples to leave him and go follow Jesus. John wasn't the possessive or jealous type.

> **John 1:40–42** Andrew, Simon Peter's brother, was one of the two who heard what John had said and who had followed Jesus. The first thing Andrew did was to find his brother Simon and tell him, "We have found the Messiah" (that is, the Christ). And he brought him to Jesus. Jesus looked at him and said, "You are Simon son of John. You will be called Cephas" (which, when translated, is Peter).

Two-For-One Special

Andrew was so impressed with Jesus that he hunted up his brother, Simon <u>Peter</u>, to tell him who Jesus was—the Messiah they were looking for. They weren't expecting God's Son but rather a king who would free them from Roman rule and set up God's kingdom of peace.

Andrew, like John the Baptist, was a good second-place player. Throughout the **Gospels**, he lived in the shadow of his brother, Peter; only here did he come first. Starting with his brother, Andrew developed a reputation for bringing people to Jesus.

When Peter met Jesus, Jesus already knew who Peter was. He didn't just glance at Peter or look at his body; he read his heart. Then he changed Simon's name to Peter (in Greek), or Cephas (in Aramaic), which means a rock, someone steady and strong. It would take a few years for Peter to live up to that name change, but he did.

Jewish people who lived in Palestine spoke Aramaic. However, most of those who lived outside of that land spoke Greek. That's why John translated the word *Messiah* and Simon's new name into other languages.

When Andrew heard what John the Baptist said about Jesus, he believed Jesus was the promised Messiah. Then he went to find his brother to tell him. If you had been there, what would you have done?

Jesus doesn't just see us how we are now. He saw us in our past. He also knows all our possibilities, what we *can* become if we trust him. And he will help us realize those possibilities to become all that God made us to be.

> **John 1:43–46** The next day Jesus decided to leave for Galilee. Finding Philip, he said to him, "Follow me."
>
> Philip, like Andrew and Peter, was from the town of Bethsaida. Philip found Nathanael and told him, "We have found the one Moses wrote about in the Law, and about whom the prophets also wrote—Jesus of Nazareth, the son of Joseph."
>
> "Nazareth! Can anything good come from there?" Nathanael asked.
>
> "Come and see," said Philip.

☞ **GO TO:**

Matthew 16:17–19 (Peter)

Gospels: Matthew, Mark, Luke, John

TITLE OF JESUS

The Messiah

CULTURE CLUE

Something to Ponder

Remember This . . .

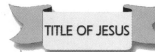
**One Whom Moses
and Prophets
Wrote About**

☞ **GO TO:**

Acts 24:5 (Nazareth)

**Something
to Ponder**

TITLE OF JESUS

Son of God

Say What?

As Jesus continued recruiting disciples, he traveled north into the region called Galilee (see appendix A). There he called Philip, who also followed him immediately. Philip in turn looked for his friend Nathanael to tell him about Jesus. Philip described Jesus in four ways. First, Philip said Jesus was the one whom Moses wrote about in the Law. Second, Philip said Jesus was the one whom the prophets wrote about. "Moses and the Prophets" is one way Jewish people referred to the whole of the Old Testament. Third, Philip said he was *"Jesus of Nazareth,"* indicating the place where Jesus grew up. Fourth, Philip said Jesus was the *"son of Joseph,"* indicating his humanity.

But Nathanael was doubtful because of where Jesus came from. People from Nazareth (see appendix A) were looked down upon. They were considered to be from the other side of the tracks. Instead of trying to convince Nathanael with arguments, Philip echoed Jesus' words, *"Come and see"* for yourself.

When Jesus began his public ministry, he called a group of men to follow him. They spent time with him, watched him work, and told others about him. Jesus is still looking for people to do the same things today. Are you one of them?

> **John 1:47–51** When Jesus saw Nathanael approaching, he said of him, "Here is a true Israelite, in whom there is nothing false."
>
> "How do you know me?" Nathanael asked.
>
> Jesus answered, "I saw you while you were still under the fig tree before Philip called you."
>
> Then Nathanael declared, "Rabbi, you are the Son of God; you are the King of Israel."
>
> Jesus said, "You believe because I told you I saw you under the fig tree. You shall see greater things than that." He then added, "I tell you the truth, you shall see heaven open, and the angels of God ascending and descending on the Son of Man."

You Ain't Seen Nothin' Yet

Even before the introductions, Jesus saw Nathanael and knew who he was—just as he knew Simon Peter the day before. In calling Nathanael an *"Israelite, in whom there is nothing false,"* Jesus was referring to one of the **fathers of Judaism**: Jacob. Jacob was a trickster, but after he met God, God changed his name to Israel, which means "prince with God" (see GWMB, pages 39–53). Jesus' knowledge of him, including the fact that deceit was not part of his lifestyle, convinced Nathanael that Jesus was who Philip claimed—God's Son, the King of Israel, or Messiah.

Jesus acknowledged Nathanael's belief in him and told him more revelations were to come. Following through on the reference to Jacob, who had a dream about angels going up and down a ladder between heaven and earth, Jesus told Nathanael that he too would see <u>angels going</u> up and down as the bridge between heaven and earth. Nathanael would witness Jesus as a ladder between man and God.

fathers of Judaism:
Abraham, Isaac, and Jacob

☞ **GO TO:**

Genesis 28
(angels going)

Leon Morris: The ascent and descent of the angels seems to be a reference to the vision of Jacob (Gen. 28:10ff.). . . . In both passages there is the thought of communication between heaven and earth. . . . In this passage the place of the ladder is taken by "the Son of man." Jesus Himself is the link between heaven and earth (3:13). . . . The expression then is a figurative way of saying that Jesus will reveal heavenly things to men, a thought which is developed throughout this Gospel.[14]

What Others
are Saying:

When was the last time you talked with someone who greeted you with a statement about your character? Nathanael's conversation with Jesus certainly wasn't one you hear every day. The fact that Jesus knew the kind of person he was, where he was, and what he had been doing drew Nathanael to him. Nate immediately recognized Jesus as God's Son, the promised Messiah. And he followed Jesus.

Conversations with Christ

Study Questions

1. How did John describe Jesus?
2. What does this passage teach about John the Baptist?
3. How do we become God's children?
4. What did John do to encourage people to focus on Jesus instead of himself?
5. How did Andrew, John, Simon, Philip, and Nathanael respond to John the Baptist's testimony about Jesus?

- Jesus existed before he was born in Bethlehem (see appendix A). He created the world and everything that is in it. (John 1:1–5)

- John the Baptist's ministry was to introduce people to Jesus, to testify to who he is. (John 1:6–9)

- Jesus came to offer eternal life to people, but many of his own Jewish people didn't recognize who he was and consequently rejected him. (John 1:10–13)

- Jesus, who is God, became a man to show us what God is like. (John 1:14–18)

- John the Baptist introduced Jesus to the Jewish people as the Lamb of God, who would later die to take away their sins. (John 1:19–34)

- Jesus recruited the first of twelve disciples to be with him, learn from him, and tell others about him. (John 1:35–51)

JOHN 2: JESUS THE AUTHORITY

CHAPTER HIGHLIGHTS

- Water with a Kick
- Cleaning Frenzy in the Temple

Let's Get Started

So many people have the wrong idea of what Jesus is like. For example, some see him as a cosmic killjoy who wouldn't know a good time if he walked into one, a scowling fanatic who thumps the Bible and preaches a down-with-good-times message. In fact, they think he spends his days—and especially his nights—looking for people who are having fun in order to make them stop.

Others think of him as gentle Jesus, meek and mild. He's the Christmas baby who grew up with that same **docile** demeanor, who doesn't have the guts to stand up to anyone. He's a God of love who agrees with everyone, who passes out hugs like they were candy, who's a typical Caspar **Milquetoast**.

Surprise! Jesus fits neither of these perceptions. John blew away these misconceptions in chapter 2 of his book by describing two events Jesus was involved in—changing water to wine and cleaning out the Temple.

The first event was also the first of seven miracles in this book. They were like road signs pointing to Jesus as God, not just a man.

docile: mild, agreeable

Milquetoast: a wimp

WATER WITH A KICK

> **John 2:1–2** On the third day a wedding took place at Cana in Galilee. Jesus' mother was there, and Jesus and his disciples had also been invited to the wedding.

The Party Goer

Jesus wasn't a stuffy religious leader who didn't know how to have to fun. Instead, people wanted him at their parties, and he accepted their invitations. On this particular day, three days after he called Nathanael to follow him, Jesus attended a wedding in Cana (see appendix A) with his mother, Mary, and his six new disciples. Since his earthly father, Joseph, is not mentioned here or in other events recorded after Jesus began his ministry, we assume he died before Jesus entered upon his ministry.

Something to Ponder

Some Christians come across as party poopers who think having a good time is a sin. Other Christians go all out to enjoy themselves and help others do the same but fail to use self-control. Mature Christians know how to have a good time without compromising their convictions. Christians should not be people who are so focused on "religious" activities that they don't have time to socialize with people who need to hear about Jesus.

> **John 2:3–5** When the wine was gone, Jesus' mother said to him, "They have no more wine."
>
> "Dear woman, why do you involve me?" Jesus replied. "My time has not yet come."
>
> His mother said to the servants, "Do whatever he tells you."

Empty Jugs

When the wine ran out, Jesus' mother knew who to go to for help: her son. Although his answer sounds harsh in English, he was not being rude or talking back to his mother. Rather, "woman" was a respectful form of address in his culture—like calling a woman "Ma'am" today. Since it wasn't normal to use this name with one's own mother, Jesus was putting distance between himself and Mary (see GWWB, pages 114–115). He was helping her understand his transition from being her child to becoming her Lord.

his time: Jesus' death and resurrection

By saying **his time** had not yet come, Jesus made it clear that he didn't do miracles on demand. However, Mary recognized his authority and had faith in his ability to remedy the problem when she told the servants to obey him.

Throughout the Gospel, Jesus and the writer of John mark events in Jesus' ministry by saying his time or hour had not yet come or had come. To check out these markers, read the following verses: John 7:30; 8:20; 12:23, 27; 13:1; 17:1.

Dig Deeper

What Others are Saying:

Warren W. Wiersbe: Certainly [Mary] knew who He was, even though she did not declare this wonderful truth to others. She must have been very close to either the bride or the bridegroom to have such a personal concern for the success of the festivities, or even to know that the supply of wine was depleted. Perhaps Mary was assisting in the preparation and serving of the meal.

Mary did not tell Jesus what to do; she simply reported the problem. . . . Jesus' reply seems a bit abrupt, [but] . . . His statement merely means, "Why are you getting Me involved in this matter?" He was making it clear to His mother that He was no longer under her supervision (it is likely that Joseph was dead), but that from now on, he would be doing what the Father wanted Him to do.[1]

Weddings typically lasted for seven days and included long guest lists. (Aren't you glad we don't celebrate weddings like that today, especially if you have to pay for it?) Although guests helped with the expenses, the host was responsible for providing enough wine for the whole week, as well as lodging for the guests. So running out of wine was a huge social embarrassment.

CULTURE CLUE

> **John 2:6–10** Nearby stood six stone water jars, the kind used by the Jews for **ceremonial washing**, each holding from twenty to thirty gallons. Jesus said to the servants, "Fill the jars with water"; so they filled them to the brim. Then he told them, "Now draw some out and take it to the master of the banquet." They did so, and the master of the banquet tasted the water that had been turned into wine. He did not realize where it had come from, though the servants who had drawn the water knew. Then he called the bridegroom aside and said, "Everyone brings out the choice wine first and then the cheaper wine after the guests have had too much to drink; but you have saved the best till now."

ceremonial washing: washing for religious reasons

Watch This

These stone jars, filled with water, were common in Jewish houses. For this wedding, the family probably borrowed the best-looking ones they could find to make a better impression. Jewish people washed their hands by pouring water over them before and after eating. This ritual cleansed them from both physical dirt as well as symbolic dirt from touching people and objects that were considered bad influences or religiously unclean.

Although he didn't have to, Jesus responded to his mother's request. He told the servants to fill six jars with water all the way up to the brim (see illustration below). Doing so would leave no room to add wine or anything else to the water. When the servants ladled it out, the water had turned into wine with instant fermentation. This was no small miracle; Jesus created about 180 gallons of wine. That's 2,880 cups of wine! Mary and the servants knew Jesus performed a miracle, but nobody else did. The servants delivered it to the **banquet master**, who tasted it before serving it to the guests. He discovered it wasn't ordinary or inferior wine; it was even better than what the bridegroom had served previously.

banquet master: person in charge of distributing wine to guests

Pharisees: religious leaders with strict rules

Craig S. Keener: The description of the stone jars indicates that they contained enough water to fill a Jewish immersion pool used for ceremonial purification. Although **Pharisees** forbade storing such water in jars, some Jews were less strict; thus these large jars

Stone Water Jar

Jews used large stone water jars such as this one to store pure water meant for ritual washing.

were being reserved for ritual purposes. Stone jars were common because they were less likely to contract ritual uncleanness than those made of other substances. Using the jars for another purpose would temporarily defile them; Jesus shows more concern for his friend's wedding than for contemporary ritual.[2]

defile: contaminate

Normally the host served the best wine at the beginning of a social gathering. Although Jewish people didn't promote or condone drunkenness, they saved inferior wine for later (in this case, later in the week), when guests' taste buds had been dulled from drinking. Thus the master of the banquet was surprised at the quality of the wine Jesus had made.

CULTURE CLUE

Jesus didn't need the servants' help to perform this miracle. He could have miraculously filled the jars with wine without their first filling them with water. But he chose to include people in his work then just as he does now. He uses us in small and large roles—when we obey him—to accomplish his purposes and demonstrate his power to the world.

Remember This . . .

Jesus' mother approached him at the wedding and reported that the wine had run out. She believed he could help since she told the servants to do whatever he told them. As a result, his disciples, who observed this miracle, believed in him.

Conversations with Christ

> **John 2:11** This, the first of his miraculous signs, Jesus performed at Cana in Galilee. He thus revealed his glory, and his disciples put their faith in him.

The First Of Many

John didn't record all the miracles Jesus performed while he was here on earth. Instead, he selected specific ones to teach specific truths: *"Jesus did many other miraculous signs in the presence of his disciples, which are not recorded in this book. But these are written that you may believe that Jesus is the Christ, the Son of God, and that by believing you may have life in his name"* (John 20:30–31).

Since turning the water into wine was Jesus' first miracle, it was important. (It also means that stories of Jesus performing miracles when he was a child and a teenager are false.) It *"revealed his* **glory***,"* showing that he is, indeed, God's Son. As a result, his disciples believed in him.

glory: unique, divine nature

☞ **GO TO:**

John 1:14 (glory)

Dig Deeper

True to his focus on belief or unbelief in Jesus as God's Son, John was careful to give the results of each miracle. The chart below shows the miracles recounted in John.

Reference	Jesus' Miracle	Result
John 2:1–11	Turned water into wine	Disciples believed.
John 4:46–53	Healed official's son	Official and his household believed.
John 5:5–16	Healed lame man	Jesus was persecuted by Pharisees.
John 6:5–13	Fed five thousand	People wanted to make Jesus king.
John 6:16–21	Walked on water	Jesus escaped and joined disciples.
John 9:1–38	Healed the blind man	Pharisees were confused. Healed man worshiped Jesus.
John 11:38–53	Raised Lazarus from the dead	Pharisees plotted to kill Jesus.

What Others are Saying:

D. Edmond Hiebert: Six of the miracles are peculiar to this gospel. . . . In John these miracles are always designated as "signs," for they point to the deeper truth concerning Jesus as Messiah and Son of God. . . . The signs were intended to reveal the true nature of the person of Jesus and to awaken faith in Him. But the signs did not automatically produce conviction.[4]

THE FAITH FACTOR—One Greek word can be translated two ways: "believe" or "have faith in." After witnessing the miracle with the wine, the disciples believed in Jesus. They put their confidence and trust in him.

TITLE OF JESUS

Divine

CLEANING FRENZY IN THE TEMPLE

> **John 2:12** After this he went down to Capernaum with his mother and brothers and his disciples. There they stayed for a few days.

☞ **GO TO:**

Matthew 13:55 (brothers)

brothers: Jesus' half brothers, children of Mary, his mother, and Joseph

Time Out

After the wedding, Jesus, his **brothers**, and his disciples went to Capernaum (see appendix A), his headquarters for ministering in Galilee. Capernaum was an important city in that time since it was on a major trade route with a customs station and a Roman military post. It had a **synagogue** and was home to several of Jesus' disciples. Jesus did many miracles here and gave some of his most famous sermons in this area.

> **John 2:13–17** When it was almost time for the Jewish Passover, Jesus went up to Jerusalem. In the temple courts he found men selling cattle, sheep and doves, and others sitting at tables exchanging money. So he made a whip out of cords, and drove all from the temple area, both sheep and cattle; he scattered the coins of the money changers and overturned their tables. To those who sold doves he said, "Get these out of here! How dare you turn my Father's house into a market!"
>
> His disciples remembered that it is written: "**Zeal** for your house will consume me."

Spring Cleaning

Passover is a Jewish holiday that comes in the spring, either March or April on our calendars. It commemorates the time when Moses freed the Jewish people from slavery in Egypt (see GWMB, pages 74–83), and its meal is the basis for the Christian communion service. It was also one of three pilgrim holidays when Jewish males were required to travel to Jerusalem to celebrate it, most often taking their families with them. Thus the city was packed with pilgrims.

Since many of the people were from out of town and did not bring animals with them to sacrifice to God in the Temple, merchants sold animals in the temple area (see illustration, page 28) at inflated prices. Imagine the noise of hundreds of creatures mooing, bleating, and cooing. And the stench! People probably had to hold their noses and watch where they walked in order to get inside the Temple to worship God.

Also, since foreign coins were not acceptable for offerings or the annual temple tax, money changers made their living by exchanging foreign money for temple currency. They charged **exorbitant** exchange rates—much better than trying to make money from the stock market.

No wonder Jesus was **livid**! All those people came to worship God, and the merchants and money changers were trying to get rich at the people's expense. Their greed made it hard for others, especially the poor people, to worship. So Jesus expressed his anger at sin but did it without losing control like we so often do.

☞ **GO TO:**

Luke 7:5 (synagogue)

synagogue: *gathering place for religious instruction and prayer*

☞ **GO TO:**

Psalm 69:9 (zeal)

zeal: *enthusiasm, jealous concern*

☞ **GO TO:**

Exodus 12 (Passover)

Deuteronomy 16:16 (pilgrim holidays)

exorbitant: *outrageously high*

livid: *intensely angry*

Temple in Jesus' Day

The Temple was more than a building in which the Jewish people worshiped God. It was a gathering place. This diagram shows several courts that surrounded the main building. Animals were bought and sold in the Court of the Gentiles.

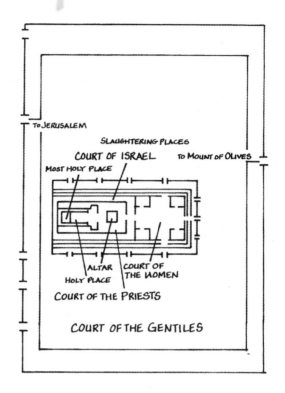

To Jerusalem

SLAUGHTERING PLACES

COURT OF ISRAEL   To Mount of Olives

MOST HOLY PLACE

ALTAR   COURT OF THE WOMEN

HOLY PLACE

COURT OF THE PRIESTS

COURT OF THE GENTILES

What Others are Saying:

Annas: Jewish high priest

☞ **GO TO:**

Exodus 30:11–16; Matthew 17:24–27 (temple tax)

CULTURE CLUE

William Hendriksen: It is true, in the abstract, that each worshipper was allowed to bring to the temple an animal of his own selection. But let him try it! In all likelihood it would not be approved by the judges, the privileged venders who filled the money-chests of **Annas**! Hence, to save trouble and disappointment, animals for sacrifice were bought right here in the outer court, which was called the court of the Gentiles because they were permitted to enter it. Of course, the dealers in cattle and sheep would be tempted to charge exorbitant prices for such animals. They would exploit the worshippers. And those who sold pigeons would do likewise, charging, perhaps, $4 for a pair of doves worth a nickel.[5]

All Jewish males over the age of nineteen, except for slaves, had to pay an annual <u>temple tax</u> of half a shekel to support their house of worship. A shekel equaled three days' wages in Jesus' time. Normally, worshipers paid this tax in person when they made the pilgrimage to Jerusalem if they didn't live there.

> **John 2:18–22** Then the Jews demanded of him, "What miraculous sign can you show us to prove your authority to do all this?"
>
> Jesus answered them, "Destroy this temple, and I will raise it again in three days."
>
> The Jews replied, "It has taken forty-six years to build this temple, and you are going to raise it in three days?"
>
> But the temple he had spoken of was his body.
>
> After he was raised from the dead, his disciples recalled what he had said. Then they believed the Scripture and the words that Jesus had spoken.

KEY POINT

Jesus demonstrated his authority as God by turning water into wine and cleansing the Temple.

Show Us The Proof

After Jesus' cleaning frenzy, people wanted to know who he thought he was: "Show us the proof." Anybody who charged in and acted like he did, claiming the Temple was his Father's house, was suspect. Either this guy was nuts or else he was the expected Messiah. They wanted proof for his claim to be Messiah.

Jesus, however, wasn't going to be manipulated into doing miracles on demand. Instead, he issued a counterchallenge, prophesying about his coming death and resurrection. But the people didn't get it. They thought he was talking about the temple building where they were standing. Three years later, after his resurrection from the dead, Jesus' disciples finally understood what he said.

D. A. Carson: As the legal authorities, these Jews had every right to question the credentials of someone who had taken such bold action in the temple complex. . . . But the way they cast their question betrays two critical deficiencies. First, they display no reflection or self-examination over whether Jesus' cleansing of the temple and related charges were foundationally *just*. They are therefore less concerned with pure worship and a right approach to God than they are with questions of precedent and authority. Second, if the authorities had been convinced that Jesus was merely some petty hooligan, or that he was emotionally unstable, there were adequate recourses; that they requested a miraculous sign demonstrates they harboured at least a suspicion that they were dealing with a heaven-sent prophet.[6]

What Others are Saying:

King Herod was renovating the Temple during this time. Work started in 20 or 21 B.C. and continued until A.D. 64. In order to gain favor with the Jews, Herod promised to beautify and enlarge the second temple so it would be greater than Solomon's original building. However, his work didn't last long; it was destroyed in A.D. 70 when Rome captured Jerusalem. The Roman soldiers knew the Temple could be a rallying point for another Jewish rebellion, and so they destroyed it.

> **John 2:23–25** Now while he was in Jerusalem at the Passover Feast, many people saw the miraculous signs he was doing and believed in his name. But Jesus would not entrust himself to them, for he knew all men. He did not need man's testimony about man, for he knew what was in a man.

Seeing To The Heart

After the temple incident, Jesus did do some miracles. As a result, some people professed to believe in him. But he knew they didn't fully understand who he was. They were looking for a political king, and he fit the bill. Other people saw him only as a miracle worker, but he knew the depth—or shallowness—of their faith. He wasn't impressed by their words.

What Others are Saying:

Warren W. Wiersbe: The word *believed* in John 2:23 and *commit* [entrust] in v. 24 are the same Greek word. These people believed in Jesus, but He did not believe in them! They were "unsaved believers"! It was one thing to respond to a miracle but quite something else to commit one's self to Jesus Christ and continue in His Word (8:30–31).[7]

Something to Ponder

Belief in Jesus comes in several varieties. Some people believe for the wrong reasons—because of what he has done for them or what they hope he'll do. Some believe with their minds; they agree he is God's Son, but that's it. Some believe with their emotions, but that initial belief fizzles when the emotional moment is gone. Others believe with their hearts; they commit their whole selves to Jesus as Savior from their sins and allow him to guide their lives. Which level of belief do you have?

Study Questions

1. Why did Jesus' mother ask him to do something when the wine was gone?
2. How did he respond to her request?
3. Why did Jesus perform this miracle?
4. What did Jesus do when he saw the scene at the Temple? Why?
5. How did Jesus respond to the Jewish leaders' demand for a miracle after he cleansed the Temple?
6. How did the people respond to Jesus' miracles?

CHAPTER WRAP-UP

- While attending a wedding, Jesus turned water into better wine than the host had already served. (John 2:1–10)

- The miracle of turning water to wine was the first of several signs that pointed to Jesus' deity. (John 2:11)

- Jesus drove the animal merchants and money changers out of the temple area, charging them with turning God's house of worship into a marketplace. (John 2:12–17)

- Jewish authorities demanded a sign from Jesus to prove his authority for cleansing the Temple. Instead of providing an immediate sign, he told them about his future death and resurrection. (John 2:18–25)

JOHN 3: JESUS THE CHOICE GIVER

Let's Get Started

"Born again." How often have you seen this phrase in a news story or magazine feature? How many times have you heard it on TV and radio? It's a phrase that has been **bandied** about a lot in the last few years.

bandied: tossed back and forth

It seems like everything and everyone is born again. A restaurant changes its menu, and it's labeled born again. A man changes jobs, and his career is born again. A quick search for "born again" on the Internet produces hundreds of sites, many of them religious in nature. But there is an odd assortment of other uses for the term "born again":

- Born Again™—a trademarked line of skin creams and oils
- Born-Again Boards—makers of surfboards and other hand-crafted wood products
- Born Again Used Books—a store in Colorado Springs, Colorado
- Born Again Records—the third biggest independent gospel record label in the United States
- Born Again—a CD title with explicit lyrics by the Notorious B.I.G.
- Born Again Card™ Recycling Program, which turns Christmas cards into ornaments
- Born Again Motorcycles, Inc.—a store that sells used parts for vintage cycles
- Born Again Creations—a company that produces one-of-a-kind dolls and other collectibles
- Born Again Bears—a company that recycles furs into teddy bears

The first time "born again" appears, however, is in John 3 when Jesus talks to Nicodemus. It's like a movie that generates a bunch of sequels. Today's phrase came from this original wording in John, even though most people aren't aware of its source.

THE ORIGINAL BORN AGAIN

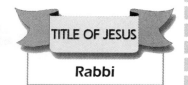

TITLE OF JESUS

Rabbi

> **John 3:1–2** Now there was a man of the Pharisees named Nicodemus, a member of the Jewish ruling council. He came to Jesus at night and said, "Rabbi, we know you are a teacher who has come from God. For no one could perform the miraculous signs you are doing if God were not with him."

Nick At Night

Many people witnessed Jesus' miracles, referred to at the end of chapter 2. One of them was Nicodemus, a religious leader. His credentials were impressive. He was both a Pharisee—a fundamentalist of his day who took Scripture seriously and taught it to the people—and a member of the Sanhedrin, the ruling body of the Jewish people.

Jesus' miracles had raised questions in his mind. He wanted to know more and probably had a hundred questions to ask. So he did the logical thing: he went directly to Jesus to get the straight scoop. He started out by flattering Jesus: *"**Rabbi**, we know you are a teacher who has come from God."* Lots of people in Nick's day claimed they came from God, but the miracles proved Jesus did.

Rabbi: teacher

What Others are Saying:

Manford George Gutzke: Nicodemus came to Jesus "by night." Some suggest that this was a cowardly thing to do, and criticize him because he did not come openly. Actually there is oftentimes more courage in quiet sincerity than in noisy approach. . . . It does not seem necessary to think that he was a furtive man, but rather his actions could show he was cautious and realistic. The night time was probably a time when Jesus was not besieged by hundreds of needy people, and so had time for the interview. Also it could be a mark of his urgent interest that he sought this interview at a time when Jesus was free to spend time in conversation with him.[1]

Philip Yancey: He [Nicodemus] comes to Jesus at night, in order to avoid detection. He risks his reputation and safety even by meeting with Jesus, whom his fellow Pharisees have sworn to kill. But Nicodemus has questions, burning questions, the most important questions anyone could ask: *Who are you, Jesus? Have you really come from God?*[2]

> **John 3:3–8** In reply Jesus declared, "I tell you the truth, no one can see the kingdom of God unless he is born again."
>
> "How can a man be born when he is old?" Nicodemus asked. "Surely he cannot enter a second time into his mother's womb to be born!"
>
> Jesus answered, "I tell you the truth, no one can enter the kingdom of God unless he is born of water and the Spirit. Flesh gives birth to flesh, but the Spirit gives birth to spirit. You should not be surprised at my saying, 'You must be born again.' The wind blows wherever it pleases. You hear its sound, but you cannot tell where it comes from or where it is going. So it is with everyone born of the Spirit."

Happy Birthday, Happy Birthday

If Jesus' statements don't seem to follow Nick's opening words and you feel like you missed part of the conversation, you're right. Jesus ignored his opening remarks and got right to the question that was on his mind: How can I get into God's kingdom? Because he's God, Jesus knew Nicodemus's problem—that even though Nick knew the Bible, he'd missed the point. God doesn't care about how much Scripture we know; he wants everyone, including religious leaders, to have a heart relationship with him—to be born again.

But Nicodemus got stuck on the literal concept of birth. He couldn't understand how someone who is old could be born a second time physically. All he could think about was how silly it is for a full-grown man to crawl back into his mother's womb. Even if he tried, he'd never fit! (And think how painful it would be to his mother!)

But Jesus camped on the spiritual meaning of **born again**. He explained that the second birth comes from *"water and the Spirit."* Water may refer to <u>God's Word</u> or to John's baptism in water that symbolized repentance from sin. *"The Spirit"* is the Holy Spirit,

born again: *born from above*

☞ **GO TO:**

Ephesians 5:25–26 (God's Word)

repent: turn away from sin

God Himself. The Holy Spirit uses the Bible to convict people of their sin. When they see their need for Jesus as Savior from that sin and **repent**, the result is the new birth. And without new birth, no one can get into heaven.

Being born again is a mysterious event—just like the wind blowing. Nobody can see the wind; we only see what it does. Similarly, nobody can see the Holy Spirit, only the effects of his work in a person's life.

What Others are Saying:

Craig S. Keener: Because Jewish teachers spoke of Gentile converts to Judaism as starting life anew like "newborn children" (just as adopted sons under Roman law relinquished all legal status in their former family when they became part of a new one), Nicodemus should have understood that Jesus meant conversion; but it never occurs to him that someone Jewish would need to convert to the true faith of Israel.[3]

AN OLD OBJECT LESSON

John 3:9–12 "How can this be?" Nicodemus asked.

"You are Israel's teacher," said Jesus, "and do you not understand these things? I tell you the truth, we speak of what we know, and we testify to what we have seen, but still **you people** do not accept our testimony. I have spoken to you of earthly things and you do not believe; how then will you believe if I speak of heavenly things?"

you people: Jewish religious leaders

Truth Or Consequences

For a Bible teacher, Nicodemus sure was dense. He didn't get what Jesus was telling him even though it wasn't a new teaching. Although he knew the events and facts in the Old Testament, he didn't understand them. In spite of what Jesus had already taught, the religious leaders refused to submit to his authority. If Nicodemus couldn't understand Jesus' earthly illustrations, how could he possibly understand deeper spiritual truths?

Roger L. Fredrikson: There is a note of sadness in Jesus' response in verse 10. How can Nicodemus be a teacher of Israel and yet not know these things? Nicodemus's being a religious leader is like the blind leading the blind. What Jesus has shared with him is not sophisticated doctrine. These are the ABCs, and if Nicodemus cannot grasp these truths taught through simple, earthly symbols, there is no way he can ever understand and accept the deeper realities.[4]

What Others are Saying:

Bill Myers: Now before we come down too hard on Nicodemus, keep in mind that for his whole life the guy has basically seen and thought in physical terms. Even though he's a religious leader and should have some understanding of what God does in the supernatural, he's thinking and living only in the natural. No wonder he's a little nervous when he's told he has to be "born again." He's obviously not real keen on breaking the news to his mom.

But the same is true today. We live and think so much in the natural that we find God's *supernatural* a little confusing. We wind up looking at Christianity as a religious code, full of do's and don'ts, instead of a supernatural relationship and empowering by God.

For most of us, trying to understand this relationship and empowering is like being blind and trying to understand the concept of color. If you've never had sight, how can you understand, say, the color blue?[5]

> **John 3:13–15** "No one has ever gone into heaven except the one who came from heaven—the Son of Man. Just as Moses <u>lifted up</u> the snake in the desert, so the Son of Man must be lifted up, that everyone who believes in him may have eternal life."

☞ **GO TO:**

Numbers 21:4–9 (lifted up)

The Snake Who Saved

To further help Nicodemus understand the new birth, Jesus used another illustration, this one from the Law Nicodemus taught. Back in Moses' day, the Israelites were traveling through the wilderness from Egypt to the land God had promised them. God gave them food from heaven and water from rocks. Still they complained about having no real food or water. Then God sent them fiery snakes that bit them and made them die. So the people asked Moses to intercede with the Lord. When Moses prayed, God told him to make a bronze snake and put it on a pole. Then when the people were bitten, they would live if they looked at that snake.

TITLE OF JESUS

Son of Man

The Israelites were given physical life as the result of believing and exercising faith in the cure God prescribed for the snakebites. So, too, people are saved from sin by exercising faith in Christ as personal Savior from that sin. The cure for the Israelites was effective only for those who looked at the serpent; healing was not automatically given to everyone. Those who refused to look at the snake died. Similarly, God's gift of salvation is effective only for those who believe. People don't go to heaven automatically.

At this point, Nicodemus faded out of the narrative, so we don't have a record of his reaction to Jesus' invitation to be born again. Jesus is concerned with all persons, not just with Nicodemus, and addresses the following remarks to a wider audience. We'll catch up with Nick later and, from his actions, find enough clues to figure out his choice for light or darkness.

GOD'S GREAT BIG LOVE

> **John 3:16–18** "For God so loved the world that he gave his one and only Son, that whoever believes in him shall not perish but have eternal life. For God did not send his Son into the world to condemn the world, but to save the world through him. Whoever believes in him is not condemned, but whoever does not believe stands condemned already because he has not believed in the name of God's one and only Son."

Love In The Dark

God **loved** the **world** so much that he took action. He sent his **one and only** son, Jesus, on a rescue mission to save those who are **perishing**. Jesus made it clear that he came into the world to save people and give them eternal life, not to **condemn** them to hell.

God's greatest act of love divides humankind into two camps: the forgiven and the condemned. Everyone starts out life condemned in God's eyes. We all like to think we're pretty good—at least better than the next guy. We all think we're good enough to go to heaven. But God says, "No way. *Nada. Nyet.*" Only those who believe in the name of Jesus and trust him to save them from their sins will be able to go to heaven. Faith in Jesus changes our location after death. It also changes our life before death.

TITLE OF JESUS

One and Only Son of God

KEY POINT

In twenty-six English words, John 3:16 summarizes most of the Bible. It contains a number of profound— yet simple—truths.

loved: unselfish and sacrificial love

world: all humankind

one and only: unique

perishing: spiritually lost

condemn: sentence

All the Greatest [6]

God	the greatest Lover
So loved	the greatest degree
The world	the greatest number
That he gave	the greatest act
His only begotten Son	the greatest gift
That whoever	the greatest invitation
Believes	the greatest simplicity
In Him	the greatest person
Shall not perish	the greatest escape
But	the greatest difference
Have	the greatest certainty
Eternal life	the greatest destiny

Something to Ponder

John 3:19–21 "This is the verdict: Light has come into the world, but men loved darkness instead of light because their deeds were evil. Everyone who does evil hates the light, and will not come into the light for fear that his deeds will be exposed. But whoever lives by the truth comes into the light, so that it may be seen plainly that what he has done has been done through God."

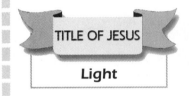

TITLE OF JESUS

Light

Light In The Dark

Light, in the form of Jesus' presence, came to earth and pierced the darkness of sin here. But people rejected him because they were comfortable in their sins and didn't want anyone to see them—like a burglar who works under cover of darkness so he won't be seen. The closer a person gets to the light of truth, the more exposed he or she is. People who live by God's truth and are trusting in Christ for their salvation are no longer afraid of God's light. They don't fear God's judgment. They know they have been saved from the penalty of sin. God's light draws them—like bugs to a lightbulb.

Though some people teach that there are many ways to go to heaven, God makes it clear that there is only one way: through faith in his Son, Jesus. Jesus is God's gift to us, but not everyone takes the gift and unwraps it.

Something to Ponder

Leon Morris: The very fact of salvation for all who believe implies judgment on all who do not. This is a solemn reality and John does not want us to escape it. Judgment is a recognized theme in contemporary Jewish thought, but it is the judgment of God, and it is thought of as taking place at the last day.[7]

Merrill C. Tenney: Notwithstanding this gloomy picture of "lost" or "perish," God's purpose toward man is positive. God's attitude is not that of suspicion or hatred but of love. He is not seeing an excuse to condemn men but is rather endeavoring to save them. His purpose in sending Jesus into the world was to show his love and to draw men to himself. If they are lost, it is because they have not committed themselves to God, the only source of life. . . .

The difference between the believer and the unbeliever does not lie in the guilt or innocence of either; it lies in the different attitudes they take toward the "light." The unbeliever shrinks from the light because it exposes his sin; the believer willingly comes to the light so that his real motives may be revealed.[8]

Conversations with Christ

Nicodemus went to Jesus to find out how to enter God's kingdom. Jesus explained it to him: *"You must be born again."* Although John did not record here how Nicodemus responded to this conversation, John 17:39 indicates he believed in Jesus. Nicodemus was probably a secret disciple until he helped Joseph of Arimathea bury Jesus' body.

Something to Ponder

God's welcome mat is always out. You can leave the darkness of sin and step into the light of God's love and eternal life at any time. But one day that opportunity will be gone without warning, either when you die or when Christ returns to take his children to heaven.

BOWING OUT FOR A NEW STAR

☞ **GO TO:**

Matthew 14:3–5
(put in prison)

> **John 3:22–26** After this, Jesus and his disciples went out into the Judean countryside, where he spent some time with them, and baptized. Now John also was baptizing at Aenon near Salim, because there was plenty of water, and people were constantly coming to be baptized. (This was before John was <u>put in prison</u>.) An argument developed between some of John's disciples

and a certain Jew over the matter of ceremonial washing. They came to John and said to him, "Rabbi, that man who was with you on the other side of the Jordan—the one you testified about—well, he is baptizing, and everyone is going to him."

Battle Of The Baptizers?

For a while, John's ministry overlapped with Jesus', but in different locations. John was baptizing at Aenon near Salim in northern Samaria. Jesus was east of him on the other side of the Jordan River. Although neither John nor Jesus saw the other as competition, some of John's disciples did see Jesus as a competitor. After arguing with an unnamed Jew (maybe Nicodemus) about **ceremonial washing**, John's disciples went to John and complained. Even though John had taught them about who Jesus is, they resented Jesus' growing popularity.

ceremonial washing:
washing for religious reasons

John 3:27–30 To this John replied, "A man can receive only what is given him from heaven. You yourselves can testify that I said, 'I am not the Christ but am sent ahead of him.' The bride belongs to the bridegroom. The friend who attends the bridegroom waits and listens for him, and is full of joy when he hears the bridegroom's voice. That joy is mine, and it is now complete. He must become greater; I must become less."

No Room For The Green-Eyed Monster

John wasn't drawn into his disciples' resentment against Jesus. He knew that everything he had, including his ministry, was from God. There is no room for the green-eyed monster of jealousy or competition in God's work. Knowing this, John was happy for Jesus' popularity, like the best man is happy for the bridegroom.

John shows an amazing level of humility in saying, *"He must become greater; I must become less."* John recognized that, because Jesus had walked on the stage, it was time for him to exit stage left. Just a few months earlier, John had top billing. Now Jesus was the new star, and John was happy about it.

KEY POINT

Jesus wants his followers to be humble.

William Barclay: Part of the aim of the writer of the Fourth Gospel is to ensure that John the Baptist received his proper place as the forerunner of Jesus, but no higher place than that. There were those who were still ready to call John master and lord; the writer of the Fourth Gospel wishes to show that John has a high place, but that the highest place was reserved for Jesus alone; and he also wishes to show that John himself had never any other idea than that Jesus was supreme.[9]

George R. Beasley-Murray: His [John's] role is likened to that of the bridegroom's "friend" at a wedding. Among the friends of the bride and groom (in Judea, at least), two had a position of trust regarding them and had to watch over the sexual relations of the young couple; they led the bride to the groom and kept watch outside the bridal chamber. The "voice of the bridegroom" is thought to be "the triumph shout by which the bridegroom announced to his friends outside that he had been united to a virginal bride." . . . The picture indicates John's selfless joy in learning of the people of God flocking to Jesus (v. 26).[10]

**Something
to Ponder**

John the Baptist wasn't jealous of Jesus. Instead, he pointed his listeners to Jesus, saying, "Jesus is the main attraction; I'm just the warm-up band." How can you have the same attitude as John and give Jesus prominence in your life this week?

A CHOICE TO MAKE

**One Who Comes
from Above**

John 3:31–33 "The one who comes from above is above all; the one who is from the earth belongs to the earth, and speaks as one from the earth. The one who comes from heaven is above all. He testifies to what he has seen and heard, but no one accepts his testimony. The man who has accepted it has certified that God is truthful."

God's Seal Of Approval

John the Baptist was through talking about himself. Instead, he focused on Jesus, who voluntarily brought the reality of heaven to earth. The fact that John said Jesus came from heaven was a claim that Jesus was God. Though the Jewish people understood this declaration, most of them rejected it. But a few people believed what Jesus had to say about God and his experiences in heaven. Those who accepted his testimony that he is the true God **certified** God's truthfulness.

People of importance wore signet rings with distinct marks or pictures. They pressed those rings into hot wax to seal documents closed after they had witnessed the writing of those papers. The seal validated its authenticity just like believers in Jesus validate or certify God's truthfulness.

> **John 3:34–36** "For the one whom God has sent speaks the words of God, for God gives the Spirit without limit. The Father loves the Son and has placed everything in his hands. Whoever believes in the Son has eternal life, but whoever rejects the Son will not see life, for God's wrath remains on him."

The Choice Is Yours

The Gospel writer John concluded this section with a challenge. Since Jesus spoke God's words and came to show us what God is like, we all face an <u>eternal choice</u>: believe him or reject him. Take eternal life or God's **wrath**. If this conclusion sounds familiar, it is. This is the same place John brought us to with the story about Nicodemus. Jesus' life on earth means we must make a choice.

R. V. G. Tasker: Belief or disbelief in the Son of God is a matter of life or death; for, while to the believer His coming is the supreme revelation of God's love bringing the assurance of eternal life, to the unbeliever it is the sign that he remains the object of God's displeasure.[11]

THE FAITH FACTOR—Believing in Jesus brings eternal life; not believing in him results in eternal death. It's a choice each person must make.

☞ **GO TO:**

John 6:27 (certified)

certified: authenticated

CULTURE CLUE

☞ **GO TO:**

Deuteronomy 30:15–20 (eternal choice)

wrath: judgment

What Others are Saying:

1. Why did Nicodemus go to see Jesus?
2. What does it mean to be born again?
3. How did Jesus' illustrations help to explain the new birth?
4. Why did God send his Son, Jesus, to earth?
5. How did John view Jesus?

CHAPTER WRAP-UP

- Jesus told Nicodemus he had to be born again to enter God's kingdom. (John 3:1–8)

- Jesus used the object lesson of the Israelites being saved from death by looking at the bronze snake to teach that spiritual salvation is the result of an individual decision to believe Jesus who died for our sins. (John 3:9–15)

- God loved the world so much that he sent his Son to save men and women, not condemn them. (John 3:16–21)

- Although John the Baptist's disciples were upset that Jesus was more popular than their leader, John acknowledged that Jesus must become greater while his own ministry diminished. (John 3:22–30)

- Jesus' appearance on earth brought an eternal choice every person must make: receive him or reject him. (John 3:31–36)

JOHN 4: JESUS THE GIVER OF SPIRITUAL LIFE

CHAPTER HIGHLIGHTS

- Contact with a Castoff
- Talking on Two Levels
- Spreading the Good News
- Long-Distance Healing

Let's Get Started

Think of the worst people you know—the kind of people you can't stand. Dirty politicians, religious bigots, murderers, groups who persecute or enslave others, drug dealers, rapists. We all categorize some groups as the scum of the earth.

The same was true in Jesus' day. Back then, Jewish people would have given the award for the worst ethnic/religious group in the world to the Samaritans. In fact, Jews hated Samaritans so much that they traveled miles out of the way to avoid them. But not Jesus—as John pointed out in chapter 4 of his book. Once again, Jesus broke the mold to meet someone's need, a Samaritan woman who came alone to a well to draw water.

CONTACT WITH A CASTOFF

> **John 4:1–3** The Pharisees heard that Jesus was gaining and baptizing more disciples than John, although in fact it was not Jesus who baptized, but his disciples. When the Lord learned of this, he left Judea and went back once more to Galilee.

The Comparison Game

And the score is: Jesus, 103; John, 45. OK, so we don't know the exact score. But the Pharisees were keeping it, trying to stir up trouble for Jesus. So Jesus left town to go north to Galilee (see appendix A).

What Others are Saying:

Merrill C. Tenney: Jesus' early ministry in the region of Judea was gaining attention, especially by the Pharisees, who constituted the ruling religious class. The growth of any messianic movement could easily be interpreted as having political overtones, and Jesus did not want to become involved in any outward conflict with the state, whether Jewish or Roman. In order to avoid a direct clash, he left Judea and journeyed northward to Galilee.[1]

> **John 4:4–6** Now he had to go through Samaria. So he came to a town in Samaria called Sychar, near the plot of ground Jacob had given to his son Joseph. Jacob's well was there, and Jesus, tired as he was from the journey, sat down by the well. It was about the sixth hour.

A Direct Detour

Instead of taking the normal roundabout, avoid-Samaria route, Jesus opted for the direct route <u>through Samaria</u> (see appendix A). Most Jewish people didn't want anything to do with Samaritans, and that included going through their territory. But then Jesus wasn't most people, as you've probably noticed. (For more of Jesus' encounters with and teaching about the Samaritans, see GWLC, pages 126–129.)

When he reached Sychar about noon, Jesus sat to rest at **Jacob**'s well (see illustration below). He'd been walking for about two days. The fact that Jesus was tired indicates he is a real man in addition to being God.

☞ **GO TO:**

Luke 9:51–56; 10:25–37 (through Samaria)

Genesis 33:18–20; 48:22 (Jacob)

Jacob: grandson of Abraham, founder of Jewish nation

Jacob's Well

The Samaritan woman met Jesus as she came to draw water from a well dug by Jacob. The well was on the main road and may have looked like this.

The feud between Jewish people and Samaritans is far older than the legendary one between the Hatfields and the McCoys. In 722 B.C., Assyria conquered the northern kingdom of Israel (see GWBI, page 83) and deported most of the Jews to Assyria. Then the king of Assyria sent other captives to live in Israel and <u>repopulate</u> the land. These Gentiles intermarried with the Jewish people who were left, resulting in the Samaritans. Because they were half-breeds, purebred Jewish people rejected them.

When the Jews returned to their land and rebuilt the Temple in Jerusalem, the Samaritans tried to **sabotage** that work. Although God had established the Temple in Jerusalem as the place to worship him, the Samaritans built their own temple on Mount Gerizim (see appendix A). The result was hatred between the two peoples.

CULTURE CLUE

☞ **GO TO:**

2 Kings 17:24–26 (repopulate)

Ezra 4 (sabotage)

sabotage: *destroy, hinder*

> **John 4:7–9** When a Samaritan woman came to draw water, Jesus said to her, "Will you give me a drink?" (His disciples had gone into the town to buy food.)
>
> The Samaritan woman said to him, "You are a Jew and I am a Samaritan woman. How can you ask me for a drink?" (For Jews do not associate with Samaritans.)

"You're Asking Me?"

Jesus was so unlike other people. Not only did he deliberately go through Samaria instead of around it, but in fact he broke all the social rules. He struck up a conversation with this woman—not just a Samaritan but a woman! This kind of action was totally unheard of. In fact, asking for water from a woman alone was like flirting today. But Jesus wasn't an ordinary Jew.

That this woman was alone at the well at noon speaks volumes about her reputation. Women didn't normally go to the well to get water at the hottest time of the day. But she didn't go with the rest of the village women because they shunned her or ridiculed her for her immoral lifestyle.

Since he was thirsty and didn't have a bucket or jar, Jesus asked this woman for a drink. His request surprised her since Jews and Samaritans didn't associate with one another.

Bruce Milne: On the issue of gender prejudice, male Jewish attitudes at the time are reflected in the following rabbinic citations: "One should not talk with a woman on the street, not even with

What Others are Saying:

his own wife, and certainly not with somebody else's wife, because of the gossip of men," and "It is forbidden to give a woman any greeting."[2]

What Others are Saying:

Brenda Quinn: Jesus came to let all people know of the love of God reaching fulfillment through his presence on earth. He came to tell us that our lives are precious to God, valuable into eternity. Jesus is looking not for a particular appearance or life story but for a heart that recognizes its need for him. Belief in Jesus and salvation through him are all that matter.[3]

TALKING ON TWO LEVELS

> **John 4:10–12** Jesus answered her, "If you knew the gift of God and who it is that asks you for a drink, you would have asked him and he would have given you living water."
>
> "Sir," the woman said, "you have nothing to draw with and the well is deep. Where can you get this living water? Are you greater than our father Jacob, who gave us the well and drank from it himself, as did also his sons and his flocks and herds?"

The Gift Of Life

Jesus began a conversation with this woman about water on two levels. The woman talked about literal water, and Jesus offered her God's gift of spiritual water, which is eternal life. When Jesus mentioned living water, the woman took him literally. She associated it with the water at the bottom of the well. It was obvious that Jesus didn't have a bucket to draw it up with.

That fact raised more questions in her mind about this Jewish stranger. Maybe she thought Jesus was putting down their ancestor who dug the well. Or maybe she was beginning to realize he was different.

KEY POINT

Jesus gives spiritual life to those who recognize their need for it.

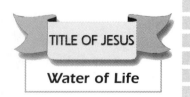

TITLE OF JESUS

Water of Life

> **John 4:13–15** Jesus answered, "Everyone who drinks this water will be thirsty again, but whoever drinks the water I give him will never thirst. Indeed, the water I give him will become in him a spring of water welling up to eternal life."

> The woman said to him, "Sir, give me this water so that I won't get thirsty and have to keep coming here to draw water."

Internal Spring

We keep drinking water because we keep getting thirsty. The water from Jacob's well would quench the woman's thirst—temporarily. She'd need to drink again in an hour or so. Jesus offered her an internal spring of water that would satisfy all her spiritual thirsts.

In the literal sense, "living water" is fresh or flowing water or the water at the bottom of a well that's fed from a spring. But Jesus used the term here to represent the spiritual water of life that permanently quenches our inner <u>thirst for God</u>. By accepting Jesus' words as God's words and believing in him as the Messiah, the woman could receive eternal life from the Holy Spirit. But the woman didn't get Jesus' meaning—not yet. She still took Jesus' words literally and wanted the water he offered, so she wouldn't have to return to the well.

☞ **GO TO:**

Psalm 42:1–2; Isaiah 55:1 (thirst for God)

Herschel H. Hobbs: She was so chained to her material existence that she could not see spiritual truth. Her spiritual density is evidenced by her reply. . . . All that she saw in Jesus' glorious offer was freedom from natural thirst and from the daily chore of this long trip to the well.[4]

What Others are Saying:

The Samaritan woman almost didn't hear what Jesus had to tell her. She was too focused on the differences between them—Jew/Samaritan, man/woman, rabbi/layperson. How have you let racial, cultural, denominational, gender, or religious ritual differences get in the way of your hearing God?

Something to Ponder

> **John 4:16–18** He told her, "Go, call your husband and come back."
>
> "I have no husband," she replied.
>
> Jesus said to her, "You are right when you say you have no husband. The fact is, you have had five husbands, and the man you now have is not your husband. What you have just said is quite true."

Serial Wife With A Serious Thirst

It may seem that Jesus threw a curve into the conversation when he abruptly switched from talking about water to talking about husbands. But he really didn't. Although Jesus was a stranger, he knew all about this woman's past and present—her five husbands and the fact that she was living with a sixth man. (For more about divorce, see WBFC, pages 300–302.) He knew she had been trying to fill up the emptiness inside with a series of relationships with men, but she still hadn't found Mr. Right. Jesus knew she thirsted for love, acceptance, and security, but she'd been looking for it in the wrong men. Instead of condemning her for her sin of immorality, he offered her the only satisfying thirst quencher for her soul—eternal life through a relationship with himself, the real Mr. Right.

What Others are Saying:

Paul N. Tassell: A person must understand he is lost before he will desire to be found. He must realize he is alienated from God before he sees the need to be reconciled to God. Jesus exposed the wickedness of the woman. . . . Jesus could have given her a lecture on the sins of divorce and adultery and sexual promiscuity. He could have railed on her for trying to evade the truth. He did instead get to the heart of the problem by getting to the problem of her heart. She was thirsty. She knew her sin did not satisfy. She knew that peace was not to be found in her sinful life-style. And Jesus tactfully brought all of that into focus for her.[5]

Remember This . . .

No matter what sins we've committed, we can still talk to Jesus. Although he hates sin, he loves us very much. He's always ready to listen to us whenever we want to talk to him about those sins. He offers us forgiveness, eternal life, and power to change.

> **John 4:19–24** "Sir," the woman said, "I can see that you are a prophet. Our fathers worshiped on this mountain, but you Jews claim that the place where we must worship is in Jerusalem."
>
> Jesus declared, "Believe me, woman, a time is coming when you will worship the Father neither on this mountain nor in Jerusalem. You Samaritans worship what you do not know; we worship what we do know, for salvation is from the Jews. Yet a time is coming and has now come when the true worshipers will worship

the Father in spirit and truth, for they are the kind of worshipers the Father seeks. God is spirit, and his worshipers must worship in spirit and in truth."

Where Do We Worship This Week?

The woman admitted that Jesus was right and that his knowledge of her was supernatural by calling him a **prophet**.

When Jesus got too close to the truth, what did she do? Like many of us, she changed the subject. She asked the question of her day: Where is *the* place to worship? The Samaritans had their own temple on Mount Gerizim partly because they had mixed their own teachings with scriptural teachings and partly because of the feud between the Samaritans and Jews. If she believed Jesus, she wouldn't be accepted in the Jewish Temple in Jerusalem. But where she worshiped wasn't the real issue. Worshiping God *"in spirit and truth"* is the issue. It is more than showing up at the right time in the right place. Real worship begins with the right heart attitude that comes from a right relationship with God.

Anne Graham Lotz: We *must* worship God as He prescribes or He won't accept it. We can't worship Him any way we choose as long as we're sincere and not hurting anyone else. We can't worship Him the way we want while Muslims worship Him the way they want and Jews worship Him the way they want and Buddhists worship Him the way they want. Jesus said we must worship God as *He* wants.[6]

The Samaritans accepted only the first division of the Jewish Scriptures—the Law, which includes the first five books of our Old Testament (Genesis through Deuteronomy). They rejected the second division called the Prophets—the rest of our Old Testament.

> **John 4:25–26** The woman said, "I know that Messiah" (called Christ) "is coming. When he comes, he will explain everything to us."
> Then Jesus declared, "I who speak to you am he."

prophet: one who speaks God's message and future events

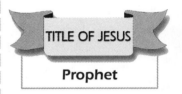

TITLE OF JESUS

Prophet

What Others are Saying:

CULTURE CLUE

Answers Are Coming

Messiah: God's anointed King

The Samaritan woman wasn't quite ready to process the truth of what real worship is. Instead, she brought up another religious issue: Who is the **Messiah**? She knew that when he came—and she was expecting him—he would have all the answers. Jesus declared forthrightly that he is the expected Messiah.

What Others are Saying:

Max Lucado: Remarkable. . . . It wasn't within the colonnades of a Roman court that he announced his identity. No, it was in the shade of a well in a rejected land to an ostracized woman. His eyes must have danced as he whispered the secret. "I am the Messiah." . . . Don't miss the drama of the moment. Look at her eyes, wide with amazement. Listen to her as she struggles for words. "Y-y-y-you a-a-a-are the M-m-m-messiah!" . . . Suddenly the insignificance of her life was swallowed by the significance of the moment. "God is here! God has come! God cares . . . for me!"[7]

When Jesus asked the Samaritan woman for a drink of water, she had no idea she'd end up with a permanent solution to the spiritual thirst inside her. But when Jesus pointed out her sin and offered forgiveness, she accepted. As a result, she told the people in her town about him, and many of them also believed he was the Messiah.

Conversations with Christ

SPREADING THE GOOD NEWS

> **John 4:27–30** Just then his disciples returned and were surprised to find him talking with a woman. But no one asked, "What do you want?" or "Why are you talking with her?"
>
> Then, leaving her water jar, the woman went back to the town and said to the people, "Come, see a man who told me everything I ever did. Could this be **the Christ**?" They came out of the town and made their way toward him.

the Christ: Greek word for Messiah

The Town Crier

No wonder Jesus' disciples were surprised when they returned with lunch. He had crossed religious, ethnic, social, moral, and gender boundaries in force at the time. Jewish rabbis didn't speak to women in public. But none of the disciples were brave enough to ask Jesus why he would do such a "horrible" thing.

Notice that the woman left her water jar. She probably did so for a number of reasons. First, she wasn't focused on physical water anymore; she had found a spiritual <u>thirst</u> quencher. Second, she was expecting to return, since water pots were not disposable items back then. Finally, she may have left it so Jesus could get a drink of water while she was gone.

Imagine being in Sychar and hearing an outcast woman crying in the streets, "Come, see Jesus, who knows all about me and wants me anyway!" They certainly knew about her immoral lifestyle and didn't want her. Although she was the least likely person in town to be saved, God used her to introduce many in the town to himself.

Leaving behind her water jar was symbolic of the woman's leaving behind her former life and inner thirst for acceptance and satisfaction. Besides, carrying it would have slowed her down when she went back to town to tell others about Jesus. Are there things in your life that you need to leave with Jesus so you can enjoy what he offers you?

☞ **GO TO:**

Isaiah 55:1–5 (thirst)

Something to Ponder

Rabbi: teacher

> **John 4:31–38** Meanwhile his disciples urged him, "**Rabbi**, eat something." But he said to them, "I have food to eat that you know nothing about." Then his disciples said to each other, "Could someone have brought him food?"
>
> "My food," said Jesus, "is to do the will of him who sent me and to finish his work. Do you not say, 'Four months more and then the harvest'? I tell you, open your eyes and look at the fields! They are ripe for harvest. Even now the reaper draws his wages, even now he harvests the crop for eternal life, so that the sower and the reaper may be glad together. Thus the saying 'One sows and another reaps' is true. I sent you to reap what you have not worked for. Others have done the hard work, and you have reaped the benefits of their labor."

Solid Soul Food

When his disciples tried to get him to eat, Jesus wasn't interested. Instead, he focused on doing <u>God's work</u>, which was far more satisfying than physical food. God's work for him then was talk-

☞ **GO TO:**

Psalm 40:8 (God's work)

ing to people like the Samaritan woman about God. That satisfied him more than food satisfies physical hunger.

Then Jesus took the subject of food back a step to the harvest, the source of food. He compared the people coming from town to fields that were ready to <u>harvest</u>. In other words, these people were ready to be told about God's gift of salvation. The disciples probably didn't think of Samaritans as being "ripe" to hear this message, because they despised the Samaritans. But the woman told them her faith story, and others before her (probably <u>John the Baptist</u>) had sown seeds of knowledge about Jesus. The disciples were there to "harvest" those seeds, to introduce the people to Jesus and a right relationship with God through him.

When we hear—or read about—people's relationships with God, our own faith grows. The Bible is full of people's faith stories—honest accounts of their failures and successes in walking with him. So reading the Bible, as well as listening to others relate what God has taught them, encourages us to trust him more. And when we tell about our faith journeys, we motivate others to get to know God better.

Real satisfaction comes from doing God's will, not from accumulating more stuff or going from relationship to relationship like the Samaritan woman did. If you're trying to fill your life with anything other than God in order to feel full and satisfied, you'll never be truly happy.

☞ **GO TO:**

Matthew 9:37 (harvest)

John 3:23 (John the Baptist)

Something to Ponder

Remember This . . .

> **John 4:39–42** Many of the Samaritans from that town believed in him because of the woman's testimony, "He told me everything I ever did." So when the Samaritans came to him, they urged him to stay with them, and he stayed two days. And because of his words many more became believers.
>
> They said to the woman, "We no longer believe just because of what you said; now we have heard for ourselves, and we know that this man really is the Savior of the world."

Ear Belief

believed in: trusted, put confidence in

Many of those Samaritans **believed in** Jesus because of what the woman had told them. Others believed when they heard him teach.

At their urging, he stayed a couple of days to teach them and help them grow spiritually.

As a result, they understood that Jesus is the Savior <u>of the whole world</u>, not just of Samaritans and Jews. Their perspective was broader than the disciples' view had been a couple of days earlier.

☞ **GO TO:**

John 3:16
(of the whole world)

What Others are Saying:

Craig S. Keener: For Jesus to lodge there, eating Samaritan food and teaching Samaritans (v. 40) would be roughly equivalent to defying segregation in the United States during the 1950s or apartheid in South Africa in the 1980s—shocking, extremely difficult, somewhat dangerous. The Jesus of the Gospels is more concerned with people than with custom.[8]

Henry Blackaby: Knowledge of God comes through experience. We come to know God as we experience Him in and around our lives.[9]

LONG-DISTANCE HEALING

> **John 4:43–47** After the two days he left for Galilee. (Now Jesus himself had pointed out that a prophet has <u>no honor</u> in his own country.) When he arrived in Galilee, the Galileans welcomed him. They had seen all that he had done in Jerusalem at the **Passover** Feast, for they also had been there.
>
> Once more he visited Cana in Galilee, where he had turned the water into wine. And there was a certain royal official whose son lay sick at Capernaum. When this man heard that Jesus had arrived in Galilee from Judea, he went to him and begged him to come and heal his son, who was close to death.

☞ **GO TO:**

Matthew 13:57
(no honor)

Passover: *spring celebration of God's delivering the Israelites from Egypt*

Back In Cana

After a brief stopover in Samaria, Jesus continued on to Galilee, where people welcomed him. He returned to Cana (see appendix A), the place of his <u>first miracle</u>, turning water to wine.

This royal official served in **Herod**'s court. He would have been wealthy but probably not religious. However, he had heard about Jesus and his first miracle. So he trekked twenty miles—almost a day's walk—to where Jesus was and begged him to heal his dying

☞ **GO TO:**

John 2:11 (first miracle)

Herod: *Roman governor of Palestine*

son. This official was desperate! But he went to the right person for help.

What Others are Saying:

Warren W. Wiersbe: Apparently Jesus had detected in Judea (His own country) the increasing hostility of the religious leaders, although the real opposition would not yet appear for some months. Our Lord was really never identified with Judea even though He had been born in Bethlehem. He was known as the Prophet from Galilee (John 7:52; Matt. 21:11). Jesus knew that the public response to His ministry in Jerusalem had been insincere and shallow (John 2:23–25), and that it was not honoring to Him at all.[10]

besought: asked

Matthew Henry: [The official showed] his great respect to our Lord Jesus, that he would come himself to wait upon him, when he might have sent a servant; and that he **besought** him, when, as a man in authority, some would think he might have ordered his attendance. The greatest men, when they come to God, must become beggars.[11]

John 4:48–54 "Unless you people see miraculous signs and wonders," Jesus told him, "you will never believe."

The royal official said, "Sir, come down before my child dies." Jesus replied, "You may go. Your son will live."

The man took Jesus at his word and departed. While he was still on the way, his servants met him with the news that his boy was living. When he inquired as to the time when his son got better, they said to him, "The fever left him yesterday at the **seventh hour**."

Then the father realized that this was the exact time at which Jesus had said to him, "Your son will live." So he and all his household believed.

This was the second miraculous sign that Jesus performed, having come from Judea to Galilee.

seventh hour: 7:00 P.M., Roman time

A Master Of Distance

Jesus lamented the fact that the Galileans subscribed to the seeing-is-believing philosophy. The official didn't get sidetracked with a philosophical or religious discussion. Instead, he kept after Jesus to go to Capernaum (see appendix A) to heal his son. Jesus told him to go home, and his son would live.

Amazingly, the man did just that! He believed Jesus and acted on his faith. On the way, his servants met him to tell him that his son was healed—at the exact time Jesus said the boy would live. This fact convinced the official that Jesus was the Son of God, and he shared his faith with the rest of his household, who also believed.

The boy's healing became the second miracle Jesus performed in Cana, demonstrating his power over distance.

Erwin W. Lutzer: Faith is contagious. The idea that Jesus, a Jew, was accepted by this Gentile as Lord and Savior was unthinkable at the time. It would not be easy for this man to profess faith in Christ in the court of Herod. But facts are facts. He had seen and experienced what Jesus could do. And he believed.[12]

What Others are Saying:

THE FAITH FACTOR—By definition, faith is believing what we cannot see. This official believed Jesus could heal his son even from a distance and had faith that he would.

Although the royal official had never met Jesus and wasn't a religious man, he demonstrated unconditional trust in Jesus. When Jesus told him to go home, he obeyed, realizing Jesus didn't need to be present to heal his son. Do you have that kind of trust in Jesus? Or are you enrolled in the seeing-is-believing school of faith?

Something to Ponder

As John wrote about Jesus' ministry, he mentioned numerous geographical locations. Plus, he identified places by events or physical markers, such as *"Jacob's well was there"* (John 4:6) and *"Cana in Galilee, where he had turned the water into wine"* (John 4:46). Recounting the journey was a popular way to teach the next generation about Jesus' ministry.

CULTURE CLUE

Study Questions

1. What was unusual about Jesus' stop in Samaria?
2. What did Jesus teach the Samaritan woman in their conversation?
3. How did the woman respond to Jesus' teaching?
4. What lessons did Jesus teach his disciples when they returned after his conversation with the woman?

5. How did the Samaritan woman influence others after she believed in Jesus?

6. How did Jesus respond to the official's request to heal his son?

7. What do you learn about Jesus from the miracle he performed for the official's son?

CHAPTER WRAP-UP

- Jesus made a detour through Samaria to talk with a woman at a well about himself and to offer her eternal life. (John 4:1–9)

- Jesus told the woman about her past and taught her about true worship. As a result, she believed he is the Messiah. (John 4:10–26)

- The Samaritan woman went back to her village to tell the people she had met the Messiah. In the meantime, Jesus explained to his disciples the principle of sowing and reaping in relation to faith. (John 4:27–42)

- Jesus demonstrated power over distance by healing an official's dying son from twenty miles away. (John 4:43–54)

JOHN 5: JESUS THE HEALER

CHAPTER HIGHLIGHTS

- Lame Man Walks
- Jewish Judgment
- The Defense Speaks
- Witnesses for the Defense

Let's Get Started

Desperate for healing, sick people will flock to any site that purports to offer a miracle cure.

For example, several years ago in Tlacote, Mexico, five thousand to ten thousand people a day stood in line for over a mile to get water from Jesus Chahin's well to cure their illnesses. When a sick farm dog recovered swiftly after lapping some of the water, Chahin started giving it away. Once the word got out, people traveled from as far away as Europe and Russia. The health department tested the water and found it to be normal. But Chahin said it weighs less than normal water, a fact to which he attributed its healing properties. It is supposed to have cured AIDS, blindness, lameness, cancer, obesity, high cholesterol, and a number of other diseases.

The following year, a spring of healing water was discovered in a cave in Germany, east of Dusseldorf. People claimed it healed blindness, bad backs, rheumatism, and high blood pressure.

A few months later, water began gushing out of a deserted well north of Delhi, India. People who bathed in it said they were healed of skin diseases, polio, and other illnesses.

The sites and healings go on and on.

But this phenomenon is not new. Even back in Jesus' day, sick people gathered at a pool in hopes of being healed, as John reported in chapter 5. When Jesus healed a lame man at that pool, the miracle led to a lot of trouble for Jesus. But he ably defended himself.

LAME MAN WALKS

> **John 5:1–3** Some time later, Jesus went up to Jerusalem for a feast of the Jews. Now there is in Jerusalem near the Sheep Gate a pool, which in Aramaic is called Bethesda and which is surrounded by five covered colonnades. Here a great number of disabled people used to lie—the blind, the lame, the paralyzed.

Poolside Party

feast: possibly the Feast of Tabernacles in the fall

As an observant Jew, Jesus went to Jerusalem to celebrate a **feast**. But that wasn't the only reason he went. He made a stop at the Pool of Bethesda (see illustration, page 61). The NIV doesn't include the last part of verse 3 nor any of verse 4 because these words are not in the most reliable manuscripts. In the New King James Version, verses 3 and 4 read, *"In these lay a great multitude of sick people, blind, lame, paralyzed, waiting for the moving of the water. For an **angel** went down at a certain time into the pool and stirred up the water; then whoever stepped in first, after the stirring of the water, was made well of whatever disease he had."*

angel: created being

Whether healing actually occurred here each year, we don't know. People were desperate to try anything that might work. So they gathered around the pool, hoping, waiting, and praying for healing.

What Others are Saying:

Anne Graham Lotz: Most passersby would have been hard-pressed to notice the bubbling water of the pool because the scene surrounding it was surely so heart-wrenching. Every reject in the city must have gathered at the pool of Bethesda, the "House of Mercy." The emaciated bodies, the pale faces, the pain-deadened eyes, the hollow cheeks all gave silent witness to the helplessness and hopelessness of the diseased and disfigured and dying who lay, crumpled and sprawled, like discarded refuse on the terrace that led to the water's edge.[1]

R. Kent Hughes: The Pool of Bethesda was a sort of shrine. The pool periodically rippled because of a subterranean spring. Long before, a sick person had been in the pool when it rippled and he had concluded that he was healed by the water. News of the "miracle" spread over the city and surrounding countryside and a legend was born: At certain seasons an angel of the Lord went

Pool of Bethesda

There were two large pools near the Sheep Gate and the present site of the Church of St. Anne. They were surrounded by porches. Archaeologists have found what they think is the site of the Pool of Bethesda. The remains are depicted here.

down into the pool, and stirred up the water. The first person to go into the pool after the stirring would be healed (v. 4). As a result, hundreds of people from the countryside came to the Pool of Bethesda to be healed. Five porticoes were built so that the sick could be shaded from the sun as they waited for the stirring of the waters.[2]

> **John 5:5** One who was there had been an invalid for thirty-eight years.

Hoping Against Hope

Imagine living by the side of a pool with a lot of other sick people, hoping to be the first one in when the water is stirred up. Imagine knowing that, even if you are the first to see the water bubbling, there's no hope of your being healed because you can't get in by yourself and there's no one to help you. Imagine straining day in and day out to keep your arm, or some part of your body, as close to the water's edge as the hordes of people around you will tolerate as they push and shove to stake out a spot for themselves. Imagine calling out to the healthy people who walked by and begging them to give you, not the person beside you, some food or money. That's what this man's life was like—for thirty-eight years. Talk about depressing.

Homer A. Kent Jr.: The man who received Christ's miraculous ministration was an adult who had been an invalid for thirty-eight years (5:5). Being incapacitated for so long, he may have been well known in the community and was an ideal person for the miracle to have the greatest impact.[3]

> **John 5:6–8** When Jesus saw him lying there and learned that he had been in this condition for a long time, he asked him, "Do you want to get well?"
>
> "Sir," the invalid replied, "I have no one to help me into the pool when the water is stirred. While I am trying to get in, someone else goes down ahead of me."
>
> Then Jesus said to him, "Get up! Pick up your mat and walk."

Who Wants To Be Healed?

The man Jesus picked out from the crowd to heal was a man who had been lame for almost four decades. When he asked the man if he wanted to be healed, the man made an excuse. He didn't give the straight answer—yes—that we would expect. Jesus ignored his excuse and told him to get up and walk, which was a ridiculous command. If the man could do that, he wouldn't be lying around waiting for someone to help him into the pool!

What Others are Saying:

Lawrence O. Richards: "Do you want to get well?" (5:6) The question is psychologically and spiritually acute. Many do not want to see their situation change, no matter how grim it is. The paralyzed man undoubtedly made his living begging. He would be responsible to make his own living.[4]

There was no welfare, Medicare, or food stamps in Jesus' day. People who were sick or injured had to beg for money, especially if they did not have family members who could care for them. Perhaps, just like today, some lazy people preferred to beg or receive handouts. Continuing in that situation was often easier than being whole and having to work for a living.

> **John 5:9** At once the man was cured; he picked up his mat and walked. The day on which this took place was a Sabbath.

Instant Cure

Amazingly, the man obeyed Jesus, a stranger. As a result, he was cured immediately and walked away on that **Sabbath**. You would think the people watching would have cheered and hoisted Jesus on their shoulders like a hero. But that's not what happened. The strict religious leaders pitched a fit about two things: (1) that Jesus did "work" by healing on the Sabbath; and (2) that the sick man did "work" by picking up his mat and carrying it.

Sabbath: Saturday, Jewish day of worship

When Jesus encountered the lame man at the pool, he asked a seemingly ridiculous question, *"Do you want to get well?"* The man's answer implied that he did. So Jesus healed him, and he walked away, not knowing who had performed this miracle. Later Jesus found the man in the Temple and told him to stop sinning or he would experience worse consequences than illness. This brief conversation made the man realize Jesus was the one who had healed him. He didn't waste any time telling others about his discovery. As a result, the Jewish leaders tried to kill Jesus.

Conversations with Christ

For this lame man to get up and walk at Jesus' command was impossible. Yet he did it. What is there in your life that seems impossible? Getting a job? Paying your bills? Finding a husband or wife? Having children? Getting healed? If it's in line with God's Word and will, it's possible with Jesus when you obey him.

Something to Ponder

JEWISH JUDGMENT

> **John 5:10–13** And so **the Jews** said to the man who had been healed, "It is the Sabbath; the law forbids you to carry your mat."
>
> But he replied, "The man who made me well said to me, 'Pick up your mat and walk.'"
>
> So they asked him, "Who is this fellow who told you to pick it up and walk?"
>
> The man who was healed had no idea who it was, for Jesus had slipped away into the crowd that was there.

the Jews: Pharisees, religious leaders

The Mystery Healer

The Jewish leaders didn't care that this man was miraculously healed. They cared that the healing had taken place on the Sabbath, the day of rest, the day of no work. They had added a lot of regulations to God's <u>law to rest</u> on the Sabbath day and so had distorted its meaning. According to these leaders, carrying a bed mat on the Sabbath was a sin, and healing on the Sabbath was outlawed as well.

As a result, they grilled the man to find out who had healed him. But he didn't know. He must have been so busy celebrating his healing that he forgot to thank Jesus. Or maybe the healed man was just too selfish to think of anyone but himself. Anyway, Jesus had disappeared before he could find out who he was.

> **John 5:14–18** Later Jesus found him at the temple and said to him, "See, you are well again. Stop sinning or something worse may happen to you." The man went away and told the Jews that it was Jesus who had made him well.
>
> So, because Jesus was doing these things on the Sabbath, the Jews persecuted him. Jesus said to them, "My Father is always at his work to this very day, and I, too, am working." For this reason the Jews tried all the harder to kill him; not only was he breaking the Sabbath, but he was even calling God his own Father, making himself equal with God.

Down With Jesus

Later Jesus looked up the man he had healed to identify himself.

Logically, the Jewish leaders should have prosecuted the healed man for breaking the law instead of going after Jesus. But they were on a mission to destroy this man who claimed to be God and who pointed out that God doesn't quit working on the Sabbath. After all, God keeps on holding the universe together, sending rain and sunshine, answering prayers, giving life, and taking life regardless of what day it is.

Although the Jews didn't believe in Jesus as the Messiah, they understood his claim to deity. Because they didn't believe Jesus was the Messiah, they regarded his claim as **blasphemy**, an offense that carried the <u>death penalty</u>. This is the first of many recorded persecutions of Jesus in the Book of John.

☞ **GO TO:**

Exodus 20:10
(law to rest)

TITLE OF JESUS

God

KEY POINT

Jesus showed he is God by healing the lame man, and then Jesus claimed to be God.

blasphemy: insulting and disrespecting God

☞ **GO TO:**

Leviticus 24:16
(death penalty)

Dana Gould: To the Jewish mind, Jesus' claim to be God was blasphemous because it suggested the idea of two Gods. Of course, nothing of the sort was in mind with Jesus' self-declaration as the Son of God. Rather, Jesus proclaimed that He was God in human form, the second person of the Trinity.[5]

Leon Morris: The expression "My Father" is noteworthy. It was not the way Jews usually referred to God. Usually they spoke of "our Father", and while they might use "My Father" in prayer they would qualify it with "in heaven" or some other expression to remove the suggestion of familiarity. Jesus did no such thing, here or elsewhere. He habitually thought of God as in the closest relationship to Himself. The expression implies a claim which the Jews did not miss.[6]

Jesus chose to heal people seven times on the Sabbath:

- Cast a demon out of a man (Mark 1:21–28)
- Healed Peter's mother-in-law (Mark 1:29–31)
- Healed a man's shriveled hand (Mark 3:1–6)
- Healed a crippled woman (Luke 13:10–17)
- Healed a man with dropsy (Luke 14:1–6)
- Healed this lame man (John 5:1–18)
- Gave a blind man sight (John 9:1–16)

Dig Deeper

Jesus deliberately challenged the Jewish leaders and their rules about what you can and can't do on the Sabbath. He wanted to point them back to God, who commanded us to rest from work one day a week in order to worship him, rest, and help others.

Remember This . . .

THE DEFENSE SPEAKS

> **John 5:19–23** Jesus gave them this answer: "I tell you the truth, the Son can do nothing by himself; he can do only what he sees his Father doing, because whatever the Father does the Son also does. For the Father loves the Son and shows him all he does. Yes, to your amazement he will show him even greater things than these. For just as the Father raises the dead and gives them

> life, even so the Son gives life to whom he is pleased to give it. Moreover, the Father judges no one, but has entrusted all judgment to the Son, that all may honor the Son just as they honor the Father. He who does not honor the Son does not honor the Father, who sent him."

All Rise For The Judge

Instead of denying the leaders' accusation of blasphemy, Jesus gave them a lot of ammunition to use against him. (He doesn't act like we would expect, does he?) He and the Father know each other intimately and love each other very much. Because of this relationship, Jesus can do only what God does.

Jesus went on to shock his audience even more. These Jewish leaders knew only God can raise people from the dead and judge them at the final judgment. When Jesus claimed he could do the same things, he was clearly claiming to be God. As such, failure to honor him equals failure to honor God. You can almost feel the anger rising from the leaders as they listened to Jesus' words.

R. V. G. Tasker: Jesus therefore at once asserts that for Him to act independently of God would be utterly impossible, because the relationship between God and Himself is a Father-Son relationship; and no son can act all the time independently of his father. In His case, moreover, the relationship is unique. . . . Without this unique relationship, none of the works of Jesus would have been possible.[7]

Roger L. Fredrikson: The Father has given His power of life to the Son. The work of the Father is revealed in the works of the Son as He freely shares life with whomever He chooses. Every devout Jew knew that God was the Source of all life—not only in the act of creation, but even in raising the dead. They accepted the accounts of life being given to the dead in the Old Testament records, but for this **itinerant** preacher to claim that gift of life was an affront to their rigid orthodoxy. Yet, specific proof that the life of God was in Him was before them in the one who had been healed.[8]

itinerant: traveling

When Jesus claimed to be equal with God, either he was joking (and it was a bad joke!), crazy (what sane person would give this much ammunition to the people who wanted to kill him?), lying (and therefore no one could trust him about anything), or telling the truth. What do you think?

No matter what anyone or any religion says, we can't have God without Jesus. They come as an indivisible set. If we reject Jesus, we also reject God. If we accept Jesus, we also accept God. There isn't an either/or option.

> **John 5:24–27** "I tell you the truth, whoever hears my word and believes him who sent me has eternal life and will not be condemned; he has crossed over from death to life. I tell you the truth, a time is coming and has now come when the dead will hear the voice of the Son of God and those who hear will live. For as the Father has life in himself, so he has granted the Son to have life in himself. And he has given him authority to judge because he is the <u>Son of Man</u>."

Dead Men Hearing

The Hebrew Scriptures teach that eternal life happens after people are raised from the dead at the last judgment. Jesus gave this concept a new spin by declaring that eternal life—a new quality of life—is available right now when people believe in him.

Jesus' second claim to being the Son of God was the fact that God gave him the authority to raise people from the dead. Later he would demonstrate that ability with <u>Lazarus</u>. Here he mentioned two resurrections: (1) people who are dead in sin made alive to eternal life, and (2) his own physical resurrection from the dead.

> **John 5:28–30** "Do not be amazed at this, for a time is coming when all who are in their graves will hear his voice and come out—those who have done good will rise to live, and those who have done evil will rise to be condemned. By myself I can do nothing; I judge only as I hear, and my judgment is just, for I seek not to please myself but him who sent me."

Something to Ponder

Remember This . . .

TITLE OF JESUS

Son of Man

☞ **GO TO:**

Daniel 7:13–14 (Son of Man)

☞ **GO TO:**

John 11:1–44 (Lazarus)

Grave-Cracking Lesson

In spite of what some people teach, death is not the end. We don't just breathe our last and go into oblivion. Rather, death is the beginning of a new life that will last forever either in heaven or in hell. Jesus continued his list of resurrections by referring to the future resurrection of dead believers to eternal life and the resurrection of dead unbelievers to judgment. Both of these will happen when he returns.

Although God the Father gave Jesus the job of judging people, he can't—and won't—do it on his own. After all, they are an inseparable team and Jesus wants to please the Father. Once more, Jesus drove home the point that he is God, which caused the Jewish leaders to accuse him of blasphemy.

☞ **GO TO:**

1 Thessalonians
    4:13–18
    (resurrection of dead
    believers)

Revelation 20:11–15
    (judgment)

WITNESSES FOR THE DEFENSE

> **John 5:31–35** "If I testify about myself, my testimony is not valid. There is another who testifies in my favor, and I know that his testimony about me is valid.
>
> "You have sent to John and he has testified to the truth. Not that I accept human testimony; but I mention it that you may be saved. John was a lamp that burned and gave light, and you chose for a time to enjoy his light."

☞ **GO TO:**

Deuteronomy 17:6;
    19:15
    (another who testifies)

Jesus Trots Out The Testimonies

Jesus' third claim to being God's Son was a roll call of witnesses. He started with his own testimony, though he realized that wasn't enough by itself. So he trotted out John the Baptist, whom the Jewish people listened to for a while. John brought God's light, but they didn't really understand his message and put their faith in Jesus, God's Son.

☞ **GO TO:**

John 1:29
    (John the Baptist)

> **John 5:36–40** "I have testimony weightier than that of John. For the very work that the Father has given me to finish, and which I am doing, testifies that the Father has sent me. And the Father who sent me has himself testified concerning me. You have never heard his voice nor seen his form, nor does his word dwell in

you, for you do not believe the one he sent. You diligently study the Scriptures because you think that by them you possess eternal life. These are the Scriptures that testify about me, yet you refuse to come to me to have life."

Miracle Defense

Jesus then brought out his miracles as a testimony to his deity. After all, who but God could change <u>water into wine</u> and <u>heal a dying boy</u> from a distance? The people involved in those miracles could testify convincingly about what Jesus had done for them.

In case these witnesses were not enough, Jesus next called God the Father and his Word as witnesses. The people to whom Jesus was speaking had not seen God or heard his voice, but they had his written Word. Both the religious leaders and the common people respected God's written Word, which testifies to Jesus and his deity. But the leaders who studied and taught the Scriptures didn't understand that the passages about the Messiah pointed to Jesus, who was finally living there among them.

☞ **GO TO:**

John 2:1–11 (water into wine)

John 4:43–54 (heal a dying boy)

William Barclay: There is only one proper way to read the Bible—to read it as all pointing to Jesus Christ. Then many of the things which puzzle us, and sometimes distress us, are clearly seen as stages on the way, a pointing forward to Jesus Christ, who is the supreme revelation and by whose light all other revelation is to be tested. The Jews worshipped a God who wrote rather than a God who acted and therefore when Christ came they did not recognize him.[9]

What Others are Saying:

Paul Little: People often ask, "If Christianity is true, why do the majority of intelligent people not believe it?" The answer is precisely the same as the reason the majority of unintelligent people don't believe it. They don't want to![10]

We can know the Bible backward and forward like the Jewish leaders in Jesus' day and still not know God and his Son. God didn't give us Scripture just so we would have something to study. Instead, he gave us his Word so we can know he exists, what he is like, that he loves us, and that he wants a personal relationship with us through faith in his Son. Bible head knowledge is useless unless we act on it—first by believing in Jesus and then by practicing the truth God tells us, so we can become more and more like him.

Something to Ponder

> **John 5:41–44** "I do not accept praise from men, but I know you. I know that you do not have the love of God in your hearts. I have come in my Father's name, and you do not accept me; but if someone else comes in his own name, you will accept him. How can you believe if you accept praise from one another, yet make no effort to obtain the praise that comes from the only God?"

Short In The Love Department

Jesus wasn't looking for praise from people. Instead, he was evaluating their love for God. This group came up short in that department although they would have sworn they did love him. In reality, they loved their religion more. That's why they didn't accept Jesus' claim to be sent by God. Sure, they would have accepted him if he had fit their preconceived notions of what the Messiah was supposed to do—like free them from the Roman rule. But Jesus didn't. So these leaders continued to seek one another's approval instead of God's.

> **John 5:45–47** "But do not think I will accuse you before the Father. Your accuser is Moses, on whom your hopes are set. If you believed Moses, you would believe me, for he wrote about me. But since you do not believe what he wrote, how are you going to believe what I say?"

☞ **GO TO:**

Numbers 21:9; 24:17
(wrote about Jesus)

Accusations As A Closing Statement

For his closing statement, Jesus pointed out that Moses, whom the people revered and quoted, would become their judge. He wrote about Jesus, whom they wanted to kill. But they didn't believe either Moses or Jesus. Case closed.

What Others are Saying:

Merrill C. Tenney: Moses, who wrote the Law, was highly revered by the Jewish nation. They would not knowingly do anything contrary to his teaching. Their obedience to him was a source of pride. In fact, their very hope in securing God's favor and blessing lay in their relationship to Moses. Jesus told the people that the law of Moses would condemn them in their rejection of him because their failure to believe in him was essentially a rejection of Moses since Moses had prefigured him.[11]

THE FAITH FACTOR—Believing what the Scriptures say about Jesus leads to belief in him as Messiah since the Bible accurately predicted many facts about him.

Study Questions

1. Why was the crowd of sick people gathered at the Pool of Bethesda?
2. Why did Jesus ask the man at the pool if he wanted to be healed?
3. How did Jesus heal him?
4. Why were the Jewish leaders upset about this healing?
5. Why did Jesus later seek out the healed man?
6. What claims did Jesus make to support his deity?
7. What witnesses did Jesus call to support his claim to be God's Son?
8. How effective was Jesus' defense for himself as the Son of God?

CHAPTER WRAP-UP

- Jesus instantly healed a man who had been lame for thirty-eight years. (John 5:1–9)

- Because Jesus healed on the Sabbath and claimed to be God, the Jewish leaders tried to kill him. (John 5:10–18)

- Jesus claimed to be able to give life like God does. (John 5:19–30)

- Jesus called five witnesses to prove his deity: himself, John the Baptist, his works, God the Father, and God's Word. (John 5:31–47)

JOHN 6: JESUS THE MIRACLE WORKER

Let's Get Started

Take a minute for these fun food facts:

The world's largest lollipop weighed 1.01 tons.

The largest cookie ever made was a chocolate chip cookie 34 feet in diameter with nearly 4 million chocolate chips.

The longest meat loaf on record was 3,491 feet, 9 inches long.

The largest omelet was 1,324 square feet and was made in a frying pan 41 feet, 1 inch in diameter.

The largest pizza ever baked was 122 feet, 8 inches in diameter.

The largest crowd fed with five loaves and two small fish lived in Jesus' day and was five thousand men plus women and children. John—as well as the other three Gospel writers—recorded this event. It must have been important, since all four of them wrote it up. It also introduced the first of Jesus' "I am" descriptions of himself. These statements point to the fact that he is God and will provide what we need for our spiritual lives.

Jesus' feeding of the more than five thousand was the peak of his popular career. Up until now, his popularity quotient had been increasing steadily. But after this miracle, he started teaching about his death. As a result, the number of his disciples began to dwindle.

ONE LUNCH FEEDS A CROWD

John 6:1–4 Some time after this, Jesus crossed to the far shore of the Sea of Galilee (that is, the Sea of Tiberias), and a great crowd of people followed him because they

> saw the miraculous signs he had performed on the sick. Then Jesus went up on a mountainside and sat down with his disciples. The Jewish Passover Feast was near.

No Time For Rest

Jesus had healed the lame man and sparred with the Jewish leaders over doing it on the Sabbath. He needed some R and R. So he crossed the Sea of Galilee (see appendix A) to get away from the crowd. But they followed him anyway, hoping for more miracles.

> **John 6:5–9** When Jesus looked up and saw a great crowd coming toward him, he said to Philip, "Where shall we buy bread for these people to eat?" He asked this only to test him, for he already had in mind what he was going to do.
>
> Philip answered him, "Eight months' wages would not buy enough bread for each one to have a bite!"
>
> Another of his disciples, Andrew, Simon Peter's brother, spoke up, "Here is a boy with five small barley loaves and two small fish, but how far will they go among so many?"

Going For Broke

You'd think Jesus' disciples, after spending time with him and watching him do miracles, would be primed for another one. Instead, they had no idea how they'd feed this huge crowd—at least fifteen to twenty thousand people, counting women and children—when Jesus asked them where they could buy enough bread.

Philip saw the problem clearly. It would take more than eight months' salary just to give everyone a bite, and they didn't have *that* kind of money.

Andrew was a bit more helpful. He rounded up five bagels and a couple of sardines from a young boy. But he knew that lunch wouldn't make a dent in the crowd's appetite.

Jesus, however, knew how they'd feed that crowd.

What Others are Saying:

Erwin W. Lutzer: Their [the disciples'] initial response, according to the account in Mark, was to say, "Send the people away so they can go to the surrounding countryside and villages and buy themselves something to eat" (Mark 6:36). They were not hardhearted, just realistic. What were they to do? Like us watching refugees on television, they felt both compassion and helplessness; a willingness to do something, along with the futility of knowing that nothing (or very little) could be done.[1]

During Jesus' time, people known as wonder workers drew large crowds. So it wasn't unusual that five thousand men and their families followed him.

Teachers taught by asking questions and putting their disciples into difficult situations to test their understanding—like Jesus did with his disciples here.

CULTURE CLUE

> **John 6:10–13** Jesus said, "Have the people sit down." There was plenty of grass in that place, and the **men** sat down, about <u>five thousand</u> of them. Jesus then took the loaves, gave thanks, and distributed to those who were seated as much as they wanted. He did the same with the fish. When they had all had enough to eat, he said to his disciples, "Gather the pieces that are left over. Let nothing be wasted." So they gathered them and filled twelve baskets with the pieces of the five barley loaves left over by those who had eaten.

men: males

☞ **GO TO:**

Matthew 14:21
(five thousand)

God & Son Catering

Since Jesus already had the problem solved, he instructed his disciples to have the people sit down on the grass for a picnic. From the other accounts of this event, we can assume the miracle took place in Jesus' hands as he gave the food to his disciples to distribute to the crowd.

As a result of a young boy's generosity, Jesus multiplied a lunch into plenty to eat for a crowd—with twelve baskets of leftovers. It's nice to know that even Jesus believed in using leftovers. (That's good news for moms everywhere!) The amount of food gathered shows that Jesus supplied more than enough for every hungry person.

the Prophet: one like Moses

☞ **GO TO:**

Deuteronomy 18:15–18 (the Prophet)

> **John 6:14–15** After the people saw the miraculous sign that Jesus did, they began to say, "Surely this is **the Prophet** who is to come into the world." Jesus, knowing that they intended to come and make him king by force, withdrew again to a mountain by himself.

Disappearing Act

manna: breadlike wafers that miraculously appeared on the ground

The people got all excited. They had visions of Moses feeding their ancestors with **manna** from heaven (see GWHN, pages 179–180). As a result of this miracle, the people wanted to use Jesus—to make him a king to gain freedom from Roman rule. Before they could try to manipulate him, however, Jesus disappeared. After all, he had come to offer spiritual, not political, salvation.

What Others are Saying:

Erwin W. Lutzer: After the feeding of the five thousand, there was a clamor to crown Jesus king. . . . What a king He would be! He could feed the country without effort, rancor, or fanfare! Goodbye fishing and baking bread. Welcome leisure and prosperity![2]

Synoptics: Matthew, Mark, and Luke

Herschel H. Hobbs: From the **Synoptics** we know that He first sent the Twelve away and then dismissed the crowd (Matt. 14:22–23; Mark 6:45–46). The fact that He first sent the disciples away allows two possible interpretations. Some see in this Jesus' desire to get them out of this revolutionary atmosphere lest they be affected by it. The other and more plausible position is that they themselves were the cause of this abortive attempt at revolution. Jesus' veiled reference to Judas the next day (vv. 70–71) suggests that he may have been at the bottom of the entire thing. If this be a correct surmise then Jesus had to send the Twelve away before He could control the crowd. Afterward, He slipped away to pray.[3]

CULTURE CLUE

Jewish teachers hated waste. Even though Jesus provided the bread miraculously and the leftovers didn't cost anything, he wouldn't have squandered what was left.

According to Roman custom, more food was to be served than needed, so there would be leftovers. Consequently, Jesus was a good host.

Remember This . . .

Jesus not only fed over fifteen thousand people enough food to satisfy them, but in addition he provided so much that there were leftovers. That's typical of Jesus. He often gives us more than enough, more than we ask for. (But not always, so we can't get in the habit of expecting an abundance of money or things.)

This young boy gave Jesus all he had even though it wasn't very much. He didn't keep it for himself or give Jesus only part of it. As a result, Jesus multiplied it to feed thousands. What do you have that you can give to Jesus? Money? Time? Possessions? Yourself? The more you give, the more he will give back to you. It's a guaranteed investment.

Something to Ponder

WINDY WAVE WALKER

> **John 6:16–18** When evening came, his disciples went down to the **lake**, where they got into a boat and set off across the lake for Capernaum. By now it was dark, and Jesus had not yet joined them. A strong wind was blowing and the waters grew rough.

lake: Sea of Galilee

Sailing Into A Storm

After the impromptu picnic, Jesus' disciples set sail without their leader across the Sea of Galilee toward Capernaum (see appendix A). However, they hadn't counted on dealing with a storm after dark.

R. Kent Hughes: The storm was raging around the disciples. The spray was dashing over the boat and the masts had begun to crack. Water was sloshing in the dark hold of the beleaguered ship. The disciples must have wondered, "Has the Lord forgotten us?"[4]

What Others are Saying:

Warren W. Wiersbe: The Lord has to balance our lives; otherwise we will become proud and then fall. The disciples had experienced great joy in being part of a thrilling miracle. Now they had to face a storm and learn to trust the Lord more. The feeding of the 5,000 was the lesson, but the storm was the examination after the lesson.[5]

The Sea of Galilee is a lake in northern Israel that's eight miles wide at the widest point and thirteen miles long. It's six hundred feet below sea level and surrounded by hills. It is known for sudden, violent storms. The disciples were probably more than halfway across the water when the storm started, so going back wasn't an option.

CULTURE CLUE

Jesus showed that he
is God by feeding five
thousand with a boy's
lunch and walking on
water.

John 6:19–21 When they had rowed three or three and a half miles, they saw Jesus approaching the boat, walking on the water; and they were terrified. But he said to them, "It is I; don't be afraid." Then they were willing to take him into the boat, and immediately the boat reached the shore where they were heading.

He Can Walk On Water!

By now, the disciples should have been ready for anything as far as Jesus was concerned. But when they saw him walking on the water in the middle of a storm, they freaked out. (Wouldn't you?) When Jesus introduced himself, they recognized his voice and welcomed him on board.

Then another miracle occurred: the boat came to shore instantly at the other side of the sea.

HOW NOT TO WIN FRIENDS AND INFLUENCE PEOPLE

John 6:22–24 The next day the crowd that had stayed on the opposite shore of the lake realized that only one boat had been there, and that Jesus had not entered it with his disciples, but that they had gone away alone. Then some boats from Tiberias landed near the place where the people had eaten the bread after the Lord had given thanks. Once the crowd realized that neither Jesus nor his disciples were there, they got into the boats and went to Capernaum in search of Jesus.

Seeking The Supplier

In the morning, the people who were still there looked for Jesus. Maybe they were expecting breakfast. Since they saw the disciples leave in the only boat available, and since they hadn't seen Jesus get in that boat, they naturally wondered where he was. After boats arrived from Tiberias, the people used them to get across the lake toward Capernaum (see appendix A) to find Jesus.

> **John 6:25–29** When they found him on the other side of the lake, they asked him, "Rabbi, when did you get here?"
>
> Jesus answered, "I tell you the truth, you are looking for me, not because you saw miraculous signs but because you ate the loaves and had your fill. Do not work for food that spoils, but for food that endures to eternal life, which the Son of Man will give you. On him God the Father has placed his seal of approval."
>
> Then they asked him, "What must we do to do the works God requires?"
>
> Jesus answered, "The work of God is this: to believe in the one he has sent."

Vain Reasons

The people were looking for Jesus for all the wrong reasons. They didn't care that the miracles authenticated his claim to be God and that he offered eternal life instead of eternal death. They were interested in physical bread.

Like so many people today, this crowd was focused on what they could do to earn God's favor. They were confident that they could earn their way into God's club of preferred members. But God doesn't want our works; he wants our faith in his Son.

What Others are Saying:

Lawrence O. Richards: So much in our relationship with Jesus remains rooted in materialism. We trust Him, hoping He'll keep us healthy. Or get us a job. We even pray for the Lord to give us the numbers so we can win Lotto! . . . It's not that God doesn't care about our material needs. God does. And He meets them, providing our "daily bread." The thing is that God cares most about our spiritual needs: the truly vital and important needs that every human being has.[6]

W. E. Vine: The sealing here signifies the authentication, the commissioning with authority, by God, of the Son of man as the sole giver of eternal life. The allusion may be to the impress of a mark by bakers upon their loaves, or, with a typical reference, to the testing and sealing of lambs for sacrifice, foreshadowing Christ as the Passover Lamb.[7]

W. Graham Scroggie: These people loved Jesus for His bread, and therefore loved the bread more than Jesus. Mark the double paradox in verse 27. The people are told that they should not labour for the perishable food, which is the very thing they must get by working; and that they should labour for the heavenly food, which is not to be earned by labour.[8]

Conversations with Christ

What started out as a seemingly innocent question, *"Rabbi, when did you get here?"* opened a conversation the people really didn't want to have. Jesus cut to the heart of the issue. They only wanted to be with him for the miracles, not for the eternal life he offered. In the end, they walked away from him. In walking away from Jesus, they were walking toward spiritual death.

Something to Ponder

Jesus invites us to come to him with our needs, and he *wants* to spend time with us. But sometimes we seek him for selfish reasons like this crowd did. They only wanted more physical food, not eternal life. Sometimes we expect miracles on demand. Neither of these reasons will get us a relationship with Jesus.

☞ **GO TO:**

Exodus 16:4
   (ate the manna)

> **John 6:30–34** So they asked him, "What miraculous sign then will you give that we may see it and believe you? What will you do? Our forefathers <u>ate the manna</u> in the desert; as it is written: 'He gave them bread from heaven to eat.' "
>
> Jesus said to them, "I tell you the truth, it is not Moses who has given you the bread from heaven, but it is my Father who gives you the true bread from heaven. For the bread of God is he who comes down from heaven and gives life to the world."
>
> "Sir," they said, "from now on give us this bread."

Real Bread

As if Jesus had not shown these people enough miracles already, they asked for a sign so they could believe in him. After all, Moses had fed their ancestors with manna for forty years. Could Jesus top that?

Sure he could. Moses hadn't provided the manna; God had. Now God was giving them true bread from heaven—Jesus himself. Jesus was offering them spiritual food. Manna had to be gathered every day. Physical food must be eaten every day. Spiritual food from Jesus, once accepted and believed in faith, lasts forever. The crowd missed the point, however. They wanted physical bread delivered hot to the breakfast table, and they boldly asked for it.

> **John 6:35–40** Then Jesus declared, "I am the bread of life. He who comes to me will never go hungry, and he who believes in me will never be thirsty. But as I told you, you have seen me and still you do not believe. All that the Father gives me will come to me, and whoever comes to me I will never drive away. For I have come down from heaven not to do my will but to do the will of him who sent me. And this is the will of him who sent me, that I shall lose none of all that he has given me, but raise them up at the last day. For my Father's will is that everyone who looks to the Son and believes in him shall have eternal life, and I will raise him up at the last day."

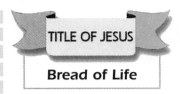

TITLE OF JESUS

Bread of Life

No Mystery In This Will

As someone who could top Moses, Jesus claimed to be *"the bread of life."* In doing so, he again pointed to his deity. When talking with Moses, God called himself "I am" (see GWBI, page 26). By using the same name, Jesus clearly said, "I am God." He had come from heaven to provide spiritual nourishment to those who will believe in him.

Jesus performed the miracle of feeding this huge crowd, then taught them that he is the bread of life in the context of Passover. This holiday celebrated God's delivering the Israelites from Egyptian slavery. The night before they left Egypt, they made unleavened bread because there wasn't time to let the dough rise. As God provided physically for his people back then, and as Jesus provided physical bread for this crowd, so Jesus, as the bread of life, provides spiritual nourishment.

The crowd could only see the miracles, not the fact that Jesus is God. They lacked the personal belief that is necessary for eternal life. But just because they didn't believe, that doesn't mean God gave up. He is in the business of drawing people to Jesus—people who are spiritually hungry. When they come to him through faith, they can never lose their salvation.

☞ **GO TO:**

Exodus 3:14 (I am)

Bruce B. Barton: What does it mean to *believe*? The first step is accepting Jesus' claim to be the Son of God. We declare in prayer to Jesus, "You are the Christ, the Son of the living God" (Matthew 16:16 **NKJV**). Accepting Jesus means giving him control of every area of life. To believe means to yield our wills, our desires, our plans, our strengths and weaknesses to Christ's direction and safe-

What Others are Saying:

NKJV: *New King James Version*

keeping. It means moment-by-moment obedience. Believing is a relationship with the one who promises to live within, trusting him to guide and direct us to do his will.[9]

Jesus' "I Am" Claims

Jesus made seven statements beginning with the words "I am." These statements were meant to show Jesus' deity. His hearers would have recalled the name of their God—Yahweh, or "I AM"—given to Moses in Exodus 3:13–15.

Dig Deeper

Reference	Jesus' Statement
John 6:35	I am the bread of life
John 8:12	I am the light of the world
John 10:7	I am the gate for the sheep
John 10:11	I am the good shepherd
John 11:25	I am the resurrection and the life
John 14:6	I am the way, the truth, and the life
John 15:1	I am the true vine

THE FAITH FACTOR—Belief in Jesus cures spiritual hunger and thirst and provides eternal life after physical death.

> **John 6:41–42** At this the Jews began to grumble about him because he said, "I am the bread that came down from heaven." They said, "Is this not Jesus, the son of Joseph, whose father and mother we know? How can he now say, 'I came down from heaven'?"

The Opposition Party

"So, who does this Jesus think he is anyway?" the people wanted to know. After all, they knew his parents, Mary and Joseph, and maybe some of them had known him since he was a baby. So, how could he say he came from heaven?

What Others are Saying:

Philip Yancey: That response shows why Jesus distrusts sensation-seeking crowds: they care far more for physical spectacle than for spiritual truth. And what happens next certainly bears out his suspicion. As he is interpreting the spiritual meaning of the miracle, all the enthusiasm of the previous day melts away. The crowd grows downright restless when he openly avows his true identity as the one sent from God. They cannot reconcile such exalted claims ("I have come down from heaven") with their knowledge that he is a local man, whose mother and father they know.[10]

> **John 6:43–51** "Stop grumbling among yourselves," Jesus answered. "No one can come to me unless the Father who sent me draws him, and I will raise him up at the last day. It is written <u>in the Prophets</u>: 'They will all be taught by God.' Everyone who listens to the Father and learns from him comes to me. No one has seen the Father except the one who is from God; only he has seen the Father. I tell you the truth, he who believes has everlasting life. I am the bread of life. Your forefathers ate the manna in the desert, yet they died. But here is the bread that comes down from heaven, which a man may eat and not die. I am the living bread that came down from heaven. If anyone eats of this bread, he will live forever. This bread is my flesh, which I will give for the life of the world."

☞ **GO TO:**

Isaiah 54:13
(in the Prophets)

A New Brand Of Bread

Note that Jesus didn't try to convince the crowd that he is God. Those who were seeking God would not need more proof; God would draw them. Those who believe in Jesus will receive eternal life. It's that easy. He offers spiritual food through himself.

Again Jesus explained that he is the bread of life in contrast to the manna, which their ancestors ate and which couldn't keep them from dying. (You'd think they'd get the point, but they didn't—not unlike a lot of people today.) This time he equated the bread to his body, which he would soon give up on the cross so the world could have life.

D. A. Carson: Readers could not help but remember that Jesus has already been presented as the Lamb of God who takes away the sin of the world (1:29, 36). Jesus himself is the one who gives his flesh: his sacrifice is voluntary (cf. Heb. 9:13–14). And since it is *for the life of the world*, his sacrifice is **vicarious**.[11]

What Others are Saying:

vicarious: on behalf of someone else

JOHN 6: JESUS THE MIRACLE WORKER   **83**

> **John 6:52–59** Then **the Jews** began to argue sharply among themselves, "How can this man give us his flesh to eat?"
>
> Jesus said to them, "I tell you the truth, unless you eat the flesh of the Son of Man and drink his blood, you have no life in you. Whoever eats my flesh and drinks my blood has eternal life, and I will raise him up at the last day. For my flesh is real food and my blood is real drink. Whoever eats my flesh and drinks my blood remains in me, and I in him. Just as the living Father sent me and I live because of the Father, so the one who feeds on me will live because of me. This is the bread that came down from heaven. Your forefathers ate manna and died, but he who feeds on this bread will live forever." He said this while teaching in the synagogue in Capernaum.

Is Jesus A Cannibal?

The Jews listening to Jesus were thinking literally. But Jesus was speaking figuratively; he was not promoting cannibalism. To make himself understood, Jesus added a new twist to the conversation: drinking his blood. This phrase, if taken literally, was even more disgusting to the Jewish people than the possibility of eating Jesus' flesh. Drinking blood was a gross sin forbidden by the law of Moses.

☞ **GO TO:**

Leviticus 17:10–14
(drinking blood)

After getting his listeners' attention, Jesus explained what he meant. He was not changing the meaning of his teaching. Again he pointed out that to get the spiritual benefits he offered we must take him completely into our lives and rely on him for everything—just as to get the benefits of bread we must eat and digest it.

Christians down through the ages have participated in a service called communion to remind them of Christ's gift of his body and blood given on the cross for the forgiveness of their sins.

The Jewish leaders began this conversation by wondering how Jesus could be greater than Moses. Jesus climaxed his talk by reminding them that Moses and the Israelites who ate manna died, but those who eat Jesus' food will never die. Jesus is indeed greater than Moses, and he wasn't afraid to say so while in a synagogue.

**What Others
are Saying:**

Warren W. Wiersbe: Being orthodox Jews, the listeners knew the divine prohibition against eating human flesh or any kind of blood (Gen. 9:3–4; Lev. 17:10–16; 19:26). Here we have another example in John's Gospel of the people misunderstanding a spiritual truth by treating it literally.[12]

James Montgomery Boice: Is he [Jesus] as real to you spiritually as something you can taste or handle? Is He as much a part of you as that which you eat? Do not think me blasphemous when I say that He must be as real and as useful to you as a hamburger and french fries. I say this because, though He is obviously far more real and useful than these, the unfortunate thing is that for many people He is much less.[13]

What Others are Saying:

Bread, to benefit us, must be taken into our lives and **assimilated**. By analogy, Jesus must be taken into our lives by faith and assimilated. It does no more good to look at Jesus and not take him into our lives than it does to look at a loaf of bread and not eat it.

Remember This . . .

assimilated: *made a part of something else*

TO LEAVE OR NOT TO LEAVE

John 6:60–65 On hearing it, many of his disciples said, "This is a **hard** teaching. Who can accept it?"

Aware that his disciples were grumbling about this, Jesus said to them, "Does this offend you? What if you see the Son of Man ascend to where he was before! The Spirit gives life; the flesh counts for nothing. The words I have spoken to you are spirit and they are life. Yet there are some of you who do not believe." For Jesus had <u>known</u> from the beginning which of them did not believe and who would betray him. He went on to say, "This is why I told you that no one can come to me unless the Father has enabled him."

hard: *hard to accept*

☞ **GO TO:**

John 2:23–25 (known)

All Or Nothing

The crowd faced a huge decision. Jesus' miracles certainly were attractive. After all, who wouldn't want free food and whole bodies? But his teaching was hard and cost much to practice. It offended them in a big way.

Jesus wasn't surprised by their reaction. He already knew which of his followers believed in him and which did not. He even knew who would later betray him. That's more proof that he is God.

followed: *walked alongside, committed to Jesus*

> **John 6:66–71** From this time many of his disciples turned back and no longer **followed** him.
>
> "You do not want to leave too, do you?" Jesus asked the Twelve.
>
> Simon Peter answered him, "Lord, to whom shall we go? You have the words of eternal life. We believe and know that you are the Holy One of God."
>
> Then Jesus replied, "Have I not chosen you, the Twelve? Yet one of you is a devil!" (He meant Judas, the son of Simon Iscariot, who, though one of the Twelve, was later to betray him.)

No One Else

disciples: *adherents who weren't committed to Jesus*

As a result of Jesus' teaching, many who claimed to be his **disciples** left. Looking at the disappearing crowd, Jesus turned to his twelve disciples and asked them if they were going to leave too. Peter had the right idea when he said to Jesus, *"Lord, to whom shall we go?"* There is no one else; Jesus is the only one who can give eternal life.

Not all the disciples agreed with Peter, however. Jesus knew that Judas would later betray him, although for now he didn't walk away with the crowd.

Remember This . . .

Jesus wasn't looking for numbers or spiritual scalps. He didn't care about fame or having a huge following. He didn't want disciples who followed him when it was convenient or when they didn't have anything better to do. He wanted followers who were committed to him wholeheartedly. It was either all or nothing. The same is true today. Jesus still wants followers who are sold out to him, not a lot of people who warm pews and play church.

Something to Ponder

How much are you like the grumbling disciples? When life gets hard and Jesus doesn't meet your expectations, do you want to walk away? Do you want him on your terms or his? Are you willing to follow Jesus no matter what?

Study Questions

1. Why were the people following Jesus?
2. How did Jesus react to them?
3. What did the miracle of feeding the crowd teach about Jesus?

4. How did the crowd respond to this miracle?

5. What happened on the Sea of Galilee?

6. What did this miracle teach about Jesus?

7. Summarize what Jesus taught the crowd.

8. How did people respond to his teaching? Why?

CHAPTER WRAP-UP

- Jesus fed five thousand men plus women and children with five loaves and two fish. (John 6:1–15)

- Jesus walked on water to help his disciples during a storm. (John 6:16–21)

- Jesus taught the crowd the necessity of believing in him for eternal life by comparing himself to bread that gives physical nourishment. (John 6:22–59)

- Most of the crowd walked away from Jesus after his speech, but his twelve disciples stuck with him. (John 6:60–71)

JOHN 7: JESUS THE DIVIDER

Let's Get Started

When the temperature soars to the nineties and above, a glass of cold lemonade or ice tea is refreshing.

When the heat is accompanied with thick humidity, an air-conditioned car or house is refreshing.

When you're feeling sluggish, a brisk walk or a dip in a pool is refreshing.

When the heat dehydrates you, a bottle of water is refreshing.

When you're tired, a twenty-minute power nap is refreshing.

When you crave chocolate, a candy bar is refreshing.

When your nerves are frazzled, a long, hot bath is refreshing.

When you've worked hard for a long period, goofing off and doing nothing is refreshing.

Refreshment takes many forms, depending on the situation and our needs.

Jesus offered spiritual refreshment to the Jewish people, but their responses varied widely, as John recorded in chapter 7. Some people said he was a good man. Some thought he was a deceiver. Some said he was demon-possessed. The Pharisees wanted to arrest him. Others believed he was the promised Messiah. One thing was clear: Jesus' offer divided the people into different camps.

THE GREAT DEBATE

John 7:1–5 After this, Jesus went around in Galilee, purposely staying away from Judea because the Jews there were waiting to take his life. But when the Jewish Feast of Tabernacles was near, Jesus' brothers said to him, "You ought to leave here and go to Judea, so that your disciples may see the miracles you do. No one who wants to become a public figure acts in secret. Since you are doing these things, show yourself to the world." For even his own brothers did not believe in him.

Unwanted Advice

Instead of getting a AAA Triptik for the most direct route between places, Jesus often determined his route by who he wanted to see (like the <u>Samaritan woman</u> at the well) or who he wanted to avoid. In this case, he was avoiding the Jewish leaders who wanted to kill him. Ever since Jesus had healed the paralyzed man by the Pool of Bethesda on the Sabbath, the religious leaders had wanted to <u>kill him</u>. From this point on, John focuses more and more on the opposition Jesus faced.

When it was time to go to Jerusalem to celebrate the Feast of Tabernacles, Jesus' half <u>brothers</u> were after him to go there and show the world who he was. The average people were gathered like the crowd waiting outside the Academy Awards ceremony. Anybody who was anybody would want to make a grand entrance. All Jesus had to do was walk in and announce, "Hey, guys! The Messiah is here, and you're looking at him!"

At this point, Jesus' brothers didn't believe he was the Messiah. But, for whatever reasons, they were concerned that Jesus was missing a huge opportunity to become even more famous and powerful than he already was. Jesus didn't need this advice. Obviously, Jesus could have done anything he wanted, including calling a staff of angels from heaven to escort him on a cloud to the feast. But Jesus didn't want to do that.

Although Jesus' half brothers tried to talk him into going public at the beginning of the Feast of Tabernacles, Jesus didn't listen to them. They must have heard at least some of his teaching and probably had more than a few conversations with him at home. But they lived in unbelief like most of the Jewish people. It wasn't until after Jesus' death that his brothers believed in him as the Son of God.

☞ **GO TO:**

John 4
 (Samaritan woman)

John 5:18 (kill him)

Matthew 13:55
 (brothers)

Conversations with Christ

> **John 7:6–9** Therefore Jesus told them, "The right **time** for me has not yet come; for you any time is right. The world cannot hate you, but it hates me because I testify that what it does is evil. You go to the Feast. I am not yet going up to this Feast, because for me the right time has not yet come." Having said this, he stayed in Galilee.

time: opportunity

I'm Sticking With My Plan

Jesus operated on his own timetable and his own terms. This wasn't the right time to go to the feast to celebrate, because of the Jewish leaders' hatred toward him even though he loved them. Jesus wanted to avoid unwelcome publicity, so he stayed behind in Galilee. He had plans of his own and was sticking with them.

J. Vernon McGee: Notice the little word *yet* in "My time is not *yet* come." Jesus did not say that He would not go down to the feast, but He was not going down with them publicly to win public favor by something spectacular, or whatever they wanted Him to do. He would go at His Father's appointed time and in His Father's way.[1]

What Others are Saying:

If your family members ridicule your faith in God, treat it as unimportant, mock it, or refuse to talk about it, you're not alone. Even Jesus' family members didn't understand his relationship with God. And they certainly didn't approve of how he lived out that relationship and what he taught about it.

Remember This . . .

The Feast of Tabernacles is a week-long thanksgiving celebration for the harvest, a commemoration of the Israelites' wandering in the wilderness, and a time to look forward to God's coming messianic kingdom. It falls in September or October on our calendar. It also was one of the three pilgrim feasts for which Jewish men were required to go to Jerusalem. They lived in temporary booths to remind themselves of how God was faithful to their ancestors in the wilderness.

CULTURE CLUE

Dig Deeper

Gospel: Matthew, Mark, and Luke

For the year that occurs between verses 1 and 2, Jesus stayed in and around Galilee. John doesn't tell us what he did during that time, but the other **Gospel** writers do. You can read the details about some of his actions in the following passages.

Reference	Miracles
Mark 7:24–30	Cast a demon out of a girl
Mark 7:31–37	Healed a deaf man
Mark 8:1–9	Fed four thousand
Mark 8:10–13	Refused to do a miracle to prove he was the Messiah
Mark 8:22–26	Healed a blind man
Mark 9:2–13	Revealed his **glory** to three disciples
Mark 9:14–29	Cast a demon out of a boy

glory: unique, divine nature

> **John 7:10–13** However, after his brothers had left for the Feast, he went also, not publicly, but in secret. Now at the Feast the Jews were watching for him and asking, "Where is that man?"
>
> Among the crowds there was widespread whispering about him. Some said, "He is a good man."
>
> Others replied, "No, he deceives the people." But no one would say anything publicly about him for fear of **the Jews**.

the Jews: Jerusalem authorities

incognito: with concealed identity

☞ **GO TO:**

Deuteronomy 13 (deceiver)

The Talk Of The Town

When the time was right, Jesus went to the feast **incognito**. The atmosphere there was tense. As usual, Jesus was the topic of conversation and whispers. The people called him a good man and a **deceiver**, anything and everything but who he said he was—God's Son, the Messiah. And no one talked about him openly because they feared what the Jewish authorities would do to them.

What Others are Saying:

deceiver: one who leads people into idolatry or forsaking God

carnal: worldly

cavil: trivial objection

Arthur W. Pink: Whenever God's truth is faithfully proclaimed, opposition will be encountered and strife stirred up. The fault is not in God's truth, but in human nature. . . . So the truth of God will yield spiritual fruit from a believing heart, but from the **carnal** mind it will evoke endless **cavil** and blasphemy.[2]

John Calvin: [The Jewish authorities] fumed with hatred against Christ so much that they would not allow anyone to speak. This was not because they minded Christ being slandered with all kinds of **malice**, but because they thought it would be better if his name was buried in oblivion. So when those who are opposed to truth find that there is nothing to be gained from their cruelty, their great longing is to eradicate Christ's memory, and this alone they seek to achieve. The fact that everyone was silent and subdued through fear was proof enough of the great tyranny the Jews imposed.[3]

malice: desire to harm

THE GREAT TEACHING

> **John 7:14–15** Not until halfway through the Feast did Jesus go up to the temple courts and begin to teach. The Jews were amazed and asked, "How did this man get such learning without having studied?"

Smart Without Studying

Halfway through the celebration, Jesus showed up in the temple court—a very public place—and began to teach. The people were surprised at how much he knew about the Scriptures since he didn't have a theological degree or training with a **rabbi**. After all, he was a carpenter, an uneducated man who didn't even profess to be a rabbi by dressing like one. Jesus didn't need formal training, because his teaching came straight from God. Everyone who wanted to do God's will would recognize his teaching as such.

rabbi: teacher, spiritual instructor

Advanced theological education didn't take place in seminaries or graduate schools in Jesus' day. Rather, recognized rabbis, who were authorities in Scripture and Jewish law, trained groups of disciples who memorized their interpretations of the law and quoted them when teaching.

CULTURE CLUE

> **John 7:16–19** Jesus answered, "My teaching is not my own. It comes from him who sent me. If anyone **chooses** to do God's will, he will find out whether my teaching comes from God or whether I speak on my own. He who speaks on his own does so to gain honor for himself, but he who works for the honor of the one who sent him is a man of truth; there is nothing false about him. Has not Moses given you the law? Yet not one of you keeps the law. Why are you trying to kill me?"

chooses: consciously determines

Discerning Right Teaching

Instead of waiting for the people to challenge his credentials, Jesus took the offensive and told them to check him out. He even challenged their lack of keeping the law although they professed to do so. Then he wanted to know why they were trying to kill him.

What Others
are Saying:

J. Carl Laney: Jesus states that a willingness to *obey* the truth is a prerequisite to an *understanding* of His message. If anyone purposes to do God's will, he will come to recognize . . . the divine origin of Jesus' teaching. [A.] Plummer remarks, "The mere mechanical performance of God's will is not enough; there must be an inclination towards Him, a wish to make our conduct agree with His will; and without this agreement Divine doctrine cannot be recognized as such." Experiential knowledge of God comes with a willingness to do His will.[4]

☞ GO TO:

John 5:1–15
(one miracle)

> **John 7:20–24** "You are demon-possessed," the crowd answered. "Who is trying to kill you?"
>
> Jesus said to them, "I did <u>one miracle</u>, and you are all astonished. Yet, because Moses gave you circumcision (though actually it did not come from Moses, but from the patriarchs), you circumcise a child on the Sabbath. Now if a child can be circumcised on the Sabbath so that the law of Moses may not be broken, why are you angry with me for healing the whole man on the Sabbath? Stop judging by mere appearances, and make a right judgment."

You Can't Judge A Book By Its Cover

You could almost see the fireworks between Jesus and the people. He certainly wasn't going to win friends and influence people the way today's politicians do.

Naturally, the people denied they were going to kill him. Accusing him of being possessed by a demon was a classic sidestep of the issue. Jesus wouldn't let them get away with it, though. He brought them back to the real issue of their false judgment. How could they accuse him of breaking the Sabbath law by healing a man when they **circumcised** infants (see GWGN, pages 143–144) on the Sabbath? What hypocrites!

circumcised: performed a rite of Jewish identity by removing the foreskin

F. F. Bruce: Jesus argues that if the sabbath law may rightly be suspended for the removal of a small piece of tissue from one part of the body, it cannot be wrong to heal a man's whole body on the sabbath day. This type of argument, in fact was used by some rabbis to justify medical treatment in a case of urgency on the sabbath, but Jesus uses it to justify an act of healing whether the case is urgent or not.[5]

As Jesus pointed out, a doctorate in theology or Bible does not guarantee a right relationship with God or even accurate knowledge about him. God isn't looking for academic credentials. Rather, he wants people with right heart attitudes, people who realize they need him and aren't too proud to confess that.

Something to Ponder

How To Spot False Teachers

- Their words don't match what the Bible teaches.
- They focus on themselves, not God.
- They want the glory instead of giving it to God.
- They don't point people to Jesus.
- They don't challenge people to live out the commands and principles of Scripture.
- They rarely talk about sin and the need for repentance.

Remember This . . .

> **John 7:25–27** At that point some of the people of Jerusalem began to ask, "Isn't this the man they are trying to kill? Here he is, speaking publicly, and they are not saying a word to him. Have the authorities really concluded that he is the Christ? But we know where this man is from; when the Christ comes, no one will know where he is from."

We Know This Man

Finally, the people realized that the man called Jesus was the center of all this controversy. They didn't think he could possibly be the **Christ**, the Messiah, since they knew where he came from. He was the son of Joseph and Mary who grew up in Nazareth, wasn't he? However, they claimed no one would know where Messiah comes from. That was a lie—or at least a lack of scriptural knowl-

Christ: anointed one

edge. After all, one of their prophets predicted the Messiah would be born in Bethlehem (see appendix A): *"But you, Bethlehem Ephrathah, though you are small among the clans of Judah, out of you will come for me one who will be ruler over Israel, whose origins are from of old, from ancient times"* (Micah 5:2). (For more about how the Messiah came to be born in Bethlehem, see GWLC, pages 21–22.)

> **John 7:28–29** Then Jesus, still teaching in the temple courts, cried out, "Yes, you know me, and you know where I am from. I am not here on my own, but he who sent me is true. You do not know him, but I know him because I am from him and he sent me."

Half Right/Half Wrong

As usual, Jesus didn't mince words. He told the people they were only half right. Sure, they knew where he came from physically. But he wasn't interested in focusing on his life history. Instead, Jesus returned again to the main issue: They didn't know God.

THE GREAT MYSTERY

> **John 7:30–32** At this they tried to seize him, but no one laid a hand on him, because his time had not yet come. Still, many in the crowd put their faith in him. They said, "When the Christ comes, will he do more miraculous signs than this man?"
>
> The Pharisees heard the crowd whispering such things about him. Then the chief priests and the Pharisees sent temple guards to arrest him.

Taking On The Jesus Movement

Jesus certainly wasn't Mr. Popularity. Telling this crowd of religious people that they didn't know God was an invitation to opposition. And the opposition from those who didn't believe in him came. They tried to grab him, and the Pharisees sent guards to arrest him, but all these attempts failed because it wasn't his time to die.

Not everyone opposed him, however. Many people put their faith in him, believing he was the Messiah because of the miracles he did.

THE FAITH FACTOR—Like the religious leaders demonstrated, sometimes too much studying gets in the way of believing who Jesus is and that God sent him to earth. He wants us to put our faith in him based on the facts of Scripture.

There is no middle ground with Jesus. Sooner or later, everyone has to take a side—believe in him or not believe in him. Have eternal life or eternal death. Be for him or against him. Which side are you on?

Something to Ponder

> **John 7:33–36** Jesus said, "I am with you for only a short time, and then I go to the one who sent me. You will look for me, but you will not find me; and where I am, you cannot come."
>
> The Jews said to one another, "Where does this man intend to go that we cannot find him? Will he go where our people live scattered among the **Greeks**, and teach the Greeks? What did he mean when he said, 'You will look for me, but you will not find me,' and 'Where I am, you cannot come'?"

Greeks: all non-Jews, Gentiles

The Last Word

Jesus got in the last word. He told the crowd that he wouldn't always be with them. Soon he would go back to God, and they wouldn't be able to find him. In their denseness, they didn't understand what he said. They thought Jesus meant he was planning a trip into gentile territory, since they didn't understand his true relationship with God.

THE GREAT THIRST QUENCHER

> **John 7:37–39** On the last and greatest day of the Feast, Jesus stood and said in a loud voice, "If anyone is thirsty, let him come to me and drink. Whoever believes in

me, as the Scripture has said, streams of living water will flow from within him." By this he meant the Spirit, whom those who believed in him were later to receive. Up to that time the Spirit had not been given, since Jesus had not yet been glorified.

Flow Of The Spirit

During the last day of the celebration, Jesus got up and shouted that he was the source of a steady stream of living <u>water</u> that would quench their spiritual thirst. In doing so, he gave new meaning to the celebration, pointing to the Holy Spirit who was yet to come. Just as water quenches our physical thirst, so the Spirit satisfies people's inner thirst for God. Water also causes seeds and cuttings to grow and produce fruit. So, too, the Spirit produces <u>spiritual fruit</u> in our lives—like love, joy, and peace.

Jesus also announced that his coming was the beginning of God's promised **kingdom**, a time of forgiveness and right relationships with the Father.

☞ **GO TO:**

Isaiah 44:3 (water)

Galatians 5:22–23 (spiritual fruit)

kingdom: God's rule on earth

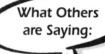
What Others are Saying:

Mitch and Zhava Glaser: Jesus invited the whole congregation of Israel to come and drink of living water, just as He had previously extended a similar invitation to the woman at the well. . . . To come to Jesus and drink is to believe in Him as the Savior and source of eternal life. The bubbling inner spring and the thundering flow of living water are references to the Holy Spirit and His ministry of indwelling all who believe.[6]

CULTURE CLUE

On the first day of the Feast of Tabernacles, a priest read Zechariah 14:8: *"On that day living water will flow out from Jerusalem."* For seven days, the priests led a procession from the Pool of Siloam through the Water Gate to the Temple. One priest carried water from the pool in a golden pitcher. Once there, they circled the altar, and the priest with the pitcher poured the water in a basin at the side of the altar. This water offering by the priests helped the Israelites remember how God had <u>provided water</u> to their ancestors during their desert wanderings. The people waved palm branches and sang psalms. On the seventh day, they circled the altar seven times. This ceremony was more than a time of praying for rain so they would have good crops; it also illustrated the prediction in Zechariah 14 and Ezekiel 47 of living water flowing from the Temple.

☞ **GO TO:**

Exodus 17:1–6 (provided water)

THE GREAT DIVIDE

> **John 7:40–44** On hearing his words, some of the people said, "Surely this man is the Prophet."
>
> Others said, "He is the Christ."
>
> Still others asked, "How can the Christ come from Galilee? Does not the Scripture say that the Christ will come from David's family and from Bethlehem, the town where David lived?" Thus the people were divided because of Jesus. Some wanted to seize him, but no one laid a hand on him.

KEY POINT

The people were divided about who Jesus was after hearing him teach at the Feast of Tabernacles.

So, Who *Is* This Man?

Jesus had a real knack for dividing people. Some thought he was the **Prophet**. Some thought he was the Messiah, while others said he couldn't possibly be. They argued over where the Messiah would come from. Jesus obviously didn't qualify, the people thought, since he came from Nazareth in Galilee. (Although Jesus had grown up there, he was born in Bethlehem, as the Scriptures predicted.) Some people wanted to grab him, but no one did.

Prophet: the one Moses predicted would come

☞ **GO TO:**

Luke 2:4–7 (born in Bethlehem)

> **John 7:45–49** Finally the temple guards went back to the chief priests and Pharisees, who asked them, "Why didn't you bring him in?"
>
> "No one ever spoke the way this man does," the guards declared.
>
> "You mean he has deceived you also?" the Pharisees retorted. "Has any of the rulers or of the Pharisees believed in him? No! But this mob that knows nothing of the law—there is a curse on them."

Thinking In Circles

The guards left Jesus alone, then had to endure the wrath of the Pharisees who sent them to make the arrest. The guards were smart enough to know that publicly arresting Jesus would probably start a riot and bring out the Roman army.

The authorities' reluctance to squash Jesus' ministry caused even more doubt in the minds of the common people. On the one hand, if Jesus really was the troublemaker that the Pharisees said he was, why didn't they just arrest him? On the other hand, since the religious leaders seemed divided in their opinions of Jesus, then maybe Jesus was who he said he was. Maybe Jesus deserved a closer look.

The Pharisees' thinking about Jesus was circular and close-minded. Since none of them believed Jesus was the Messiah, then he couldn't be. Case closed. If any of these people in the crowd wanted to believe, it was because they didn't know the law. They were obviously too ignorant to make the right decision.

> **John 7:50–53** Nicodemus, who had gone to Jesus earlier and who was one of their own number, asked, "Does our law condemn anyone without first hearing him to find out what he is doing?"
>
> They replied, "Are you from Galilee, too? Look into it, and you will find that a prophet does not come out of Galilee."
>
> Then each went to his own home.

Nicodemus Speaks Up

☞ **GO TO:**

John 3:1–21
(Nicodemus)

<u>Nicodemus</u> stood up for Jesus before his fellow Pharisees. According to Deuteronomy 1:16, an accused person gets a hearing before being judged. These teachers of the law were ignoring the law. Nicodemus raised the question of a legal technicality, no doubt hoping the other Pharisees would say, "Oh, you're right. We forgot about that. Well, we'll have to give the man a fair hearing." For Nicodemus to risk his reputation to speak out for Jesus is a good indication that he was a secret believer in Jesus.

The Pharisees rejected Nicodemus out of hand and ridiculed him. To be called a Galilean was like being called stupid. And in the Pharisees' minds, only dumb Galileans believed this "idiot" from Galilee.

Without reaching a final decision about Jesus, they all went home.

What Others are Saying:

Merrill C. Tenney: The reappearance of Nicodemus is difficult to explain unless he afterward became a believer, and reported this story himself. The discussion among the Pharisees must have taken place in private, especially since a scheme to arrest or kill Jesus was being considered. It is hardly conceivable that the Pharisees would have planned the matter openly when Jesus had a large number of sympathizers. Only one on the inside would report this, and he was the only insider who would do it.[7]

Study Questions

1. What problem did Jesus have with his brothers? Why?
2. Who did people think Jesus was?
3. Why were the Jewish people so divided on who Jesus was?
4. How can we know that Jesus' teaching is true?
5. What is significant about Jesus' speech on the last day of Tabernacles?
6. Why did Nicodemus stand up for Jesus before the Pharisees?

CHAPTER WRAP-UP

- Jesus' brothers, who didn't believe in him, tried to get him to show himself publicly at the Feast of Tabernacles. But he didn't go until the time was right according to God's timetable. (John 7:1–13)

- Jesus claimed his teaching was from God and challenged the leaders' claims that they were following the law when they accused him of breaking it. (John 7:14–29)

- As the people divided over Jesus' teaching, he told them he would be going back to God. (John 7:30–36)

- Jesus offered living water to spiritually thirsty people when they believe in him. (John 7:37–39)

- Jesus' teaching divided the people. Some believed; others wanted to kill him. (John 7:40–53)

JOHN 8: JESUS THE FREEDOM GIVER

CHAPTER HIGHLIGHTS

- Woman Caught in Adultery
- Light in the Darkness
- Free at Last

Let's Get Started

Freedom. We all want it. But it has different meanings for different people.

To a child, freedom is being grown up and not having to obey parents and teachers.

To a teen, freedom is having a driver's license and a car.

To a mother, freedom is an afternoon or evening with a babysitter to watch the kids.

To a businessperson, freedom is a weekend with no work.

To a teacher, freedom is summer vacation with no classes.

To a person in jail, freedom is parole or the end of the sentence pronounced by a judge.

In this chapter, we learn that freedom runs deeper than a change in circumstances or location. A woman caught in adultery and brought to Jesus learns that freedom is forgiveness of her sin—instead of being stoned for it. Later Jesus taught that freedom begins with a relationship with him. As a result, we'll know the truth that will set us free spiritually.

WOMAN CAUGHT IN ADULTERY

> **John 8:1–2** But Jesus went to the Mount of Olives. At dawn he appeared again in the temple courts, where all the people gathered around him, and he sat down to teach them.

An Early-Morning Class

One thing about Jesus—he never missed an opportunity to teach. He was up and at 'em early. When people gathered to listen, he always had something to say. This day was no exception.

Warren W. Wiersbe: John 7:53–8:11 is not found in some of the ancient manuscripts; where it is found, it is not always in this location in John's Gospel. Most scholars seem to agree that the passage is a part of inspired Scripture ("a fragment of authentic Gospel material," says Dr. F. F. Bruce) regardless of where it is placed.[1]

> **John 8:3–5** The teachers of the law and the Pharisees brought in a woman caught in adultery. They made her stand before the group and said to Jesus, "Teacher, this woman was caught in the act of adultery. In the Law Moses commanded us to stone such women. Now what do you say?"

Almost A Perfect Trap

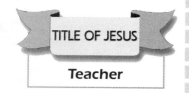

TITLE OF JESUS

Teacher

Imagine being the center of attention, teaching important stuff about God to people who are actually interested in what you have to say. Class is going along well when suddenly a group of religious leaders crash the group, dragging a woman with them. And not just any woman. They had caught her in bed with a man who wasn't her husband.

Their interruption raises some interesting questions. How did they know where to find someone who was committing adultery? (Normally, Pharisees wouldn't have much contact with a common woman like her.) How were they able to catch her in the act of having sex? (The context implies that witnesses had seen that act.) Why didn't they bring the man too? (He was just as guilty as the woman.) Smells like a setup, doesn't it?

These were men with a mission. According to the law, stoning to death was the punishment for both parties for sleeping with someone else's spouse. There was no way Jesus could wriggle out of this dilemma. If he said to let her go, he'd be disobeying God's Word and would lose his credibility as a teacher. If he agreed to stone her, the religious leaders would accuse him of having none of the **mercy** or love he taught about.

☞ **GO TO:**

Leviticus 20:10 (stoning to death)

mercy: *not getting what we deserve*

> **John 8:6–8** They were using this question as a trap, in order to have a basis for accusing him.
>
> But Jesus bent down and started to write on the ground with his finger. When they kept on questioning him, he straightened up and said to them, "If any one of you is without sin, let him be the first to throw a stone at her." Again he stooped down and wrote on the ground.

Words In The Dirt

Those religious leaders had Jesus trapped. No matter which choice he took, he gave them ammunition to use against him. So Jesus chose option C; he ignored them. (He's hard to keep in a box!) No doubt about it—being ignored takes all the fun out of an execution. But these men weren't going to give up easily. *They kept on questioning him,* no doubt hoping to break down his resistance.

When that didn't work, Jesus went to option D, pointing the finger at the accusers. "If you want to kill her, go ahead," he said. "But be sure the first one to throw a stone at her has never sinned." Whoa! That remark wasn't what those self-righteous men wanted to hear.

What Others are Saying:

Bill Myers: To this day no one's sure what Jesus wrote when He bent down and scribbled on the ground. Some think it was a list of each of the Pharisees' sins.[2]

Craig S. Keener: God wrote the Ten Commandments with his finger (Ex 31:18; Deut 9:10); perhaps Jesus writes the first line of the tenth commandment in the **Septuagint** of Exodus 20: "You shall not covet your neighbor's wife."[3]

Everett F. Harrison: In His own manner, Jesus matched their rudeness with deliberate preoccupation, as He wrote on the ground. He was ignoring them as a rebuke to their harsh spirit. In His method, He contrived to embarrass the intruders, turning the tables on them. Through it all He had in view an educative motive, showing that the touching of the conscience of men was more potent than the debating of the requirements of the Law.[4]

Septuagint: Greek translation of the Hebrew Old Testament

> **John 8:9–11** At this, those who heard began to go away one at a time, the older ones first, until only Jesus was left, with the woman still standing there. Jesus straightened up and asked her, "Woman, where are they? Has no one condemned you?"
>
> "No one, sir," she said.
>
> "Then neither do I condemn you," Jesus declared. "Go now and leave your life of sin."

Caught In Their Own Trap

Naturally none of these men could confess to never having sinned. So they all went home. Jesus had caught them in their own trap. When only the woman was left, Jesus stood up, looked at her, and asked the obvious question: "Where is everybody?" Then Jesus showed her his love by forgiving her instead of **condemning** her. He didn't say she was innocent. Neither did he hammer home her guilt or read her a laundry list of sins. She knew she had sinned against God, and Jesus wanted her to quit making sin a habit.

condemning: saying someone is guilty

What Others are Saying:

Yeshua: *Hebrew for Jesus*

Torah: *first five books of Old Testament*

Conversations with Christ

Remember This . . .

David H. Stern: **Yeshua**'s response showed four things: he was not against the **Torah**, he was merciful toward the woman, he opposed her sin (Exodus 20:13(14)), and he could silence hecklers and put them to shame.[5]

Although Jesus and the adulterous woman did not exchange a lot of words—at least words that are recorded here—this was a significant conversation. She learned that no one is perfect except Jesus, and therefore we do not have the right to condemn others for their sin. Jesus offers forgiveness, not condemnation, when we bring that sin to him. Although we don't have a record of the woman after this event, I doubt she slept with someone else's husband again.

No matter what you've done wrong—even if the legal penalty is death—Jesus wants to forgive you. There is no sin that's so bad he can't forgive it, as he demonstrated with the woman caught in adultery.

LIGHT IN THE DARKNESS

> **John 8:12** When Jesus spoke again to the people, he said, "I am the light of the world. Whoever follows me will never walk in darkness, but will have the light of life."

A Shining Light

Intermission's over. The short drama with the woman caught in adultery had a happy ending. Now John picks up the dialogue from 7:52 between Jesus and the Jewish leaders during the Feast of Tabernacles.

Jesus uttered this bold statement of being *"the light of the world"* against the backdrop of the light in the Temple and the court around it. That short sentence set off fireworks as Jesus' use of *"I am"* made it clear that he is God. The Jewish people understood that light stood for God's holiness. As if that wasn't enough, Jesus claimed to be light for all people, not just Jews. As the light that pierces darkness, Jesus shed light on God, showing people what he is like and what he does. Jesus' presence and teachings also shed light on the darkness of people's sin and separation from God. So people who follow Jesus don't walk blindly in sin anymore. Instead, they can see their sin and need for forgiveness.

In the Temple, a menorah, or golden candlestick (see illustration, page 108), burned constantly. During the Feast of Tabernacles, four huge menorahs lit up the outside court at night while men danced and sang praises to God. This light commemorated the pillar of fire that led the Israelites when they wandered in the wilderness in Moses' day. At the end of the celebration each night—or rather, early morning—two priests faced the Temple and proclaimed, "Our fathers who were in this place turned their backs to the Temple of God and their faces eastward and threw themselves down eastward before the sun, but we direct our eyes to Yahweh." It was in this context that Jesus declared, *"I am the light of the world."*

KEY POINT

Jesus gave freedom to the woman caught in adultery and claimed to be God by using the Father's name, I am.

☞ GO TO:

Isaiah 42:6 (light of the world)

Psalm 27:1; 36:9 (light)

Isaiah 49:6 (all people)

CULTURE CLUE

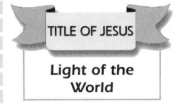

TITLE OF JESUS

Light of the World

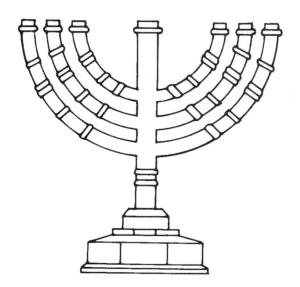

> **John 8:13–18** The Pharisees challenged him, "Here you are, appearing as your own witness; your testimony is not valid."
>
> Jesus answered, "Even if I testify on my own behalf, my testimony is valid, for I know where I came from and where I am going. But you have no idea where I come from or where I am going. You judge by human standards; I pass judgment on no one. But if I do judge, my decisions are right, because I am not alone. I stand with the Father, who sent me. In your own Law it is written that the testimony of two men is valid. I am one who testifies for myself; my other witness is the Father, who sent me."

Time For Testimony

Instead of seeing Jesus' light, the Pharisees saw red. They understood what he was saying, but they didn't want to believe it. So they challenged him with the law: For a valid testimony, two witnesses are needed.

Jesus didn't disagree. He pointed out that his testimony was true even without a second witness because he knew where he came from (eternity past with God) and where he was going (back to God). These leaders were judging him by their own standards as though he were another man. If they really needed a second witness, he had one—God the Father.

☞ **GO TO:**

Deuteronomy 19:15 (two witnesses)

> **John 8:19–20** Then they asked him, "Where is your father?"
>
> "You do not know me or my Father," Jesus replied. "If you knew me, you would know my Father also." He spoke these words while teaching in the temple area near the place where the offerings were put. Yet no one seized him, because his time had not yet come.

The Great Unknown

Since Jesus said he had a second witness, the leaders asked him to produce this mystery man. They couldn't get out of their literal rut, refusing to consider that Jesus' Father was God. Obviously, they didn't know either Jesus or the Father.

This discussion took place out in the open in the Court of Women (see illustration, page 28) outside the temple building near the offering boxes. These were thirteen trumpet-shaped collection boxes, inscribed with the use for money deposited in them. Seven were for the temple tax and six for offerings. The leaders could easily have grabbed Jesus there, but it wasn't time yet for his arrest.

Dana Gould: Jesus' assertion that if people knew Him, they would know His Father is one of the most striking in all the New Testament. He was speaking to some of the most educated, most religious people who have ever lived. They were confident they knew God and understood His ways. But their rejection of Jesus shows they didn't know God. They knew only their own ideas about God.[6]

> **What Others are Saying:**

> **John 8:21–24** Once more Jesus said to them, "I am going away, and you will look for me, and you will die in your sin. Where I go, you cannot come."
>
> This made the Jews ask, "Will he kill himself? Is that why he says, 'Where I go, you cannot come'?"
>
> But he continued, "You are from below; I am from above. You are of this world; I am not of this world. I told you that you would die in your sins; if you do not believe that I am the one I claim to be, you will indeed die in your sins."

Too Much Thinking Inside The Box

If these religious leaders weren't going to believe in Jesus while he was there with them, they had no chance for salvation from their sins. As usual, they didn't have a clue as to what he was talking about. They thought he was going to commit suicide.

Instead of trying to correct their misinterpretation, Jesus told them why they didn't get it. They were tied to the earth with no understanding of spiritual truths; he was from heaven with a perspective outside their closed box of thinking.

THE FAITH FACTOR—Not believing in Jesus equals spiritual death. It's only when we place our faith in him as Savior from our sin that we gain spiritual life.

> **John 8:25–26** "Who are you?" they asked.
>
> "Just what I have been claiming all along," Jesus replied. "I have much to say in judgment of you. But he who sent me is reliable, and what I have heard from him I tell the world."

Maximum Density

This conversation was way over the heads of these leaders. They were dense to the max! Their direct approach—"Who are you?"—didn't get an answer they wanted. Jesus insisted he was exactly who he had said he was. Instead of continuing this fruitless discussion, Jesus took the high road and didn't say any more that would condemn them. Instead, he would speak what God told him to tell the world (not just the Jewish people).

TITLE OF JESUS

Son of Man

> **John 8:27–30** They did not understand that he was telling them about his Father. So Jesus said, "When you have lifted up the Son of Man, then you will know that I am the one I claim to be and that I do nothing on my own but speak just what the Father has taught me. The one who sent me is with me; he has not left me alone, for I always do what pleases him." Even as he spoke, many put their faith in him.

The Ultimate Proof

The Pharisees still didn't understand what Jesus told them about his relationship with God the Father. So Jesus mentioned the ultimate proof: his resurrection after crucifixion. When that happened, they would know for sure that he was telling the truth and that he wasn't operating alone. Note that some of that hardhearted, dense group finally believed in him.

FREE AT LAST

> **John 8:31–33** To the Jews who had believed him, Jesus said, "If you hold to my teaching, you are really my disciples. Then you will know the truth, and the truth will set you free."
>
> They answered him, "We are Abraham's descendants and have never been slaves of anyone. How can you say that we shall be set free?"

Offended On The Defensive

Turning his attention to those who believed, Jesus urged them to continue in his teaching. As a result, they'd learn God's truth (Jesus himself as well as God's words), which would set them free from slavery to sin.

The Jewish leaders in the crowd took offense at Jesus' words. The very idea of telling them they needed to be set free was ridiculous! They weren't slaves. Never had been.

What they conveniently forgot, however, was that their ancestors had been slaves in Egypt and later were taken into captivity by a couple of other countries. Furthermore, they currently lived under Roman rule.

Dana Gould: *Hold to* is a verb that means to "abide," "continue." Here it is used of holding to Jesus' teachings. Literally, "my teaching" is "my word." This is an active, not a passive, activity. To "hold to" the word means not only knowing the truth, but *living* it.[7]

Charles U. Wagner: Abraham had never been a slave to any man, and because he was declared righteous by God, the Jews knew that He was not enslaved by sin. Since Abraham's descendants had been God's Chosen People from the beginning, how could anyone suggest that they needed to be made free? These

What Others are Saying:

people thought their family background and national heritage were enough to make them acceptable to God.[8]

> **John 8:34–38** Jesus replied, "I tell you the truth, everyone who sins is a slave to sin. Now a slave has no permanent place in the family, but a son belongs to it forever. So if the Son sets you free, you will be free indeed. I know you are Abraham's descendants. Yet you are ready to kill me, because you have no room for my word. I am telling you what I have seen in the Father's presence, and you do what you have heard from your father."

Wrong Father, Wrong Family

So much for just the Pharisees squirming under Jesus' teaching. Jesus made everybody uncomfortable when he said, *"Everyone who sins is a <u>slave to sin</u>."* (He doesn't play favorites.) While sin can be fun, it eventually controls us. We all know what it's like to want to do something right but instead to do what we know is wrong. We don't have to let sin pull us down, however. Jesus can break the choke hold it puts on us and make us part of his family forever. Even though the Jews believed their family line from Abraham guaranteed them a place in God's family, they were wrong. The fact that they wanted to kill Jesus proved they had a different father—the devil.

☞ **GO TO:**

Romans 6:14–23 (slave to sin)

Remember This . . .

Real freedom isn't being able to do what we want when we want. (Remember as a child knowing you'd have that kind of freedom when you grew up—and later discovering it doesn't exist even in adulthood?) Real freedom is getting out of the darkness of sin into the light of a relationship with Jesus.

> **John 8:39–41** "Abraham is our father," they answered.
> "If you were Abraham's children," said Jesus, "then you would do the things Abraham did. As it is, you are determined to kill me, a man who has told you the truth that I heard from God. Abraham did not do such things. You are doing the things your own father does."
> "We are not illegitimate children," they protested. "The only Father we have is God himself."

Thinking In A Rut

No matter what Jesus said, the Jewish people couldn't get past their ingrained belief that they were fine because they were Abraham's children. Their actions proved them wrong, and Jesus said so. Changing their tactic a bit, they claimed God as their only father.

Jesus' arguments hinge on the principle that one's relationship with Abraham is dependent not on physical descent but on having a personal faith in God that is modeled on Abraham's faith. Jesus pointed out that relationship with God is indicated by belief in him. Abraham foresaw Christ's coming and believed in him, for Jesus is the I Am who spoke to Abraham in the first place.

The hatred that the religious elite showed toward Jesus mirrored the reaction of Satan to God, not the response of Abraham.

> The Jews relied on their own efforts to keep the law and on the merits of Abraham to guarantee their salvation. Jewish theology held that, by obeying God's call, Abraham had **accrued** enough merit to cover the deficiencies of all his descendants throughout history. Thus to claim Abraham as father was to claim a special relationship with God that was guaranteed by physical descent from that patriarch.

CULTURE CLUE

accrued: *accumulated*

James Montgomery Boice: Jesus taught this truth in a **parable** once, pointing out that good fruit does not come from a bad tree. It takes a good tree to produce it. Similarly, bad fruit does not come from a good tree. A bad tree creates it. In the same way, you can come to know the true nature of your spiritual family tree by the fruit found on it. What is the fruit in your life? How about your speech? How about your actions?"

What Others are Saying:

☞ **GO TO:**

Luke 6:43–45 (parable)

parable: *a story that teaches spiritual truth through familiar events or objects*

> **John 8:42–44** Jesus said to them, "If God were your Father, you would love me, for I came from God and now am here. I have not come on my own; but he sent me. Why is my language not clear to you? Because you are unable to hear what I say. You belong to your father, the devil, and you want to carry out your father's desire. He was a murderer from the beginning, not holding to the truth, for there is no truth in him. When he lies, he speaks his native language, for he is a liar and the father of lies."

The Devil's Children

For anyone who thinks Jesus is Caspar Milquetoast, this encounter with the Jewish people blows away that image. He didn't mince words. If they really were God's children, they would love Jesus, not try to kill him. Their actions make it clear that they are of the family line of Satan rather than the family line of Abraham. It wasn't a matter of not understanding his words; it was a matter of the heart and will. Their hearts belonged to the devil, who is a murderer and a <u>liar</u>.

☞ **GO TO:**

Genesis 3:4 (liar)

> **John 8:45–47** "Yet because I tell the truth, you do not believe me! Can any of you prove me guilty of sin? If I am telling the truth, why don't you believe me? He who belongs to God hears what God says. The reason you do not hear is that you do not belong to God."

Deaf Ears

Unlike the devil, Jesus spoke the truth. But the people didn't believe him, nor could they point out any sin in his life. They were deaf to the truth because their hearts were hard and they were not God's children.

Something to Ponder

It's easy for God and his Word to get drowned out by the noise around us, by our busy schedules, by our selfishness, and by what we read, watch, and listen to. If you really want to hear God, find a quiet place without distractions, read the Bible with an open mind and heart, listen to what he says, then obey him.

> **John 8:48–51** The Jews answered him, "Aren't we right in saying that you are a Samaritan and demon-possessed?"
>
> "I am not possessed by a demon," said Jesus, "but I honor my Father and you dishonor me. I am not seeking glory for myself; but there is one who seeks it, and he is the judge. I tell you the truth, if anyone keeps my word, he will never see death."

Watch Where You're Looking

Having run out of arguments, the leaders resorted to name-calling like children. They used the two worst insults they could think of—Samaritan and demon-possessed—likely in reaction to what Jesus had just said about them. In spite of what they thought and said about him, Jesus honored God. He wasn't seeking glory for himself; he was seeking to introduce people to the Father so they wouldn't spend eternity in hell.

When you have a choice to make, do you think about how the options will affect you and make you look good—or bad? Or do you consider how your actions will put God in the limelight? Jesus always chose the second option, seeking to bring glory to God the Father, not himself.

Something to Ponder

> **John 8:52–56** At this the Jews exclaimed, "Now we know that you are demon-possessed! Abraham died and so did the prophets, yet you say that if anyone keeps your word, he will never taste death. Are you greater than our father Abraham? He died, and so did the prophets. Who do you think you are?"
>
> Jesus replied, "If I glorify myself, my glory means nothing. My Father, whom you claim as your God, is the one who glorifies me. Though you do not know him, I know him. If I said I did not, I would be a liar like you, but I do know him and keep his word. Your father Abraham rejoiced at the thought of seeing my day; he saw it and was glad."

He Must Be A Madman

These Jews thought Jesus was crazy, claiming to be better than men of God like Abraham and the Old Testament prophets. They all died. Nobody could prevent death; it was inevitable.

The Jewish leaders stuck to their conviction that they were God's children by descent from Abraham. Likewise, Jesus never wavered in pointing them back to his relationship with God. God is the one who sent him and shows people his **glory**. Their physical ancestor Abraham saw the time when Jesus would be there on earth.

glory: *unique, divine nature*

☞ **GO TO:**

Exodus 3:14 (I am)

> **John 8:57–59** "You are not yet fifty years old," the Jews said to him, "and you have seen Abraham!"
>
> "I tell you the truth," Jesus answered, "before Abraham was born, I am!" At this, they picked up stones to stone him, but Jesus hid himself, slipping away from the temple grounds.

A Young Old Man

Abraham lived two thousand years before, and Jesus was only in his mid thirties. How could Abraham have seen someone who wouldn't be born for a couple of millennia? All this talk was enough to drive anyone mad. But what Jesus meant was that he didn't have a beginning; he existed before Abraham.

The people understood exactly what Jesus was saying—that he is God. Consequently, they tried to stone Jesus for blasphemy. But Jesus was able to hide in the crowd and escape.

What Others are Saying:

George R. Beasley-Murray: "Not yet fifty years" is not intended to suggest that Jesus was almost that age. . . . It simply indicates the common view of the end of a man's working life (see Num 4:2–3, 39; 8:24–25); Jesus has not yet reached seniority, and he claims to have seen Abraham![10]

Matthew Henry: Dr. Lightfoot will tell you how they came to have stones so readily in the temple; they had workmen at this time repairing the temple, or making some additions, and the pieces of stone which they hewed off served for this purpose.[11]

Study Questions

1. Why did the religious leaders bring the adulterous woman to Jesus?
2. How did Jesus' attitude toward her differ from theirs?
3. What did Jesus mean when he said he is the *"light of the world"*?
4. What witnesses did Jesus offer to prove his words were true?
5. What does knowing the truth do for us?
6. Why did Jesus say the religious leaders weren't Abraham's children?
7. Who did he say their father was?
8. Why did the Jews try to stone Jesus?

- When the religious leaders brought a woman caught in adultery to Jesus, he forgave her sins instead of punishing her. (John 8:1–11)

- Jesus is the Light of the World who shows people their sins and what God is like. (John 8:12–20)

- People who don't believe in Jesus will die in their sins instead of gaining eternal life. (John 8:21–30)

- Freedom from slavery to sin comes from knowing Jesus and the truth of God's Word. (John 8:31–47)

- When Jesus claimed deity by saying he existed before Abraham, the religious leaders tried to stone him. (John 8:48–59)

JOHN 9: JESUS THE SIGHT GIVER

CHAPTER HIGHLIGHTS

- Sight for the Blind
- Seeing Men Go Blind
- Seeing the Messiah

Let's Get Started

When was the last time you noticed the fiery reds and oranges of a sunrise? Layers of blue in the sky? Shades of pink in a flower bed? Constellations in the night sky? Our world is full of color, yet too often we don't see it.

A man born blind in Jesus' day spent most of his life without being able to see colors or anything else. But when Jesus saw him and gave him sight, his world changed—in more than one way. He met the Messiah and stirred up even more controversy between the Jewish religious leaders and Jesus.

SIGHT FOR THE BLIND

> **John 9:1–2** As he went along, he saw a man blind from birth. His disciples asked him, "Rabbi, who sinned, this man or his parents, that he was born blind?"

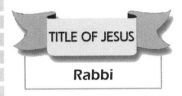

TITLE OF JESUS

Rabbi

Whose Fault Is It?

He had never seen his parents' faces, nor his own in a reflection. He had never seen the beauty of a sunset, the red of a rose, the twinkling of stars, the greenness of grass. But when Jesus and his disciples met him, the disciples weren't concerned about helping this man. They were only curious about why he was blind, assuming his disability was punishment for someone's sin.

GO TO:

Exodus 34:7
(parent's sin)

Since blind people could support themselves only by begging, they tended to hang out around the Temple. That was the best location because a lot of people would pass by them and because people would be more charitable when they came to worship.

According to Jewish teachers, a lot of suffering and physical deformities, like blindness and deafness, were caused by sin. Even a <u>parent's sin</u> could be passed on to a child in the form of suffering or sickness.

What Others are Saying:

Roger L. Fredrikson: We humans persist in wanting to know who to blame. We discuss the matter endlessly, sometimes earnestly, but often foolishly. However, Jesus brushes this question aside. He does not focus on the past, nor is He interested in answering theological speculation, for He sets the needs of this man in the context of what God can do.[1]

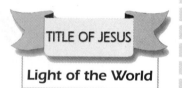

Something to Ponder

Jesus' disciples had probably seen so many blind beggars that they were calloused to that man's situation. It's easy for us to have the same attitude today toward people who are sick, out of work, or homeless. Instead of viewing them with curiosity, ask God to show you ways to help them.

TITLE OF JESUS

Light of the World

> **John 9:3–5** "Neither this man nor his parents sinned," said Jesus, "but this happened so that the work of God might be displayed in his life. As long as it is day, we must do the work of him who sent me. Night is coming, when no one can work. While I am in the world, I am the light of the world."

God On Display

The disciples were only concerned about the cause of the man's blindness. Jesus was concerned about the purpose for it. (He usually was on a different wavelength than other people.) According to Jesus, God allowed the blindness (he didn't deliberately inflict it) so Jesus could demonstrate his power in healing him. Jesus wasn't a grandstander, but he liked to put God's power on display. There wasn't a lot of time to do that. His time on earth was short, so there was an urgency to what he could do before his death.

Matthew Henry: The consideration of our death approaching should **quicken** us to improve all the opportunities of life, both for doing and getting good.[2]

What Others are Saying:

quicken: hurry

> **John 9:6–7** Having said this, he spit on the ground, made some mud with the saliva, and put it on the man's eyes. "Go," he told him, "wash in the Pool of Siloam" (this word means Sent). So the man went and washed, and came home seeing.

A Real Eye-Opener

Often Jesus used unconventional means to produce supernatural results. If a doctor today tried to restore sight with mud pies made with his saliva, he'd be laughed out of medicine—or sued for malpractice. But Jesus got away with it. The blind man must have been quite a sight, walking across town with mud pies on his eyes. He probably felt foolish. Certainly people would have stared at him, and he could have felt their stares even though he couldn't see them. Maybe he debated with himself about whether washing away the mud would work. Nevertheless, he went to the pool. That took a lot of faith! It also gave him his sight.

What Others are Saying:

Lawrence O. Richards: Jesus usually healed simply by speaking the word. Here He told the blind man to "go" and did not even promise healing. The blind man however did set out to do as Jesus said. And in obeying he gained his sight.

The incident is an illustration of the truth Christ expressed to His disciples in John 8:31–32. We come to know the truth by putting Jesus' words into practice. We who are blind and cannot see spiritual reality not only come to see reality, but we experience it as well.[3]

Anne Graham Lotz: It's another miracle that he ever even arrived home; each moment of discovery must have been distracting as well as thrilling! Surely the stupendous excitement that was welling up in his chest and spilling out in every pore of his being propelled him to seek out those who knew him that they might share in his incredible joy! But if he was expecting a neighborhood celebration, he was in for a rude awakening! Instead, he encountered hostile, **incredulous** interrogation.[4]

incredulous: skeptical, questioning

CULTURE CLUE

In ancient days, people thought spit had the power to heal. Since it was linked to magical arts, Jewish people were suspicious of it. If this man knew what Jesus used to make the mud he put on his eyes, he would have been very uncomfortable, not to mention grossed out.

Something to Ponder

This blind man didn't know who Jesus was. Nor did he have any assurance that what Jesus asked would restore his sight. There was always the possibility that he would make a fool of himself. If you had been this blind man, would you have let Jesus put mud on your eyes and then obeyed his command to wash it off in the Pool of Siloam?

Remember This . . .

Even though it may seem hard to believe Jesus' miracles, they were easy for him to perform. After all, he invented the laws of nature. We serve a powerful God! So don't be afraid to ask for his help, no matter how big your problem seems.

SEEING MEN GO BLIND

> **John 9:8–12** His neighbors and those who had formerly seen him begging asked, "Isn't this the same man who used to sit and beg?" Some claimed that he was.
> Others said, "No, he only looks like him."
> But he himself insisted, "I am the man."
> "How then were your eyes opened?" they demanded.
> He replied, "The man they call Jesus made some mud and put it on my eyes. He told me to go to Siloam and wash. So I went and washed, and then I could see."
> "Where is this man?" they asked him.
> "I don't know," he said.

Talk Of The Town

This healing caused a lot of talk. Some people wondered if the man who could see was the same one who was blind. Some said he was. Others thought he was a look-alike. He cleared up the confusion by insisting he was that man. So then people wanted to know how he could see. He told them the story but couldn't tell them who the healer was.

> **John 9:13–15** They brought to the Pharisees the man who had been blind. Now the day on which Jesus had made the mud and opened the man's eyes was a Sabbath. Therefore the Pharisees also asked him how he had received his sight. "He put mud on my eyes," the man replied, "and I washed, and now I see."

Tell It Again

It was customary to involve the Pharisees, as keepers of the faith, in investigating questionable situations. The fact that Jesus healed the man on the Sabbath made this one worth looking into. So a group of people took the former blind man to the Pharisees for inspection. Once more the man had to tell his story.

> **John 9:16–17** Some of the Pharisees said, "This man is not from God, for he does not keep the Sabbath."
>
> But others asked, "How can a sinner do such miraculous signs?" So they were divided.
>
> Finally they turned again to the blind man, "What have you to say about him? It was your eyes he opened."
>
> The man replied, "He is a prophet."

Blind Man Sees, Seeing Men Don't

As far as the Pharisees were concerned, evidence was irrelevant. They had already made up their minds about Jesus, and they weren't about to let the facts change their opinions. Instead of having the spiritual sight you'd expect from religious leaders, they were the ones who were blind. After discussing the situation and failing to reach a verdict, they asked the former blind man who he thought the healer was. *"A prophet"* was all he could think to call him.

Everett F. Harrison: These leaders could be expected to raise the issue of violation of the Sabbath rest. From the man's report they felt they had ample evidence for their complaint. The only catch was that the work was so humane and so unique. Could a sinner accomplish such a result? No wonder some of the Pharisees shook their heads. They were really perplexed.[5]

What Others are Saying:

Kneading, whether it was dough or clay, was one of the thirty-nine kinds of work that the Pharisees forbade on the Sabbath. So was building, and clay was a building material. Sure, it's a stretch, but those Pharisees were nitpickers.

> **John 9:18–23** The Jews still did not believe that he had been blind and had received his sight until they sent for the man's parents. "Is this your son?" they asked. "Is this the one you say was born blind? How is it that now he can see?"
>
> "We know he is our son," the parents answered, "and we know he was born blind. But how he can see now, or who opened his eyes, we don't know. Ask him. He is of age; he will speak for himself." His parents said this because they were afraid of the Jews, for already the Jews had decided that anyone who acknowledged that Jesus was the Christ would be put out of the synagogue. That was why his parents said, "He is of age; ask him."

When In Doubt, Go To The Parents

Since the Pharisees couldn't agree on the man's situation, they decided to review the case. First, they checked with the man's parents, hoping that he hadn't been born blind. If his blindness was the result of an illness or accident, they could probably come up with an explanation other than a miracle.

The parents were no help. They confirmed that the man had been born blind and now could see. Since they couldn't explain the miracle, they sent the Pharisees back to their son, who could speak for himself. In reality, they were chicken, afraid the religious leaders would kick them out of the **synagogue**.

synagogue: gathering place for religious instruction and prayer

CULTURE CLUE

Being *"put out of the synagogue"* equals excommunication. The whole family would be excluded from the community socially and religiously. Depending on the "crime," this punishment could be temporary or long-term. Sometimes it was accompanied by beatings.

> **John 9:24–25** A second time they summoned the man who had been blind. "Give glory to God," they said. "We know this man is a sinner."
>
> He replied, "Whether he is a sinner or not, I don't know. One thing I do know. I was blind but now I see!"

One More Time

The Pharisees called the former blind man in for more cross-examination. They commanded him to admit the truth and tell them his healer was a sinner. The man hadn't gone to Bible school. He probably was not a great intellect. But he had an experience that no one could deny, and he repeated it—again.

What Others are Saying:

☞ **GO TO:**

Joshua 7:19
(give glory to God)

Gerald L. Borchert: The statement "Give glory to God" is not a praise statement but the equivalent of a Jewish oath, which the authorities employed to call the man to give an honest witness and confess any sinfulness in his testimony. . . . Then they defined the closed parameters in which further investigation was to take place.[6]

> **John 9:26–27** Then they asked him, "What did he do to you? How did he open your eyes?"
> He answered, "I have told you already and you did not listen. Why do you want to hear it again? Do you want to become his disciples, too?"

Give Us An Answer

The man must have been running out of patience. He had already told the Pharisees how he gained his sight. And here they were asking him again. They were worse than children who tune out their parents or teachers. Exasperated, the man asked them if they wanted to become Jesus' followers too. What a joke!

> **John 9:28–29** Then they hurled insults at him and said, "You are this fellow's disciple! We are disciples of Moses! We know that God spoke to Moses, but as for this fellow, we don't even know where he comes from."

We're Moses' Men

Not only did the Pharisees cross-examine the former blind man; they also insulted him when he didn't provide the answers they wanted. They accused him of being a disciple of an unknown man, which makes no sense. But when your mind is made up in spite of the facts, you grasp for anything. Once more the Pharisees trotted out their relationship with Moses, claiming to be his followers, as though that would settle the issue.

> **John 9:30–34** The man answered, "Now that is remarkable! You don't know where he comes from, yet he opened my eyes. We know that God does not listen to sinners. He listens to the godly man who does his will. Nobody has ever heard of opening the eyes of a man born blind. If this man were not from God, he could do nothing."
>
> To this they replied, "You were steeped in sin at birth; how dare you lecture us!" And they threw him out.

A Thinking Man's Relationship

 **GO TO:**

Proverbs 15:29 (listen)

Even this uneducated man figured out that the Pharisees' reasoning was illogical. Tired of being grilled and insulted, he tried teaching them. His logic made sense. The fact that the healer gave him sight proved he was from God. Since God doesn't <u>listen</u> to sinners, Jesus must not be one.

It doesn't take a great mind to put the facts together. But these teachers weren't teachable. They hated being taught by this common man, so they threw him out of the synagogue.

What Others are Saying:

R. V. G. Tasker: By being content with the law that came by Moses and by shutting their eyes to the grace and truth which came by Jesus Christ, the Pharisees are being plunged into the darkness of unbelief as surely as the once-blind beggar is waking more and more towards the illumination of faith.[7]

SEEING THE MESSIAH

TITLE OF JESUS

Son of Man

> **John 9:35–38** Jesus heard that they had thrown him out, and when he found him, he said, "Do you believe in the Son of Man?"
>
> "Who is he, sir?" the man asked. "Tell me so that I may believe in him."
>
> Jesus said, "You have now seen him; in fact, he is the one speaking with you."
>
> Then the man said, "Lord, I believe," and he worshiped him.

20/20 Vision

One thing about Jesus—he doesn't abandon people when they are persecuted. When he heard the Pharisees had thrown the former blind man out of the synagogue, he looked him up. Jesus asked him if he believed in the "*Son of Man*" (one of Jesus' names). When the man wanted to know more, Jesus introduced himself, and the man told him he believed.

What a day this had been for the blind man! He woke up seeing nothing, met Jesus, walked across town with mud pies on his eyes, got his sight, was grilled by the Pharisees, and ended up worshiping Jesus! Yes, it was a great day.

THE FAITH FACTOR—Faith is based on evidence. When the blind man found out who Jesus was, he believed he was the Messiah because of the miracle he had done in giving him sight.

When Jesus hunted up the man who was no longer blind, he introduced himself as the "*Son of Man*"—a term derived from Daniel 7:13 (see GWDN, page 192) that emphasizes the true humanity of the Messiah. It was a short step from being healed to believing in Jesus for this man. He had an irrefutable experience that only God could give him. He responded with worship, the most appropriate action when meeting God.

Conversations with Christ

No matter what trouble you're going through, Jesus will stick with you if you've put your trust in him. You might feel like you're alone, but you're not. He's always there with enough strength and hope to get you through the hard times.

Remember This . . .

> **John 9:39–41** Jesus said, "For judgment I have come into this world, so that the blind will see and those who see will become blind."
>
> Some Pharisees who were with him heard him say this and asked, "What? Are we blind too?"
>
> Jesus said, "If you were blind, you would not be guilty of sin; but now that you claim you can see, your guilt remains."

Blind By Choice

The blind man believed and gained physical and spiritual sight. The Pharisees, who supposedly had spiritual sight, were blind. To this latter group, Jesus preached a short sermon on blindness. Although Jesus came to earth to save people, those who do not believe in him will receive judgment. That judgment is the result of their choices.

In nature, the same sun that causes watered plants to grow also hardens dry clay. In the spiritual realm, Jesus brings salvation to spiritually blind people who see their need of a Savior. At the same time, he blinds religious people who think they know it all but reject him. The Pharisees got the point but wanted Jesus to exempt them. "You're not talking about us, are you?" they asked. They were sure they weren't part of that <u>blind group</u>. But they were. And they weren't willing to admit it, so they'd never see spiritually.

☞ **GO TO:**

Matthew 15:14 (blind group)

What Others are Saying:

Homer A. Kent Jr.: Judgment was not the primary purpose of Christ's coming (3:17), but it was an inevitable result, for men were forced to make a decision either for or against, and this in turn would determine their destiny.[8]

R. Kent Hughes: Through their acquaintance with the Law, the Pharisees believed they were sinners, but they did not understand how deeply infected with sin they were. They adopted the external appearance of having dealt with the sin when, indeed, they had never faced the darkness of their hearts. In their self-satisfaction, they said, "We see," when they were really blind.[9]

Erwin W. Lutzer: Jesus used the blind man to illustrate His purpose for coming into the world. To put it simply, He came to give spiritual sight to those who admit that they are spiritually blind, and He came to confirm the blindness of those who self-righteously think they can see. . . . The self-righteous hate the light, withdrawing to their own secret deeds, more determined than ever that they will not be exposed.[10]

Dig Deeper

Giving sight to the blind without doing surgery should have convinced both the laypeople and the religious leaders that Jesus was God. Read the following verses.

• Exodus 4:11: *"The Lord said to him [Moses], 'Who gave man his mouth? Who makes him deaf or mute? Who gives him sight or makes him blind? Is it not I, the Lord?' "*

- Psalm 146:8: *"The Lord gives sight to the blind."*
- Isaiah 42:6b–7a, a passage spoken to the Messiah: *"I [the Lord] will keep you and will make you to be a covenant for the people and a light for the Gentiles, to open eyes that are blind."*

Study Questions

1. What did Jesus' disciples want to know about the blind man?
2. How did Jesus view the man's blindness?
3. How did Jesus heal the man?
4. How did people react to the man gaining his sight?
5. When the Pharisees questioned the man, how did he respond?
6. What convinced the man that Jesus was from God?
7. Why did Jesus look up the former blind man and introduce himself?
8. How did the man react to knowing who Jesus is?
9. What did Jesus tell the Pharisees about their blindness?

CHAPTER WRAP-UP

- Jesus told his disciples that the man was born blind so Jesus could display God's power in healing him. Then he gave the man sight. (John 9:1–7)

- Some people didn't believe the man who could see was the same one who had been born blind. (John 9:8–12)

- The Pharisees grilled the man and his parents to determine who the healer was. When they didn't like the answers, they threw the man out of the synagogue. (John 9:13–34)

- Jesus looked up the man and introduced himself. As a result, the man believed in him. (John 9:35–38)

- Jesus told the Pharisees that they were spiritually blind and would stay that way unless they believed in him. (John 9:39–41)

JOHN 10: JESUS THE GOOD SHEPHERD

CHAPTER HIGHLIGHTS

- Jesus the Gate
- Jesus the Shepherd
- Jesus the Son

Let's Get Started

Sheep are such stupid animals that they can't fend for themselves. Even when standing within a few feet of grass to eat and water to drink, they can't find either. They need a shepherd to lead them to food and drink.

Sheep are directionally impaired. They get lost easily. When lost, they have no hope of finding their way back. They need a shepherd to look for them and guide them home.

Sheep are helpless, too. They can't defend themselves, so they are easy prey for wild animals. They need a shepherd to protect them.

People are a lot like sheep. We all do stupid things now and then. Some of us get lost just going up or down an escalator. And spiritually we are all lost and defenseless. We need a shepherd. Enter Jesus, the Good Shepherd who does for us what a shepherd does for short, woolly critters. This chapter of John describes Jesus' role as our shepherd.

JESUS THE GATE

> **John 10:1–3** "I tell you the truth, the man who does not enter the sheep pen by the gate, but climbs in by some other way, is a thief and a robber. The man who enters by the gate is the shepherd of his sheep. The watchman opens the gate for him, and the sheep listen to his voice. He calls his own sheep by name and leads them out."

Beware Of Wall Climbers

When John wrote this book, he didn't divide it into chapters and verses. So there was no break between these verses and the ones that end chapter 9. Without missing a beat, Jesus switched topics from blindness to sheep tending as he sought to put the Pharisees in their place. As the religious leaders, they were supposed to shepherd God's people. But they flunked in this department. Instead, they were false shepherds, driving people away from God. To make his point, Jesus used this illustration.

Though shepherds and sheep may be unfamiliar to most of us today, Jesus' audience knew all about them. Sheep were like money in the bank. People raised them to earn a living. When in town, shepherds herded their sheep into pens with a gate (see illustration below). Often there was a community sheepfold that one man guarded while the other shepherds went home to sleep. The guard knew each shepherd and let him in through the gate, but unknown thieves couldn't get in that way. They'd have to climb over the wall and hoist lambs over it—a lot of work to steal some sheep. Since sheep know their shepherd's voice, all the shepherd had to do was call his sheep <u>by name</u> when he entered the pen, and the animals followed him out to the hillside to graze.

☞ **GO TO:**

Exodus 33:12, 17
(by name)

What Others are Saying:

Phillip Keller: His [the shepherd's] voice is used to announce his presence; he is there. It is to allay their fears and timidity. Or it is to call them to himself so they can be examined and counted care-

Sheep Pen

A sheep pen is an area enclosed with high rock walls and a gate. Rural pens often had no gates.

fully. He wants to make sure that they are all well, fit, and flourishing. Sometimes the voice is used to announce that fresh feed is being supplied, or salt, minerals, or water. He might call them up to lead them into fresh pastures or into some shelter from an approaching storm. But always the master's call conveys to the sheep a positive assurance that he cares for them and is acting in their best interests.[1]

> **John 10:4–6** "When he has brought out all his own, he goes on ahead of them, and his sheep follow him because they know his voice. But they will never follow a stranger; in fact, they will run away from him because they do not recognize a stranger's voice." Jesus used this figure of speech, but they did not understand what he was telling them.

Trailing Behind The Shepherd

"Black Ear!" "Whitey!" "Peewee!" The sheep recognize their shepherd's voice and follow him anywhere and everywhere. They ignore everyone else.

Although sheep appear to trail blindly behind the shepherd, people-sheep are a little different. They follow a shepherd deliberately. As sheep, we'll learn to tell God's voice from those of the religious crooks if we truly seek him.

In Jesus' day, these crooks, or "strangers," were the Pharisees who were leading the people astray. Even though the leaders understood sheep tending, they didn't understand the point Jesus was making with this illustration. They were as stupid as the four-legged variety.

Phillip Keller: To follow Christ means I become intimately identified with His plans and purposes for the planet and for me as a person. His wishes become my wishes. His work becomes my work. His words become my words. His standards, values, and priorities become mine. His interests become my interests. His life becomes my life.[2]

What Others are Saying:

> **John 10:7–8** Therefore Jesus said again, "I tell you the truth, I am the gate for the sheep. All who ever came before me were thieves and robbers, but the sheep did not listen to them."

Over My Dead Body

When the shepherd was out on the hillside with his sheep, he rounded them up at night in a sheepfold similar to the one in town. But it didn't have a gate or guard. To keep thieves out and sheep in, the shepherd lay down across the opening. Thus he literally was the gate. Since no one could get in or out unless the shepherd was dead, this action gives new meaning to the phrase "over my dead body."

As the gate, Jesus is the only way to God and heaven. The religious leaders who claimed to lead people to God were, in reality, *"thieves and robbers."* They had added their own rules to God's— so many, in fact, that no one could keep them all. But God's sheep— those who belong to him—didn't listen to the false teachers.

TITLE OF JESUS

Gate

> **John 10:9–10** "I am the gate; whoever enters through me will be saved. He will come in and go out, and find pasture. The thief comes only to steal and kill and destroy; I have come that they may have life, and have it to the full."

Through The Gate

To make his point, Jesus again claimed to be the gate. Because he is the real Messiah, faith in him is the only way to salvation and eternal life. The religious thieves didn't care about the people's spiritual welfare. They only cared about themselves and taking what they could from the people. (Sound familiar? We have all kinds of religious "thieves" today.) They even killed and destroyed others.

Jesus, on the other hand, came to give life to his people—eternal life in the future and a satisfying, joyful, <u>full life</u> now.

☞ **GO TO:**

Psalm 23:5 (full life)

What Others are Saying:

Manford George Gutzke: Living in faith is like the marriage relationship. When a young couple gets married, they have a wedding day of much excitement and joyous celebration. But that day of celebration is not the last day! It is only the beginning. It would be a sad story if it were the last day. It is the days that follow, which are bright and rich with promise as they live with each other, and grow to know each other more deeply, that make the wedding day so important.

So it is with coming to the Lord Jesus Christ. The sinner receives forgiveness, is accepted as a child of God, and from then on puts his trust in the Lord Jesus. It is then that He can live as he goes in and out of that precious door and finds pasture.[3]

True happiness and fulfillment come from following Jesus, the Good Shepherd. They don't come from living by the bumper sticker that reads "He who dies with the most toys wins." (To learn more about how God views money and possessions, see WBFC, pages 249–252.)

Remember This . . .

JESUS THE SHEPHERD

> **John 10:11** "I am the good shepherd. The good shepherd lays down his life for the sheep."

A Volunteer Sacrifice

For people who want to know what a dedicated, loving leader looks like, they need only look at Jesus. He is the model for others to follow. As the *"good shepherd,"* he is good from the inside out. Goodness is part of his character, not a **veneer** or mask he puts on. As the model shepherd, Jesus would voluntarily give his life so people could have eternal life.

☞ **GO TO:**

Mark 10:17–18 (good)

veneer: thin layer

What Others are Saying:

Philip Yancey: "I am the gate," Jesus says in this chapter; "I am the good shepherd." Jews who hear those words undoubtedly think back to Old Testament kings like David, who are known as the shepherds of Israel. . . . As he [Jesus] explains, a truly good shepherd, unlike a hired hand, "lays down his life for the sheep." He is the only person in history who chooses to be born, chooses to die, and chooses to come back again. This chapter explains why he makes those choices.[4]

Dig Deeper

Old Testament References To Sheep

Jesus didn't dream up the image of shepherd and sheep. It's used throughout the Old Testament. You can read more about it in the following passages.

Reference	Image
Psalm 23	God's actions as shepherd
Psalm 74:1	Israel as sheep
Psalm 78:70–72	David as shepherd
Psalm 79:13	People as the flock of God's pasture
Psalm 95:7	People as God's sheep
Isaiah 40:11	God the Messiah as a shepherd
Isaiah 53:6	People like sheep going their own way
Ezekiel 34	False and true shepherds contrasted

> **John 10:12–13** "The hired hand is not the shepherd who owns the sheep. So when he sees the wolf coming, he abandons the sheep and runs away. Then the wolf attacks the flock and scatters it. The man runs away because he is a hired hand and cares nothing for the sheep."

Only For The Money

In contrast to the good shepherd, the hired hand is in the sheep business only for the money. He doesn't have any personal interest in the flock. So he flees instead of fights when a wolf or other wild animal comes around, leaving the flock defenseless. After all, why should he risk his own life for someone else's property? Without stating the obvious, Jesus was comparing the Pharisees to these hired hands. They were concerned about themselves and their reputations instead of caring about the people's spiritual well-being.

TITLE OF JESUS

Good Shepherd

> **John 10:14–16** "I am the good shepherd; I know my sheep and my sheep know me—just as the Father knows me and I know the Father—and I lay down my life for the sheep. I have other sheep that are not of this sheep pen. I must bring them also. They too will listen to my voice, and there shall be one flock and one shepherd."

The Extended Flock

When the shepherd calls, his sheep follow because they know his voice. When Jesus the shepherd calls, his people follow him because they know he is God. We have the same loving, trusting relationship with Jesus that he has with the Father. But it's not an exclusively Jewish family. There are people outside Judaism—the world of Gentiles—who believe in Jesus, too, and become part of the flock of God's family.

☞ **GO TO:**

John 3:16 (the world)

What Others are Saying:

Matthew Henry: It is the character of Christ's sheep that *they know him;* know him from all pretenders and intruders; they know his mind, know his voice, know by experience the power of his death.[5]

William Barclay: One of the hardest things in the world to un-learn is exclusiveness. Once a people, or a section of a people, gets the idea that they are specially privileged, it is very difficult for them to accept that the privileges which they believed belonged to them and to them only are in fact open to all men. That is what the Jews never learned. They believed that they were God's chosen people and that God had no use for any other nation. . . . But here Jesus is saying that there will come a day when all men will know him as their shepherd.[6]

Something to Ponder

Everyone is following someone or something. It might be self, Jesus, Satan, Muhammad, Buddha, atheism, agnosticism, family, money, materialism, horoscopes, the crowd, or any one of several hundred religions, people, philosophies, and things. The big question is, who are *you* following? If your answer is anyone or anything other than Jesus, you'll never have a full, satisfying life here and eternal life after you die unless you put your faith in God's only Son.

Remember This . . .

Jesus our shepherd promises to protect us, fight off our enemies, lead us, give us a satisfying life, and die for us. The picture of Jesus as a shepherd is comforting and encouraging and has drawn many people to Christ.

> **John 10:17–18** "The reason my Father loves me is that I lay down my life—only to take it up again. No one takes it from me, but I lay it down of my own accord. I have authority to lay it down and authority to take it up again. This command I received from my Father."

Life After Death

Few people volunteer to die. But Jesus did. When he was killed—as we will see later—it may have appeared that Jesus was powerless against the Roman soldiers who crucified him. In reality, Jesus chose to die. Only he wouldn't stay dead—he would rise again! That was a daring claim related to having the authority to control his death and life. But it wasn't an exaggeration. God gave him that authority.

Something to Ponder

When we think of power, it's usually in one of these contexts: having enough money to buy and do what we want, having political clout, being bigger than other people, or being in charge of a group or organization. Jesus gave power another definition. He taught that real power is choosing to give your life for others.

> **John 10:19–21** At these words the Jews were again divided. Many of them said, "He is demon-possessed and raving mad. Why listen to him?"
>
> But others said, "These are not the sayings of a man possessed by a demon. Can a demon open the eyes of the blind?"

Split Decision

Jesus had a way of bringing out the best—and worst—in people. In this case, it was both. The unbelieving Jews in the crowd accused Jesus of <u>having a demon</u> and being insane. (Back then, people thought demon possession always drove people mad.) But others disagreed. They took Jesus' words seriously and remembered his healing of the <u>blind man</u>.

☞ **GO TO:**

John 7:20; 8:48
(having a demon)

John 9:1–9 (blind man)

JESUS THE SON

> **John 10:22–24** Then came the Feast of Dedication at Jerusalem. It was winter, and Jesus was in the temple area walking in Solomon's Colonnade. The Jews gathered around him, saying, "How long will you keep us in suspense? If you are the Christ, tell us plainly."

Do Tell

December is a festive month in the Jewish calendar. The big holiday is the Feast of Dedication, or Hanukkah, as it's called today. During this eight-day celebration, Jesus was in Jerusalem. One day, when he was walking on the east side of the Temple, a group of Jewish people surrounded him. They'd seen Jesus heal, do all kinds of other miracles, and say that he is God so many times that he must have sounded like a broken record. So, what comes out of their mouths? "Don't keep us in suspense. Just tell us who you really are."

The Feast of Dedication celebrates the cleansing of the Temple in 164 B.C. after Antiochus Epiphanes, the king of Syria, sacrificed a pig on the altar. The event is recorded in the books of Maccabees, which are not part of Scripture but which record events that happened between the Old and New Testaments. It is also called the Feast of Lights since lighting the menorah (see illustration, page 108) is a central part of the celebration.

What Others are Saying:

commemorates: *celebrates*

consecrated: *made holy*

Louis Goldberg: Hanukkah **commemorates** a great and decisive victory over the Syrian king, preserving not only the land and the liberty of the Jewish people but, of far more significance, their religion and worship and the knowledge of the one true God.[7]

Victor Buksbazen: Hidden in one of the nooks of the Temple the Jews found a small jar of **consecrated** oil, used in former days for the perpetual light in the Temple. The oil was sufficient only for one night, but lo and behold the little cruse of oil lasted for eight days, until a new supply could be prepared and consecrated.

In memory of the wonderful redemption from the hands of the wicked enemy, and the rededication of the Temple, it was decreed that for eight days eight candles should be lit in every Jewish household, beginning with one on the first day, two on the second, progressively until the eighth day.[8]

David R. Veerman: These leaders were waiting for the signs and answers *they* thought would convince them of Jesus' identity. Thus they couldn't hear the truth Jesus was giving them. Jesus tried to correct their mistaken ideas, but they clung to the wrong idea of what kind of Messiah God would send. Such blindness still keeps people away from Jesus. They want him on their own terms; they do not want him if it means changing their whole life.[9]

The Jewish people did not recognize Jesus as the Messiah because they were looking for a political leader. He didn't live up to their expectations, which got in the way of seeing who he really was. We have the same problem today. We put God in a box and expect him to act a certain way. When he doesn't, we're disappointed or disillusioned.

Something to Ponder

> **John 10:25–26** Jesus answered, "I did tell you, but you do not believe. The miracles I do in my Father's name speak for me, but you do not believe because you are not my sheep."

You Should Know Me

Jesus has to be the most patient person who ever lived on earth. He had told the Jewish people over and over who he was. In addition, he showed them by performing miracles. How much more proof did they need? Still, they didn't believe he was God. It wasn't a matter of having all the facts and understanding them; it was a matter of the heart. And their hearts did not belong to God.

What Others are Saying:

attributes: characteristics, qualities

J. Carl Laney: In ancient times a person's name was believed to reflect something of his person. People were often named or renamed on the basis of a developing character trait. . . . The "Father's name" refers to all that God stands for in terms of His reputation and **attributes**. The miracles done "in my Father's name" were consistent with God's character and in accord with all that He stands for.[10]

W. Graham Scroggie: These Jews were always trying to throw upon Jesus a responsibility which was their own. They attributed their uncertainty to His indefiniteness, instead of to their own stupidity (24): but He faced them with two facts: His works, and their alienation (25, 26).[11]

> **John 10:27–30** "My sheep listen to my voice; I know them, and they follow me. I give them eternal life, and they shall never perish; no one can snatch them out of my hand. My Father, who has given them to me, is greater than all; no one can snatch them out of my Father's hand. I and the Father are one."

Godly Security

Jesus offers the best guarantee in the world: eternal life with God in heaven that will never end for those who follow him. This guarantee comes with an ironclad clause that we can never lose our salvation. No, never, ever, in no way. God the Father holds believers in his hand, and no one can pry open his fingers! Then for the umpteenth time Jesus tells the people he is God.

Herschel H. Hobbs: Note that we do not hold on to Jesus or the Father. We are held by them. And before either man, thing, or devil can recapture to destroy us, such must overcome both the Son and the Father. And, of course, that is impossible.[12]

What Others are Saying:

Promises For Following Jesus

When we sign up to follow Jesus, we get an unusual guarantee. For the fine print, read the following verses.

Dig Deeper

Reference	Promise
1 John 5:11–12	Eternal life with God
Ephesians 1:7	Forgiveness of sins
Romans 5:1	Peace with God
1 John 1:7	Fellowship with God and other believers
2 Thessalonians 3:3	Protection from Satan
Romans 8:35–39	Security
1 Peter 4:12–13	Suffering
2 Timothy 3:12	Persecution

John 10:31–33 Again the Jews picked up stones to stone him, but Jesus said to them, "I have shown you many great miracles from the Father. For which of these do you stone me?"

"We are not stoning you for any of these," replied the Jews, "but for blasphemy, because you, a mere man, claim to be God."

A Stoning Obsession

For as many times as the Jewish leaders tried to stone Jesus, you'd think they were getting paid by the stone. The rocks weren't for any of the miracles Jesus had done. They understood well that he was claiming to be God, and that was a sin punishable by stoning. Apparently it never occurred to them that Jesus could be who he said he was.

☞ **GO TO:**

John 5:17–18; 8:58–59 (stone Jesus)

John 10:34–36 Jesus answered them, "Is it not written in your Law, 'I have said you are gods'? If he called them 'gods,' to whom the word of God came—and the Scripture cannot be broken—what about the one whom the Father set apart as his very own and sent into the world? Why then do you accuse me of blasphemy because I said, 'I am God's Son'?"

A Brilliant Defense

In his defense, Jesus pulled out Psalm 82, a passage his stoners were acquainted with. Set in the context of a court, this psalm tells about God warning the gods, or judges, of the earth that they will be judged someday. Jesus' argument is that God calls humans "gods" because in serving as judges they participate in a function that is reserved for God. If Scripture gives human judges this honorary title, how much greater right to the title "God" does Jesus have, who is God *by nature*!

It was a brilliant defense. But Jesus didn't stop there. He boldly and plainly told them that God had sent him and that he was God's Son.

KEY POINT

When Jesus taught that he is the good shepherd who cares for his people and claimed to be one with the Father, the religious leaders tried to seize him.

> **John 10:37–39** "Do not believe me unless I do what my Father does. But if I do it, even though you do not believe me, believe the miracles, that you may know and understand that the Father is in me, and I in the Father." Again they tried to seize him, but he escaped their grasp.

Whatever It Takes

Once more, Jesus urged the people to believe in him. If they weren't going to believe his words, then he wanted them to believe on the basis of the miracles he performed. Whatever it took, he wanted them to look at the evidence so they'd know he really was God. But did they? No, they went into arrest mode. But Jesus slipped away from them.

THE FAITH FACTOR—Jesus performed miracles so people would believe he is God, as well as a man, and put their faith in him.

What Others are Saying:

Paul Little: There are only four possible conclusions about Jesus Christ and his claims. He was either a liar, a lunatic, a legend or the Truth. The person who doesn't believe he was the Truth must label him as a liar, a lunatic or a legend.[13]

This conversation between Jesus and the Jewish leaders at Hanukkah wasn't a typical one for the holiday. They asked for proof that Jesus was the Messiah, proof that would satisfy their preconceived notions. Jesus repeatedly told them he was God the Messiah, but they refused to believe. In the end, they attempted to stone and arrest him.

Conversations with Christ

> **John 10:40–42** Then Jesus went back across the Jordan to the place where John had been baptizing in the early days. Here he stayed and many people came to him. They said, "Though John never performed a miraculous sign, all that John said about this man was true." And in that place many believed in Jesus.

Retreat To Regroup

Since the leaders were trying to arrest him, Jesus retreated from the area. He crossed the Jordan River (see appendix A) to return to where <u>John the Baptist</u> had preached and baptized when Jesus first started his ministry. He didn't return to Jerusalem until Palm Sunday. But Jesus didn't retreat from people; he continued to teach. As a result, many people had a lightbulb moment. They realized that what John said about Jesus was true, and they believed in Jesus.

☞ **GO TO:**

John 1:19–28
(John the Baptist)

Study Questions

1. Who are the sheep?
2. Who is the shepherd?
3. Who are the thieves and robbers?
4. In what ways is Jesus the model shepherd?
5. How is Jesus the gate?
6. Why do people-sheep follow Jesus?
7. At the Feast of Dedication, what did the Jewish leaders ask Jesus?
8. How did he answer them?
9. What was their response?

CHAPTER WRAP-UP

- Jesus compared people to sheep, and the religious leaders to thieves and robbers. (John 10:1–6)
- Jesus called himself the Gate who protects his people. (John 10:7–10)

- Jesus called himself the Good Shepherd who leads people to God, protects them, and gives his life for them. (John 10:11–18)
- The people were divided over who Jesus was. (John 10:19–21)
- During the Feast of Dedication, Jesus claimed again that he was God and challenged the Jews to believe in him. (John 10:22–30)
- The Jewish leaders tried to stone Jesus for blasphemy and arrest him, but he escaped. (John 10:31–42)

JOHN 11: JESUS THE RESURRECTION AND THE LIFE

CHAPTER HIGHLIGHTS

- The Case of the Delayed Healer
- Back from the Dead
- The Plot Thickens

Let's Get Started

Death. It's the one sure thing we can count on in life. (Taxes are a close second.) We hate it, but we can't avoid it. We call it something else, like "passing away," so it doesn't sound so bad. But death still brings pain, grief, heartache, and years of loss.

In the whole history of the world, only two people (<u>Enoch</u> and <u>Elijah</u>) have ever escaped dying. That's because God took them to heaven before they quit breathing. And only a few people have ever come back from the grave. Lazarus is one of them.

In this chapter, John described Lazarus's death and how Jesus brought him back from the dead. This miracle is the turning point in the Book of John. It's the last of the seven sign miracles that pointed to Jesus' deity, proving that he has power over life and death. It also ended Jesus' public ministry.

☞ **GO TO:**

Genesis 5:21–24 (Enoch)

2 Kings 2:1–11 (Elijah)

THE CASE OF THE DELAYED HEALER

> **John 11:1–2** Now a man named Lazarus was sick. He was from Bethany, the village of Mary and her sister Martha. This Mary, whose brother Lazarus now lay sick, was the same one who poured perfume on the Lord and wiped his feet with her hair.

The Bethany Trio

☞ **GO TO:**

Luke 10:38–42
(Mary, Martha)

John 12:1–3
(poured perfume)

Mary, Martha, and Lazarus, who lived in Bethany, a suburb of Jerusalem (see appendix A), were all close friends of Jesus. He and his disciples often visited in the sisters' home (see GWWB, pages 257–260). Although this is John's first mention of the trio, they were well known to his readers. John specifically identified Mary as the one who poured perfume on Jesus' feet, an event he didn't record until after this one. At this point, Lazarus was sick, but John leaves us with questions about what was wrong with him.

> **John 11:3–4** So the sisters sent word to Jesus, "Lord, the one you love is sick."
> When he heard this, Jesus said, "This sickness will not end in death. No, it is for God's glory so that God's Son may be glorified through it."

Plea To A Friend

glory: display of God's nature

☞ **GO TO:**

John 9:1–12
(blind man)

Lazarus must have been seriously ill for Mary and Martha to send word to Jesus, who was about twenty miles away. Certainly, they wouldn't have bothered if it were a cold or the flu. Whatever it was, Jesus wasn't concerned. Since he is God, he knew Lazarus was going to die but not stay dead—at least this time. Instead, he'd become another poster person for God's **glory**, like the blind man Jesus healed.

What Others are Saying:

attributes: characteristics

omnipotence: having all power

James Montgomery Boice: To glorify God means to acknowledge Him as being who He truly is; and, since one of God's **attributes** is **omnipotence**, clearly the resurrection of Lazarus caused many to acknowledge that great power and so glorify Him.[1]

> **John 11:5–6** Jesus loved Martha and her sister and Lazarus. Yet when he heard that Lazarus was sick, he stayed where he was two more days.

Two-Day Delay

Lest we think Jesus' delay was heartless, John states that Jesus loved Lazarus and his sisters. You'd expect your brother's friend to come when he heard your brother was sick, wouldn't you? Yet

Jesus waited two days. Maybe Mary and Martha looked up the road every few hours, hoping to see him. Surely his disciples thought he was crazy for not dropping everything and trekking back to Jerusalem.

But Jesus wasn't indifferent to the sisters' plea to come. Nor was he preoccupied with a lot of other work and couldn't get away. Instead, he had his reasons for delaying. As always, he lived by his own timetable.

What Others are Saying:

Bruce Milne: This story teaches us two things about God's delays. The first is that they are inevitable. . . . The second point about God's delays is that they are not final. He will come, in his own time and way. No doubt that will frequently be later than we would have chosen. From his divine perspective, however, it will be the right time. God is the best of time-keepers. He created time; he is never late for his appointments.[2]

Erwin W. Lutzer: Though Jesus loved Lazarus, that did not prevent his death. God's love toward us does not mean we will be spared that experience of passing through the iron gate of death. We might feel forsaken by God, but He is there; His love abides with us into eternity. Our suffering is not inconsistent with the love of God.[3]

Remember This . . .

God rarely operates on our timetable. We want things to happen right away and have no patience for waiting. God, on the other hand, usually doesn't work as fast as we want. But he's never late, and he's always worth waiting for.

> **John 11:7–10** Then he said to his disciples, "Let us go back to Judea."
>
> "But Rabbi," they said, "a short while ago the Jews tried to stone you, and yet you are going back there?"
>
> Jesus answered, "Are there not twelve hours of daylight? A man who walks by day will not stumble, for he sees by this world's light. It is when he walks by night that he stumbles, for he has no light."

Walking Into The Face Of Death

Finally, after what must have seemed like an eternity to the disciples, it was God's time for Jesus to leave. Just in case Jesus forgot, his disciples reminded him about the leaders' plot to get rid of him that had been hatched back in Judea. But Jesus wasn't a bit concerned.

He didn't expect an answer to his question about daylight. It was obvious. Work and walking were done while there was daylight so people wouldn't run into obstacles. (Remember, there was no electricity back then.) Likewise, Jesus had only a limited amount of time to do God's work while he was here on earth. So, regardless of the death threat, he had to go back to Jerusalem. On another level, Jesus was reminding his disciples that, as the Light of the World, his presence would keep them from stumbling spiritually. But they had to stay close to him.

☞ **GO TO:**

I Corinthians 15:51;
1 Thessalonians
4:13–15 (asleep)

> **John 11:11–13** After he had said this, he went on to tell them, "Our friend Lazarus has fallen <u>asleep</u>; but I am going there to wake him up."
>
> His disciples replied, "Lord, if he sleeps, he will get better." Jesus had been speaking of his death, but his disciples thought he meant natural sleep.

A Waking Plan

When Jesus announced he was going to wake up Lazarus, his disciples took him literally. Naturally, they thought that sleep would help him get better. But Jesus used "sleep" to mean death. His plan was to go to Lazarus and raise him from the dead.

> **John 11:14–16** So then he told them plainly, "Lazarus is dead, and for your sake I am glad I was not there, so that you may believe. But let us go to him."
>
> Then Thomas (called Didymus) said to the rest of the disciples, "Let us also go, that we may die with him."

Let's Get Going

Because his disciples missed the point, Jesus told them clearly that Lazarus was dead. In fact, it was likely Lazarus was dead by the time Jesus got the message about his illness. Jesus then went on to focus on the big picture. Lazarus's death wasn't a waste. God had allowed it so that Jesus could show his power over death and so that people would believe in him.

Although Thomas has a reputation as a <u>doubter</u> (you'll see why

☞ **GO TO:**

John 20:24–25
(doubter)

in John 20), here he showed a lot of loyalty and courage. This twin (which is what Didymus means) spoke up first and expressed the disciples' willingness to die with Jesus. They didn't have a clue as to what was ahead, but they were willing to follow Jesus anyway.

What Others are Saying:

Charles H. Spurgeon: Christ is not glad because of sorrow, but on account of the result of it. He knew that his temporary trial would help His disciples to a greater faith, and He so prizes their growth in faith that He is even glad of the sorrow which occasions it. . . . He sets so high a value upon His people's faith that He will not screen them from those trials by which faith is strengthened.[4]

Hudson Taylor: Trials afford God a platform for his working in our lives. Without them I would never know how kind, how powerful, how gracious he is.[5]

When we suffer in some way, we tend to focus on the moment. We want the pain to be over quickly, to feel good, to have the problem solved immediately. But God is working from a bigger picture. He uses the pain and problems to glorify himself.

Something to Ponder

> **John 11:17–20** On his arrival, Jesus found that Lazarus had already been in the tomb for four days. Bethany was less than two miles from Jerusalem, and many Jews had come to Martha and Mary to comfort them in the loss of their brother. When Martha heard that Jesus was coming, she went out to meet him, but Mary stayed at home.

Dead And Buried

Jesus didn't arrive until Lazarus had been buried for four days. After that length of time, everyone would be sure Lazarus was dead when Jesus raised him. No one could claim that Lazarus had a near-death experience or that he only *seemed* dead.

Jewish family members visited the tomb of a loved one for three days to make sure the person buried was really dead and not in a coma. In the hot climate a dead body would have begun to decay by that time.

When Mary and Martha heard that Jesus had finally come,

Martha ran out to greet him while her sister continued mourning with the friends and neighbors who had come to grieve with them.

D. A. Carson: The implication is that the *many Jews* who came to comfort Martha and Mary were from Jerusalem, which in turn suggests that the family was rather prominent. Although comforting the bereaved was almost universally regarded as a religious and social responsibility. . . , not every villager would have been consoled by "many" Jews from the nearby city.[6]

CULTURE CLUE

Back then in the Middle East, dead people were buried within twenty-four hours of their deaths. Bodies were not embalmed as they are today. Instead, they were covered with spices and perfumes and wrapped with long lengths of cloth. Mourning the loss of the dead was so important that the family hired professional mourners—at least one wailing woman and two flute players, many more if they were rich. After the burial, family members, friends, and neighbors came to the house to mourn with the bereaved for seven days. Jewish people still practice this custom; it's called sitting *shivah.*

> **John 11:21–22** "Lord," Martha said to Jesus, "if you had been here, my brother would not have died. But I know that even now God will give you whatever you ask."

Faith That Didn't Waver

Martha would never have said, "It's your fault, Jesus, that my brother died, because you didn't come when I asked." (People in the Middle East weren't as direct as Americans tend to be.) But that's what she meant. However, she was also sure that Jesus could bring Lazarus back to life if he chose to do so. She knew all about his other miracles, and she believed in him.

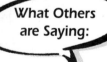

F. F. Bruce: This is not a complaint; it is an expression of her faith in Jesus' power. It is the same faith that finds voice in her assurance that God will grant Jesus whatever request he makes. She does not say, "If you ask God to restore my brother to life, he will grant your request"; but it is implied that she had this in her mind.[7]

Max Lucado: Something about death makes us accuse God of betrayal. "If God were here there would be no death!" we claim. You see, if God is God anywhere, he has to be God in the face of death. . . . Only God can deal with our ultimate dilemma—death. And only the God of the Bible has dared to stand on the canyon's edge and offer an answer. He has to be God in the face of death. If not, he is not God anywhere.[8]

> **John 11:23–27** Jesus said to her, "Your brother will rise again."
>
> Martha answered, "I know he will rise again in the resurrection at the last day."
>
> Jesus said to her, "I am the resurrection and the life. He who believes in me will live, even though he dies; and whoever lives and believes in me will never die. Do you believe this?"
>
> "Yes, Lord," she told him, "I believe that you are the Christ, the Son of God, who was to come into the world."

The Source Of Life

In response to Martha's plea, Jesus told her that Lazarus would rise from the dead. Jesus was talking about the present for a change; Martha thought he was talking about the <u>future resurrection</u> of believers. She may also have interpreted his statement as a common way of comforting the grieving, much as we say, "Your loved one is in a better place."

In the light of Lazarus's death, Jesus spoke his fifth "I am" statement: *"I am the resurrection and the life."* When we believe in him, he guarantees a future resurrection of our bodies from the grave and eternal life for our souls. Both of these come only through a relationship with him, since he is the source of resurrection and life. It was clearly a statement of deity, and Martha affirmed that fact and her belief in him.

☞ **GO TO:**

Daniel 12:2–3 (future resurrection)

Bruce B. Barton: Her statement of faith is exactly the response that Jesus wants from us. This confession presents a high point in John's Gospel, for here we see a believer acknowledging that Jesus is the Messiah, the Son of God. In recognizing Jesus as the Messiah, she saw him to be God's **envoy** appointed to deliver God's people; in recognizing Jesus as the Son of God, she saw his divinity.[9]

envoy: representative

Conversations with Christ

When Jesus finally arrived in Bethany for Lazarus's funeral, Martha was eager to talk with him. She wanted to know why he didn't show up in time to heal her brother before he died. At the same time, she expressed her faith in him. Jesus reassured her that Lazarus would rise from the dead, that he has power over life and death. Then he proved it by raising Lazarus four days after he died.

THE FAITH FACTOR—Faith in Jesus guarantees that, after death, our bodies will be raised from the dead and we will have eternal life. This is possible since Jesus is the source of resurrection and life.

> **John 11:28–32** And after she had said this, she went back and called her sister Mary aside. "The Teacher is here," she said, "and is asking for you." When Mary heard this, she got up quickly and went to him. Now Jesus had not yet entered the village, but was still at the place where Martha had met him. When the Jews who had been with Mary in the house, comforting her, noticed how quickly she got up and went out, they followed her, supposing she was going to the tomb to mourn there.
>
> When Mary reached the place where Jesus was and saw him, she fell at his feet and said, "Lord, if you had been here, my brother would not have died."

Private Meeting

After the roadside chat with Jesus, Martha went back to her house to get Mary. She talked with her sister privately so the whole mourning crowd wouldn't follow. But when Mary disappeared, the mourners followed anyway, thinking she was going to the tomb.

Martha and Mary must have talked about how Jesus could have saved Lazarus from dying, since they both gave him the same speech. Like Martha, Mary believed Jesus is God. She didn't say it like her sister, but she fell down at his feet—an act of worship reserved for God alone.

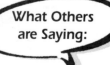

What Others are Saying:

Anne Graham Lotz: Just as a diamond seems to sparkle more brilliantly when displayed in a black velvet case, so the radiant beauty of Christlike character seems to shine more splendidly against the backdrop of suffering. Even in Martha's grief, the jewel of hope that seemed to have been birthed in her spirit sparkled. She eagerly went to Mary.[10]

Like Martha and Mary, we tend to deal in "if only's." If only this had happened. If only I hadn't done that. If only God had done what I asked. The next time you're tempted to say, "If only God . . . ," remember that God is bigger than your circumstance or problem. He's working even when you can't see him.

Something to Ponder

> **John 11:33–35** When Jesus saw her weeping, and the Jews who had come along with her also weeping, he was deeply moved in spirit and troubled. "Where have you laid him?" he asked.
> "Come and see, Lord," they replied.
> Jesus wept.

When God Cried

These verses prove again that Jesus wasn't a wimpy, unfeeling man. Mary's and the people's grief affected him greatly. The Greek word for *"deeply moved"* is the same word used for a horse's snorting and an outburst of anger. Jesus was outraged at death—and he was going to do something about it. So he asked to see Lazarus's tomb.

Verse 35, *"Jesus wept,"* may be the shortest verse in the Bible, but it packs a powerful punch. Those two words tell us Jesus mourned his friend's death deeply. They also tell us that Jesus is like us and understands what we go through. When we hurt, God hurts.

> **John 11:36–37** Then the Jews said, "See how he loved him!"
> But some of them said, "Could not he who opened the eyes of the blind man have kept this man from dying?"

A Crowd Splitter

It seems like, whatever Jesus did, he split the crowd. This time it was his emotions that divided the people. Some commented on how much Jesus loved Lazarus. Others complained because he didn't arrive in time to heal him. (Sound familiar?) They reasoned that since Jesus gave the blind man sight, surely he could heal a sick man before he died.

BACK FROM THE DEAD

> **John 11:38–40** Jesus, once more deeply moved, came to the tomb. It was a cave with a stone laid across the entrance. "Take away the stone," he said.
>
> "But, Lord," said Martha, the sister of the dead man, "by this time there is a bad odor, for he has been there four days."
>
> Then Jesus said, "Did I not tell you that if you believed, you would see the glory of God?"

The Stench Will Knock You Out

Still angry, Jesus arrives at the tomb. So, what does he do? Something utterly ridiculous. He tells them to roll away the entrance stone.

Confusion reigns. People must have been thinking, *What does he think he's doing? He must be crazy! The man's dead.* Dead is dead, whether it's one minute, one hour, one day, or four days after he takes his last breath.

Martha, the practical one, pointed out how bad the stench would be. After four days, it was probably strong enough to knock over the entire crowd. But it didn't keep Jesus from doing what he came to do: show them God's glory.

What Others are Saying:

Max Lucado: Jesus has intruded on the enemy's turf; he's standing in Satan's territory, Death Canyon. His stomach turns as he smells the sulfuric stench of the ex-angel, and he winces as he hears the oppressed wails of those trapped in the prison. Satan has been here. He has violated one of God's creations.[11]

John Calvin: Christ does not come to the tomb as an idle spectator, but like a wrestler preparing for the contest. So it is no wonder that he groans again, for the violent tyranny of death which he had to overcome stands in front of his eyes.[12]

CULTURE CLUE

Instead of burying dead bodies in holes in the ground, it was normal for people to be buried in caves. The body was wrapped tightly in long cloth strips, like covering someone with a roll of toilet paper. Faces were covered with square cloths. A huge round stone covered the entrance to the cave; it moved in a groove that was dug in the front of the opening.

After a year, when the flesh had rotted off the bones, the family entered the tomb, put the bones in a box, and kept the box in a slot in the cave wall.

> **John 11:41–44** So they took away the stone. Then Jesus looked up and said, "Father, I thank you that you have heard me. I knew that you always hear me, but I said this for the benefit of the people standing here, that they may believe that you sent me."
>
> When he had said this, Jesus called in a loud voice, "Lazarus, come out!" The dead man came out, his hands and feet wrapped with strips of linen, and a cloth around his face.
>
> Jesus said to them, "Take off the grave clothes and let him go."

KEY POINT

Jesus proved he is the resurrection and the life by raising Lazarus from the dead.

Return Of The Living Dead

We don't know who moved the stone, but at least two people didn't hesitate. Maybe Mary and Martha. They weren't turned off by the prospect of a stench. They didn't consider the possibility of embarrassment if Jesus didn't come through. They weren't afraid they'd look like idiots. They just backed up their belief in him with obedience.

After the stone was moved, Jesus thanked God for hearing him. Most of us would have been holding our noses and keeping our mouths shut. But not Jesus. He prayed out loud so the people would hear him and know the source of the miracle he was about to perform.

Then Jesus called Lazarus to come out of the tomb. If he hadn't called him by name, he would have emptied the whole graveyard! And Lazarus waddled out the best he could (see illustration, page 156). Jesus easily could have zapped the grave clothes and made them disintegrate. Instead, he involved people in the miracle, telling them to unwrap Lazarus. And somebody did.

F. L. Godet: The Jews had said of the healing of the man born blind: As an infraction of the Sabbath, this cannot be a divine work. By **rendering** thanks to God on this day in presence of all the people, even before performing the miracle, Jesus positively calls upon God to grant or to refuse Him His cooperation. In the face of such a prayer God must be recognized either as the guarantor of His mission or as the accomplice in His imposture.[13]

What Others are Saying:

rendering: giving

Lazarus in Grave Clothes

Lazarus was wrapped in strips of cloth. When Jesus commanded him to come out, he did so despite his wrappings.

What Others are Saying:

Dig Deeper

Erwin W. Lutzer: This seventh miracle in John's gospel offers proof that Jesus is not just Lord of this world, but also Lord of the next. He is not just Lord of today, but also the Lord of the most distant tomorrows. He is there when we need Him the most.[14]

Raising people from the dead wasn't a onetime gig for Jesus. Read about other back-from-the-grave events in the following passages:

- Luke 7:11–15: widow's son
- Luke 8:41–56: Jairus's daughter
- Matthew 28:1–10: Jesus himself

THE PLOT THICKENS

John 11:45–48 Therefore many of the Jews who had come to visit Mary, and had seen what Jesus did, put their faith in him. But some of them went to the Pharisees and told them what Jesus had done. Then the chief priests and the Pharisees called a meeting of the **Sanhedrin**.

"What are we accomplishing?" they asked. "Here is this man performing many miraculous signs. If we let him go on like this, everyone will believe in him, and then the Romans will come and take away both our place and our nation."

Sanhedrin: *supreme court of Israel*

Panic Among The Pharisees

Seeing a dead man live again ought to be enough to make anybody believe in Jesus. And many of the eyewitnesses to Lazarus's resurrection did believe. Some who didn't believe blabbed the event to the Pharisees, who called a meeting. (Isn't that how we try to solve a lot of problems?) The religious leaders had had trouble with Jesus all along, but now he proved he had the ultimate power—the power over death. How could they maintain control with him around? They panicked. They were afraid that Jesus would start a religious revolution—that everyone in the country would believe in him—and the Romans would take away *their* freedom.

Charles U. Wagner: All through the Lord's ministry, the Pharisees had tried to discredit the Lord Jesus on the basis of His humble origin, His home or His disregard for their legalistic restrictions. But here was a miracle they could not discount. Notice, they did not even deny that He had raised Lazarus (v. 47). They accepted the historical fact, but they rejected the One Who is the Resurrection and the Life because of the threat He posed to their position among men.[15]

What Others are Saying:

Alexander MacLaren: The holy things were, in their eyes, their special property. And so, at this supreme moment, big with the fate of themselves and of their nation, their whole anxiety is about personal interests. They hesitate, and are at a loss what to do.[16]

A variety of people gathered around Lazarus's tomb. Mary and Martha had believed in Jesus before they went there. After Jesus raised Lazarus from the dead, many more believed. Others refused to believe in spite of what they witnessed. Which group of people are you most like?

Something to Ponder

> **John 11:49–53** Then one of them, named Caiaphas, who was high priest that year, spoke up, "You know nothing at all! You do not realize that it is better for you that one man die for the people than that the whole nation perish."
>
> He did not say this on his own, but as high priest that year he prophesied that Jesus would die for the Jewish nation, and not only for that nation but also for the scattered children of God, to bring them together and make them one. So from that day on they plotted to take his life.

Out Of The Mouths Of Priests

That meeting must have been chaotic. Imagine seventy-one men talking among themselves, debating what to do with Jesus, arguing in loud voices. Finally, Caiaphas, the **high priest**, said, *"You know nothing at all!"* In other words, he told them they didn't know what they were talking about. Tactful he wasn't. He had a reputation for being ruthless and proud. No one or nothing was going to get in his way. So naturally Jesus had to be eliminated—sacrifice the one for the good of the many.

Caiaphas was only thinking about how to save his position and the status quo in his own country when he said that. But John added a bigger perspective to the remark. In God's plan, Jesus was going to die for the sins of Israel as well as the whole world. One man's death would save them spiritually and bring all of God's children together in the future.

Earlier the religious leaders had wanted Jesus to give them a <u>sign</u> to prove that he was God. What better sign than raising Lazarus from the dead after four days? So, what do they do? Plot to kill Jesus.

high priest: chief religious leader

☞ **GO TO:**

John 6:30 (sign)

> **John 11:54** Therefore Jesus no longer moved about publicly among the Jews. Instead he withdrew to a region near the desert, to a village called Ephraim, where he stayed with his disciples.

Crowd Withdrawal

Jesus was no dummy. He knew when it was wise to move on. With the religious leaders plotting to kill him with increasing intensity, he took his disciples to Ephraim (see appendix A) for a private retreat. This town was close to the desert, and if necessary Jesus could run into the desert to get away from his enemies.

> **John 11:55–57** When it was almost time for the Jewish Passover, many went up from the country to Jerusalem for their ceremonial cleansing before the Passover. They kept looking for Jesus, and as they stood in the temple area they asked one another, "What do you think? Isn't he coming to the Feast at all?" But the chief priests and Pharisees had given orders that if anyone found out where Jesus was, he should report it so that they might arrest him.

The Talk Of The Town

John marked time in Jesus' ministry with the Jewish feasts. It was <u>Passover time</u> again—the third one mentioned in this book, making it the third year of Jesus' ministry. Since it was one of the three times when Jewish males were required to go to Jerusalem to celebrate, a huge crowd of people filled the city. One of the rituals of Passover was <u>ceremonial cleansing</u>, immersion in water to make people religiously clean after touching a dead body. This ceremony took place at the Temple. While people waited in line for their turn, naturally they talked to those around them. The number one topic of conversation was Jesus and whether or not he would show up for Passover.

Everybody knew the religious leaders had a warrant out for Jesus' arrest. It was as though WANTED posters were tacked to every tree in the country with a reward for turning him in to the religious leaders.

☞ **GO TO:**

John 2:23; 6:4
(Passover time)

Numbers 9:6
(ceremonial cleansing)

Study Questions

1. Why didn't Jesus go to Lazarus as soon as he got word that his friend was sick?
2. What did Martha say to Jesus when he arrived after Lazarus died?
3. How is Jesus *"the resurrection and the life"*?
4. How did Jesus respond to Mary's mourning?
5. How did Jesus raise Lazarus from the dead?
6. What were the people's reactions to Jesus' raising Lazarus from the dead?

- When Lazarus was sick, his sisters asked Jesus to come, but he waited two days. (John 11:1–16)

- In light of Lazarus's death, Jesus told Martha that he is *"the resurrection and the life."* (John 11:17–27)

- Jesus joined the mourners in crying because Lazarus had died. (John 11:28–37)

- Jesus raised Lazarus from the dead. (John 11:38–44)

- As a result of this miracle, the religious leaders plotted to kill Jesus, so he withdrew from the city. (John 11:45–57)

JOHN 12: JESUS THE KING WHO WILL DIE

CHAPTER HIGHLIGHTS

- Pour on the Perfume
- A Royal Welcome
- It's Time to Die
- The Danger of Unbelief

Let's Get Started

Even though we don't like to think about death, wouldn't it be great if we knew when we were going to die? We could write the date in the reference section of our schedule planners. Then we could take care of what needs to be done, like preparing our loved ones, writing a will, reconciling with estranged friends and relatives, and cleaning out the attic or basement. We could also schedule in the fun things we never seem to find time for—hiking in the Rockies, walking along the seashore, learning to hang glide, riding roller coasters.

Only one person has ever known when he would die. That's Jesus. As the time drew near, he returned to Jerusalem, and Mary, Lazarus's sister, anointed him for burial before he was welcomed back in a Palm Sunday parade. Once more he taught about the necessity of believing in him and explained why many of the Jewish people didn't.

POUR ON THE PERFUME

> **John 12:1–2** Six days before the Passover, Jesus arrived at Bethany, where Lazarus lived, whom Jesus had raised from the dead. Here a dinner was given in Jesus' honor. Martha served, while Lazarus was among those reclining at the table with him.

Thanksgiving In April

Ignoring the death plot against him, Jesus and his disciples ended their retreat and headed back to Bethany, where Jesus raised Lazarus from the dead. To show their gratitude for this miracle, Martha and her siblings threw a dinner in Jesus' honor. Matthew tells us the party was in <u>Simon the Leper</u>'s home, although Martha did her usual gig of <u>serving</u>.

☞ **GO TO:**

Matthew 26:6
(Simon the Leper)

Luke 10:40 (serving)

> **John 12:3** Then Mary took about a pint of pure nard, an expensive perfume; she poured it on Jesus' feet and wiped his feet with her hair. And the house was filled with the fragrance of the perfume.

Jesus Gets Smelly Feet

What a weird act of love Mary performed! Most of us would be extremely uncomfortable if we went to dinner and our friend's sister suddenly poured perfume on our feet and then wiped them dry with her hair. But not Jesus. He saw her heart of devotion and understood what she was doing. By kneeling at Jesus' feet, Mary also showed her humility.

What Others are Saying:

Lawrence O. Richards: There is always something beautiful and fragrant about what we do out of love. No act performed out of a mere sense of duty, or out of obligation, can fill the air with that kind of fragrance.[1]

CULTURE CLUE

alabaster: hard, white mineral

The perfume Mary used was made from spikenard, an herb grown in the mountains of India and exported in **alabaster** bottles (see illustration, page 163). It was so expensive that people bought it for an investment, not to be used every day to smell good.

Married women kept their hair covered in mixed company. Since Mary used her hair to wipe off Jesus' feet, she must have been single or widowed. Nevertheless, her action would have raised a lot of eyebrows among people of both genders.

Alabaster Jar

Perfume was typically kept in a jar with a long, narrow neck. Alabaster was commonly used because it was soft enough to be carved yet hard enough to be polished.

> **John 12:4–6** But one of his disciples, Judas Iscariot, who was later to betray him, objected, "Why wasn't this perfume sold and the money given to the poor? It was worth a year's wages." He did not say this because he cared about the poor but because he was a thief; as keeper of the money bag, he used to help himself to what was put into it.

Follow The Money

Since Jesus and his disciples weren't working at regular jobs, they had to have some means of buying food and paying for lodging between invitations to dinner and overnight stays. They were sup-ported, at least in part, by several wealthy women. Judas was the treasurer of this group, and he was stealing from the money bag.

Judas's heart was on the money. He couldn't see Mary's love for Jesus because his eyes were blinded by dollar signs. He was only concerned about the fact that she wasted a whole year's salary on—of all things—foot perfume. If she had given that money to Jesus to help the poor, Judas would have had more to help himself to.

Mary was extravagant with her love, not stingy. She gave Jesus the best she had, although others at the party thought it was a waste of money—and probably an embarrassment in the way she gave it. Our best may not be something worth a year's salary. It may be a couple of hours a week teaching children the Bible; being a faithful, honest, hardworking employee; running errands for a shut-in; fixing cars for widows and single moms; or any of dozens of other acts of love and service. How can you give Jesus your best this week?

☞ **GO TO:**

Luke 8:1–3 (supported)

☞ **GO TO:**

Mark 14:4 (others)

Something to Ponder

> **John 12:7–8** "Leave her alone," Jesus replied. "It was intended that she should save this perfume for the day of my burial. You will always have the poor among you, but you will not always have me."

The Time Is Now

Mary understood that Jesus would die; that's why she anointed him with her perfume. It was an act of preparing a body for burial.

Jesus knew Judas's heart, but those around him did not. (John wrote his book after the true state of Judas's heart had been revealed—and probably after the disciples began realizing their money was disappearing.) But just in case folks in the group might misunderstand and think that Judas was sincere about wanting to help the poor, Jesus' words would remind them of a sad truth. Even after Jesus was gone, there would still be plenty of <u>poor people</u> that Judas could help. Jesus was the one who would soon be leaving this earth.

☞ **GO TO:**

Deuteronomy 15:11 (poor people)

What Others are Saying:

James Montgomery Boice: How did Mary understand these things when the others, particularly the disciples, failed? The answer is: by being often in the place where we find her now. Where? She is at the feet of Jesus, anointing Him and wiping His feet with her hair. Where is she always? At the feet of Jesus! . . . Mary is at His feet worshiping Him and learning from Him.[2]

Remember This . . .

Jesus cares more about our hearts than our wallets. We can't buy off God by giving money to poor people or good causes. He doesn't even care if we have no money to give. He just wants our love and devotion.

> **John 12:9–11** Meanwhile a large crowd of Jews found out that Jesus was there and came, not only because of him but also to see Lazarus, whom he had raised from the dead. So the chief priests made plans to kill Lazarus as well, for on account of him many of the Jews were going over to Jesus and putting their faith in him.

Contract On Lazarus

Jesus wasn't the only attraction in town. Large numbers of people came to see Lazarus. Any man who was raised from the dead would have become an immediate celebrity. The first-century media would have been camped outside his house. They would have been interviewing Lazarus and everyone who ever knew him. With Lazarus running around as proof of Jesus' deity and causing more people to believe in Jesus, the chief priests decided they had to get rid of the evidence. They decided to kill Lazarus too.

Arthur W. Pink: It was not the Pharisees but the "chief priests," who were Sadducees, (cf. Acts 5:17), that "consulted that they might also put *Lazarus* to death": They would, if possible, kill him, because he was a striking witness *against* them, denying as they did the truth of resurrection. But how fearful the state of their hearts: they had rather commit murder than acknowledge they were wrong.[3]

Lazarus attracted people because he was walking evidence of Jesus' power at work in a person's life. The actions and words of those who believe in Jesus can either attract others or drive them away. We can carry with us the <u>smell</u> of eternal death or eternal life.

A ROYAL WELCOME

> **John 12:12–13** The next day the great crowd that had come for the Feast heard that Jesus was on his way to Jerusalem. They took palm branches and went out to meet him, shouting,
> "Hosanna!"
> "Blessed is he who comes in the name of the Lord!"
> "Blessed is the King of Israel!"

Palm Branch Parade

Passover brought great crowds of people to Jerusalem, many of whom had seen Jesus perform miracles or at least heard about his ministry. Word of the raising of Lazarus spread quickly. Everyone wanted to see the man who had done this unbelievable thing.

Caught up with excitement and expectation, they lined Fifth Avenue for a ticker-tape parade, except that this was Israel and not New York City. So they did the next best thing. They lined the road into Jerusalem and waved palm branches and quoted Psalm

What Others are Saying:

Something to Ponder

☞ **GO TO:**

2 Corinthians 2:14–16 (smell)

TITLE OF JESUS

King of Israel

118:25–26. *Hosanna* is Hebrew for "save now." They thought Jesus was the king who would deliver them from Roman rule. Unfortunately, they had the wrong idea about who their Messiah-King would be.

What Others are Saying:

provocative: *tending to provoke or excite*

David E. Garland: This staged arrival in Jerusalem . . . deviates from Jesus' previous attempts to avoid calling attention to himself. . . . Jesus encourages public rejoicing by his **provocative** entrance. [Ched] Myers goes so far as to call it "political street theater." His actions encourage the crowd to blazon his name jubilantly from street corners and rooftops. Passover crowds tended to be expectant during this season that celebrated Israel's deliverance from Egypt, but they will be sadly mistaken if they expect Jesus to mastermind some military coup.[4]

Norval Geldenhuys: The moment has arrived when He is going to announce Himself as the promised King in the centre of the Holy Land so that the people can finally take sides for or against Him. Nevertheless He is not going to appear with outward power, but will enter the holy city as Prince of Peace.[5]

CULTURE CLUE

Palm branches were used for several occasions: to celebrate military victories, to welcome out-of-towners for the Passover celebration, and as part of the observance of the Feast of Tabernacles.

During the Passover dinner, Jewish people sang Psalms 113–118, the first two before eating and the other four after the meal. They are called the *Hallel*, which means "praise," because most of these psalms begin or end with the sentence *"Praise the Lord."*

> **John 12:14–15** Jesus found a young donkey and sat upon it, as it is written,
> "Do not be afraid, O Daughter of Zion;
> see, your king is coming,
> seated on a donkey's colt."

☞ **GO TO:**

Zechariah 9:9
(prophecy)

Jesus' Grand Entrance

The crowd treated Jesus as a military hero, but those great men rode on horses or in chariots. In contrast, Jesus rode a donkey to fulfill Old Testament <u>prophecy</u>. Israel's king would come on a donkey as a servant.

The way John states *"Jesus found a young donkey"* suggests that, after seeing the crowd and hearing the shouts of the people, Jesus deliberately chose to ride as he did (see also GWLC2, pages 145–147). Jesus knew that most of the people were thinking of him as an earthly leader rather than a heavenly king. But he probably enjoyed this moment of triumph.

William Barclay: A king came riding upon a horse when he was bent on *war;* he came riding upon an ass when he was coming in *peace.* This action of Jesus is a sign that he was not the warrior figure men dreamed of, but the Prince of Peace.[6]

What Others are Saying:

> **John 12:16** At first his disciples did not understand all this. Only after Jesus was glorified did they realize that these things had been written about him and that they had done these things to him.

No Comprendo

The significance of Jesus' triumphal entry into Jerusalem was lost on the disciples. It wasn't until after his resurrection that they understood he was fulfilling prophecy in the way he entered the city.

John was honest as he wrote his Gospel. He often admitted that the true meaning of events had been beyond him and his friends. Just as is the case when we look back on events, John and the other disciples understood things much more clearly in hindsight.

> **John 12:17–19** Now the crowd that was with him when he called Lazarus from the tomb and raised him from the dead continued to spread the word. Many people, because they had heard that he had given this miraculous sign, went out to meet him. So the Pharisees said to one another, "See, this is getting us nowhere. Look how the whole world has gone after him!"

Curious Crowds Close In

As the news spread about Jesus' raising Lazarus from the dead, curious crowds closed around Jesus as he rode into Jerusalem. This situation disturbed the Pharisees no end. How were they going to grab Jesus and get rid of him when he was surrounded by people who adored him? It may have looked like the whole Jewish world was following him, but most of the people didn't believe in Jesus. They were simply curiosity seekers, swept along by the excitement of the day.

IT'S TIME TO DIE

> **John 12:20–22** Now there were some Greeks among those who went up to worship at the Feast. They came to Philip, who was from Bethsaida in Galilee, with a request. "Sir," they said, "we would like to see Jesus." Philip went to tell Andrew; Andrew and Philip in turn told Jesus.

Any More Appointments Available?

Jesus was popular not only with the Jewish set; even Gentiles wanted to see him. Those Greeks were possibly God-fearers, people who attended Jewish worship services and celebrations but had not yet converted to Judaism. Or they may have been tourists. The Jerusalem Temple was one of the wonders of the ancient world, and many pagans came to see it.

One thing was for sure—they were brave. Either they didn't know the Pharisees were after Jesus because they were from out of town or else they didn't care. They just wanted to talk with Jesus. So they looked up Philip, who relayed the request to Andrew, who went with Philip to see if Jesus was taking appointments.

KEY POINT

After Mary anointed Jesus with costly perfume, he rode into Jerusalem to a palm-branch welcome and taught that he was about to die.

> **John 12:23–26** Jesus replied, "The hour has come for the Son of Man to be glorified. I tell you the truth, unless a kernel of wheat falls to the ground and dies, it remains only a single seed. But if it dies, it produces many seeds. The man who loves his life will lose it, while the man who hates his life in this world will keep it for eternal life. Whoever serves me must follow me; and where I am, my servant also will be. My Father will honor the one who serves me."

Dying To Live

All through this Gospel, John wrote that Jesus didn't do something because his time had not yet come. Finally, the time had come for Jesus' death when he would be honored as the Son of Man, the Messiah. To illustrate his death, he talked about wheat, which his listeners were familiar with. In order to have a wheat harvest, the kernels have to be planted, or die. Then they grow and multiply into a harvest of seed-producing grain. So, too, Jesus calls his followers to give up their own priorities, desires, and self-interests—to die to self or hate their lives. Then they will gain eternal life. Loving ourselves, focusing on our physical lives, and ignoring Jesus will result in spiritual death. True disciples follow Jesus even if it means physical death—and gain God's approval.

TITLE OF JESUS

Son of Man

Warren W. Wiersbe: If we are looking for comfortable lives, then we will protect our plans and desires, save our lives, and never be planted. But if we yield our lives and let God plant us, we will never be alone but will have the joy of being fruitful to the glory of God.[7]

What Others are Saying:

Bill Myers: When a grain of wheat falls and "dies" in the ground it eventually sprouts and bears more grain, which sprout and bear more, and so on and so forth until, before you know it, the initial "death" has led to life a thousand times greater.

When we give God our talents, our hopes, our lives—when we die to them (either emotionally or literally)—they too return in greater portion and abundance than we can possibly imagine.

Don't ask me how it happens, but it does . . . *always.*[8]

Follow the Leader is not a game for children only. If we're going to get anywhere spiritually and get anything done for God, Jesus has to be out in front. He doesn't follow us; we follow him. He leads; we don't.

Remember This . . .

> **John 12:27–29** "Now my heart is troubled, and what shall I say? 'Father, save me from this hour'? No, it was for this very reason I came to this hour. Father, glorify your name!"
>
> Then a voice came from heaven, "I have glorified it, and will glorify it again." The crowd that was there and heard it said it had thundered; others said an angel had spoken to him.

A Word From Our Sponsor

Jesus knew long before he was born here on earth that he would die. That's a heavy burden to live with all your life. As a man, he was not looking forward to being crucified—a painful way to die. No wonder he was troubled. Although he would have liked to be spared that death, that's why he came. So he asked the Father to glorify, or draw attention to, his name.

In response, God spoke audibly. He would glorify himself through his Son's death and resurrection. The people standing around Jesus heard God's voice. But they downplayed the supernatural, saying it was thunder or an angel speaking.

What Others are Saying:

Bruce B. Barton: *Glorify* is one of those biblical terms we often use without understanding its true meaning. The Greek root word . . . refers to brightness, beauty, and even fame. One helpful way to think of the word is to substitute the word spotlight. Jesus was consciously giving God, the Father, permission to spotlight himself through what would happen to Christ, God's Son. The Father responded by affirming that he had already spotlighted his name in Jesus and would continue to do so.[9]

> **John 12:30–33** Jesus said, "This voice was for your benefit, not mine. Now is the time for judgment on this world; now the prince of this world will be driven out. But I, when I am lifted up from the earth, will draw all men to myself." He said this to show the kind of death he was going to die.

A Planned Death

God the Father didn't need to speak from heaven for Jesus' sake. He did it for the benefit of the people standing there. His words were an introduction to Jesus' death, which would bring judgment on unbelievers, break Satan's stranglehold on the world, and eventually <u>drive him out</u> of the world altogether.

Jesus described his death as being "<u>*lifted up,*</u>" meaning crucifixion. The religious leaders were trying to stone Jesus to death, but he knew that wouldn't be the method.

His death is the means by which he offers salvation from sin and eternal life in heaven. That offer is open to all people, not just the Jewish people.

☞ **GO TO:**

Revelation 20:10 (drive him out)

Isaiah 52:13 (lifted up)

Names For Satan

Besides *"prince of this world,"* Satan has a number of other descriptive names. This table lists some of them.

Name	Reference
Tempter	Matthew 4:3
Beelzebub	Matthew 12:24
Evil one	Matthew 13:19
Devil	Matthew 13:39
Murderer	John 8:44
Liar, father of lies	John 8:44
God of this age	2 Corinthians 4:4
Ruler of the kingdom of the air	Ephesians 2:2
Dragon	Revelation 12:7
Serpent	Revelation 12:9

Dig Deeper

Beelzebub: *lord of the dung*

serpent: *snake*

> **John 12:34** The crowd spoke up, "We have heard from the Law that the Christ will remain forever, so how can you say, 'The Son of Man must be lifted up'? Who is this 'Son of Man'?"

Clarification, Please

Many of the Jewish people believed Jesus' claims to be the promised Messiah. Their palm-branch welcome was for a Messiah who would free them from Roman rule and set up a never-ending, earthly kingdom. They knew from the Scriptures that Messiah would <u>reign forever</u>. They also knew the title Son of Man was another name for Messiah. One thing they weren't expecting was a Messiah who was going to die by crucifixion. So naturally they wanted to know if the Son of Man was someone else and, if so, who he was.

☞ **GO TO:**

Isaiah 9:6–7
(reign forever)

> **John 12:35–36** Then Jesus told them, "You are going to have the light just a little while longer. Walk while you have the light, before darkness overtakes you. The man who walks in the dark does not know where he is going. Put your trust in the light while you have it, so that you may become sons of light." When he had finished speaking, Jesus left and hid himself from them.

Take Advantage Of The Light

Instead of debating theology, Jesus reminded the people that, as the Light of the World, he would be with them only a little while longer. Now was the time to believe in him, to walk in the light of his presence. If they did so, they would be able to live honestly and sincerely. After this warning, Jesus disappeared.

What Others are Saying:

Conversations with Christ

R. Kent Hughes: Our Lord was saying, "You have heard my message. Light or darkness—take your choice." Which will *we* choose?[10]

As the time of his death drew near, Jesus told the crowd he was going to die and asked the Father to glorify himself through his death. God the Father got in on this conversation with a confirmation from heaven. But the people couldn't comprehend a Messiah who would be crucified instead of bringing them an earthly kingdom. After urging them to believe in him while he was still with them, Jesus left.

THE DANGER OF UNBELIEF

> **John 12:37–38** Even after Jesus had done all these miraculous signs in their presence, they still would not believe in him. This was to fulfill the word of Isaiah the prophet:
>
> "Lord, who has believed our message
> and to whom has the arm of the
> Lord been revealed?"

Ignoring The Evidence

Jesus had done enough miracles, including raising a man from the dead, to convince the most hard-hearted person to believe in him. But still the religious leaders and most of the common people refused to do so. This response came as no surprise to Jesus or anyone else who understood the Old Testament Scriptures. Seven hundred years before, the prophet Isaiah predicted this reaction.

☞ **GO TO:**

Isaiah 53:1
(Isaiah predicted)

> **John 12:39–41** For this reason they could not believe, because, as Isaiah says elsewhere:
>> "He has blinded their eyes
>> and deadened their hearts,
>> so they can neither see with their eyes,
>> nor understand with their hearts,
>> nor turn—and I would heal them."
> Isaiah said this because he saw Jesus' glory and spoke about him.

Eyes Wide Shut

John explained the people's unbelief with another quote from Isaiah. Walking a path of unbelief is a dangerous route. The more people resist believing in Jesus, the closer they get to not being able to believe. Eventually they become so hardened in unbelief that God confirms their choices and they *can't* believe. Isaiah could predict the people's response because he saw what this crowd saw—Jesus' glory.

THE FAITH FACTOR—People who continue to reject Jesus finally will reach the point of *not* being able to believe in him. Their hearts will get hardened against him. We don't know where that point is for any of us.

J. Vernon McGee: They [the crowd] were like a man who wakes up in the morning and says to himself, "Today I won't see and I will keep my eyes closed all day." He is just as blind as the man who cannot see. . . . Jesus has presented Himself to them as the Messiah and as their King. They have rejected Jesus personally. Now He rejects them![11]

Everett F. Harrison: It was not arbitrary, but rather a judicial hardening. Opportunity long neglected evokes no responses. The conscience seared by repeated violation ceases to function. Thus the nation, steeled to resist the claims of Jesus, *could not believe.*[12]

William Hendriksen: When people, of their own accord and after repeated threats and promises, reject him [God] and spurn his messages, then—and not until then—he hardens them, *in order that* those who were *not willing* to repent may *not be able* to repent.[13]

What Others are Saying:

God expects us to believe and act on the truth of his Word as we read and hear it. If we don't, eventually we reach the point of no return and are unable to believe. None of us knows where that point is.

> **John 12:42–43** Yet at the same time many even among the leaders believed in him. But because of the Pharisees they would not confess their faith for fear they would be put out of the synagogue; for they loved praise from men more than praise from God.

Fear Of Peers

If we're honest, most of us will admit to wanting other people's approval. It was no different in Jesus' day. While most of the religious leaders had hardened their hearts against Jesus, some were secret believers. They were afraid of being excommunicated from the synagogue if they stood up for Jesus. We know from other passages that two of them were <u>Nicodemus and Joseph</u> of Arimathea, who finally showed their belief after Jesus died.

☞ **GO TO:**

John 19:38–39
(Nicodemus and
Joseph)

> **John 12:44–46** Then Jesus cried out, "When a man believes in me, he does not believe in me only, but in the one who sent me. When he looks at me, he sees the one who sent me. I have come into the world as a light, so that no one who believes in me should stay in darkness."

A Package Deal

Many Bible scholars say the rest of this chapter is John's summary of Jesus' public ministry, pulling quotes from a variety of occasions. Others say Jesus returned from hiding to speak once more. Regardless of when Jesus said these words, they are a last appeal to believe in him.

Because Jesus is God with flesh, when people saw Jesus, they saw the Father. When people believe in him, they also believe in the Father. And when they believe, they step from the darkness of Satan's territory into the light of Jesus' kingdom.

> **John 12:47–50** "As for the person who hears my words but does not keep them, I do not judge him. For I did not come to judge the world, but to save it. There is a judge for the one who rejects me and does not accept my words; that very word which I spoke will condemn him at the last day. For I did not speak of my own accord, but the Father who sent me commanded me what to say and how to say it. I know that his command leads to eternal life. So whatever I say is just what the Father has told me to say."

Savior, Not Judge

Three years before, when Jesus was talking with Nicodemus, he emphasized the fact that he came to save people from their sins, not condemn them. Here, before his final withdrawal from the public, he said the same thing. Someday, however, Jesus will return to judge people for rejecting him and his words. The message that either saves or condemns is not Jesus' alone; it came from the Father.

F. F. Bruce: The message which proclaims life to the believer is the message which proclaims judgment to the disobedient. To bestow life, not to execute judgment, was the purpose of the Son's coming into the world; nevertheless, judgment is the inevitable effect of his coming for those who turn their backs on life.[14]

> **What Others are Saying:**

Study Questions

1. What did Mary do for Jesus? Why?
2. How did Judas respond to her action? Why?
3. How did the crowd greet Jesus when he entered Jerusalem?
4. What was significant about how he entered the city?
5. What did Jesus teach about losing our lives?
6. Why didn't many of the Jewish people believe in Jesus?

CHAPTER WRAP-UP

- Mary poured perfume on Jesus' feet to anoint him for burial, but Judas said it was a waste of money. (John 12:1–8)

- When Lazarus started attracting attention, the religious leaders plotted to kill him, too. (John 12:9–11)

- Jesus rode into Jerusalem on a donkey and was greeted by crowds waving palm branches. (John 12:12–19)
- Jesus taught that we must die to our own self-interests and put our trust in him in order to gain eternal life. (John 12:20–36)
- Many Jewish people did not believe in Jesus because they had hardened their hearts against God's truth. (John 12:37–43)
- Jesus made one last appeal to believe in him. (John 12:44–50)

Part Two

JESUS' PRIVATE MINISTRY

REVEREND FUN

"I don't think that is what Jesus had in mind in his teachings on being fruitful."

JOHN 13: JESUS THE SERVANT

Let's Get Started

When asked what we want to be when we grow up, nobody answers, "A servant." It's not on the list of preferred or popular occupations. Jesus had a different view of servanthood, however. (Isn't that just like him?)

His death on the cross was close. He had less than twenty-four hours left on earth. So, what did he do? He spent Thursday evening demonstrating servanthood and teaching his disciples in private. This chapter begins what Bible students have called the upper-room discourse, which continues through chapter 17 and is named after the place where they were (a large upstairs room). Other Gospel writers recorded details of the Passover meal; John recorded Jesus' demonstration of servanthood and his teachings.

At this juncture, John slowed down in telling the story of Jesus' life. Chapters 1–12 cover three years; chapters 13–18, one night. In fact, John devoted about one-third of the book to Jesus' last two days, starting here.

A PORTRAIT OF GREATNESS

> **John 13:1** It was just before the Passover Feast. Jesus knew that the time had come for him to leave this world and go to the Father. Having loved his own who were in the world, he now showed them the full extent of his love.

KEY POINT

Jesus demonstrated that true greatness comes from serving others.

Picture Of Love

In the previous chapter, we saw how Jesus rode into Jerusalem on Sunday. John skipped the events of Monday through Wednesday and picked up the story on Thursday with the Passover dinner. Again he noted that Jesus operated on his own timetable, and it was time for him to die and go back to heaven with the Father. But he continued to show love to his disciples right up until the end.

Some commentators have disagreed about <u>the timing</u> of the meal John describes compared to the accounts in the other Gospels. Some believe that the four accounts refer to different meals. By closely examining all accounts, and by understanding that John's use of the word "before" does *not* mean twenty-four hours before, it is clear that John and the other disciples ate the Passover meal together on Thursday.

For a rundown of what Jesus did during the last week of his life before this meal, read the following passages:

Sunday:	Triumphal entry into Jerusalem (John 12:12–19)
	Wept over Jerusalem (Luke 19:41–44)
Monday:	Cursed the fig tree (Matthew 21:18–19)
	Cleansed the Temple (Matthew 21:12–13)
	Healed in the Temple (Matthew 21:14–17)
Tuesday:	Teaching (Matthew 21:19–25:46)
	Anointed by Mary (John 12:2–8)
Wednesday:	Nothing recorded

> **John 13:2** The evening meal was being served, and the devil had already prompted Judas Iscariot, son of Simon, to betray Jesus.

Betrayal Ahead

The food was on the table and everyone reclined around it. This meal was the traditional Passover *seder*, or dinner, from which came the communion service that Christian churches celebrate. Although there was no outward indication yet that Judas would betray Jesus, Satan had already set that course of action.

☞ **GO TO:**

Matthew 26:17; Mark 14:12; Luke 22:7 (the timing)

Dig Deeper

Philip Yancey: Leonardo da Vinci immortalized the setting of the Last Supper in his famous painting, arranging the participants on one side of the table as if they were posing for the artist. John avoids physical details and presents instead the **maelstrom** of human emotions. He holds a light to the disciples' faces and you can almost see the awareness flickering in their eyes. All that Jesus has told them over the past three years is setting in.[1]

> **What Others are Saying:**

maelstrom: *whirlpool*

> **John 13:3–5** Jesus knew that the Father had put all things under his power, and that he had come from God and was returning to God; so he got up from the meal, took off his outer clothing, and wrapped a towel around his waist. After that, he poured water into a basin and began to wash his disciples' feet, drying them with the towel that was wrapped around him.

Real Greatness

Jesus always had a true sense of who he was. He knew where he came from, he knew where he was going, and he knew that God had given him power over everything. With that kind of confidence, he could do the unexpected.

Before the meal, the disciples had been arguing over who is greatest. When they arrived at the house and there was no servant to wash their feet, none of them volunteered to do this demeaning job. Jesus may have gotten tired of waiting for one of them to volunteer. Finally, he did a shocking thing. He stripped down to his inner tunic and did the job himself. God, the Creator of the whole universe, stooped to wash stinky, dirty feet! What a powerful example of humility, which is true greatness!

☞ **GO TO:**

Luke 22:24–26
(who is greatest)

Fritz Ridenour: When Jesus did this most inferior of acts, He was certainly saying that humility is the absence of pride. Jesus was saying that humility is not only "putting pride in your pocket"; it is getting down on your knees—physically (if necessary) and psychologically (which is often hardest to do).[2]

> **What Others are Saying:**

John MacArthur Jr.: Christ's love and His humility are inseparable. He could not have been so consumed with a passion for serving others if He had been primarily concerned with Himself.[3]

When we think of great men and women, we don't put servants on our lists. But God does. From his viewpoint, real greatness is shown in serving others. As Jesus taught, *"Whoever wants to become great among you must be your servant, and whoever wants to be first must be your slave"* (Matthew 20:26–27).

CULTURE CLUE

In Jesus' day, people wore sandals and walked on dusty, unpaved roads. So their feet were always dirty when they entered someone's house. A basin of water and towel sat near the entrance, and a servant greeted guests with a foot washing. The lowliest servant in each household was given the job of foot washing—and didn't enjoy it.

> **John 13:6–9** He came to Simon Peter, who said to him, "Lord, are you going to wash my feet?"
>
> Jesus replied, "You do not realize now what I am doing, but later you will understand."
>
> "No," said Peter, "you shall never wash my feet."
>
> Jesus answered, "Unless I wash you, you have no part with me."
>
> "Then, Lord," Simon Peter replied, "not just my feet but my hands and my head as well!"

Don't Stop With The Feet

Peter was so shocked that Jesus would want to wash his feet that he strongly protested against it. As usual, Jesus was teaching something beyond the surface meaning. If Peter didn't let Jesus wash him spiritually clean, he'd never be clean from his sins and would not be part of his kingdom. Peter didn't get it, though. His mind stayed on physical cleaning, so he asked for a bath.

Peter never did anything halfway. It was either all or nothing. He went from rejecting Jesus' foot washing to asking for a whole bath.

What Others are Saying:

J. Carl Laney: Peter's refusal of His service was in essence a rejection of Christ's Person. Jesus was saying, "Peter, if you do not receive My ministry, of which this foot washing is a mere token, then you are guilty of rejecting my Person and cannot be My disciple."[4]

Like Peter, we usually find it hard to let others serve us, don't we? Most of us find it much easier—and less embarrassing—to be the one doing the serving. We can't be proud when another person does something nice for us. So the next time someone wants to do something for you, don't protest; accept it graciously.

Something to Ponder

> **John 13:10–11** Jesus answered, "A person who has had a bath needs only to wash his feet; his whole body is clean. And you are clean, though not every one of you." For he knew who was going to betray him, and that was why he said not every one was clean.

One Man Didn't Bathe Today

On a physical level, most people who take a bath in the morning don't take another one when their feet get dirty. They just wash their feet. On the spiritual level, when we believe in Jesus, he washes away our sins. We are saved forever. But when we sin after that—and we will—we don't need to get saved again. We just need to ask for <u>forgiveness</u> for that particular sin, like getting our feet washed, so we stay in fellowship with Jesus.

Not all the disciples in that room had experienced the initial cleansing of salvation, however. Judas had hung around with the group for three years but had never believed in Jesus. It was no surprise to Jesus that Judas was going to betray him.

☞ **GO TO:**

1 John 1:9 (forgiveness)

> **John 13:12–13** When he had finished washing their feet, he put on his clothes and returned to his place. "Do you understand what I have done for you?" he asked them. "You call me 'Teacher' and 'Lord,' and rightly so, for that is what I am."

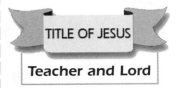

TITLE OF JESUS

Teacher and Lord

Love In Action

With the salvation lesson over, Jesus returned to what he was doing. As Teacher and Lord, or Master, he was above the disciples on the social ladder. Yet he humbled himself and did the job of a servant, showing them in a practical way what love is all about.

In those days, out of respect for Jesus' teaching role, many called him both "Teacher" and "Lord." But here Jesus is hinting at the events to come when he would die for the sins of the world. After his death and resurrection, Christians would use the word "Lord" to mean the one whom God had raised from the dead and placed above every other name.

> **John 13:14–15** "Now that I, your Lord and Teacher, have washed your feet, you also should wash one another's feet. I have set you an example that you should do as I have done for you."

Open Membership For The Towel Society

Notice that Jesus didn't scold them, saying, "Shame on you! You should have humbled yourselves and washed each other's feet." Although the disciples would have felt rebuked by his actions, Jesus was gentle and loving.

Now that Jesus had shown them how to serve, he expected them to follow his example. Some churches have taken Jesus' words literally and regularly perform foot-washing services. Whether or not we do that, we are to throw out our pride and humbly serve others as we can.

What Others are Saying:

Arthur W. Pink: The "teacher" is *believed*; the "Lord" is *obeyed*.[5]

Brenda Quinn: Jesus' demonstration of love and servanthood lives on as a reminder to believers that nothing we could do for another person is beneath something Jesus would do. No matter what we feel we deserve from others, we can't bend too low in caring for them. Service doesn't demean one's dignity; rather, as Jesus shows, it defines it.[6]

Remember This . . .

Foot washing can take many forms, such as cleaning up after a party, painting a house, walking a dog, providing a meal, or doing baby-sitting. The tasks may be menial. But if we do them out of love for Jesus, they'll be a lot easier. It's all in the attitude.

> **John 13:16–17** "I tell you the truth, no servant is greater than his master, nor is a messenger greater than the one who sent him. Now that you know these things, you will be blessed if you do them."

The Blessing's In The Doing

In the social order, servants are never above their masters, nor are messengers above their senders. Never. So if Jesus, the Master of the universe, could serve his disciples, then his disciples, in turn, can serve others. In the process, they will be blessed, or made happy.

This promise has two conditions: (1) we must remember as we serve that we will never be elevated to a position above our leader, Jesus; and (2) we must act on what we know and get busy serving. Sitting around talking about the great things we could do for Christ just doesn't cut it. To be blessed or made happy, we have to roll up our sleeves and get dirty.

R. Kent Hughes: Jesus did not say we will be happy if we think about these things or learn about them or, as is so often thought, have them done to us. "Happy are you if you *do* them." . . . We do not need to learn more about this. We need to do it.[7]

What Others are Saying:

Remember This . . .

Jesus' act of foot washing gave dignity to service. He made servants more important, rather than discounting their work. Then he threw in a bonus: real joy and satisfaction in serving other people.

Chapter 13 begins a long conversation between Jesus and his disciples that lasts for four chapters in our Bibles. Two of the topics were greatness and spiritual cleansing, which Jesus illustrated by washing the disciples' feet. We know from the Book of Acts that they learned what he taught.

Conversations with Christ

> **John 13:18–20** "I am not referring to all of you; I know those I have chosen. But this is to fulfill the scripture: 'He who shares my bread has lifted up his heel against me.'
>
> "I am telling you now before it happens, so that when it does happen you will believe that I am He. I tell you the truth, whoever accepts anyone I send accepts me; and whoever accepts me accepts the one who sent me."

An After-Dinner Kick

Judas spent three years with Jesus, eating together, traveling together, seeing the miracles and Jesus' power, hearing his teaching,

☞ **GO TO:**

Psalm 41:9
(lifting up the heel)

2 Samuel 15:12; 16:23
(betrayal)

and watching him in private. Still, he didn't believe. However, Jesus wasn't surprised. He related what Judas was about to do to Scripture. Lifting up the heel in Hebrew means "has made his heel great against me." It was a phrase used to show the pain caused by a friend's betrayal. The scripture portion Jesus quoted is in the context of David's betrayal by Ahithophel, his trusted advisor, making it more significant. Jesus warned the others, so they wouldn't be surprised when Judas betrayed him and would remember the prophecy from Scripture.

Once more Jesus emphasized that he comes as a package deal. When people received Jesus' representatives, they also received him. And when they accept Jesus, they also accept the Father.

THE FAITH FACTOR—The Bible is full of predictions about the future. God didn't give us these prophecies to satisfy our curiosity but to strengthen our belief in him when we see that they came true.

A TRAITOR AMONG US

> **John 13:21–22** After he had said this, Jesus was troubled in spirit and testified, "I tell you the truth, one of you is going to betray me."
>
> His disciples stared at one another, at a loss to know which of them he meant.

So, Who Is It?

Judas must have put on a good front, since only Jesus knew he was a hypocrite. He looked and talked like a believer. Most of us would have been mad and wanted to curse out Judas even if we didn't act on our feelings. But not Jesus. He was sad but told the group outright that one of them was the betrayer. The disciples could only look at one another, wondering who it was.

What Others are Saying:

Synoptics: Matthew, Mark, Luke

Herschel H. Hobbs: The **Synoptics** note that one after another they began to ask, "Lord, is it I?" (Matt. 26:22). Each question asked for a negative answer. Finally, Judas, lest his silence betray him, asked, "Rabbi, is it I?" (Matt. 26:25; "Rabbi," not "Lord"). Again inviting a negative answer. He still hoped that Jesus did not know of his purpose.[8]

> **John 13:23–25** One of them, the disciple whom Jesus loved, was reclining next to him. Simon Peter motioned to this disciple and said, "Ask him which one he means."
>
> Leaning back against Jesus, he asked him, "Lord, who is it?"

Who's The Traitor?

Peter had a lot of practice speaking up. So it's not surprising that he said what was on everyone's mind. What is surprising is that he didn't ask Jesus directly instead of going through John. Maybe he didn't want everyone to hear him, so he asked John, *"the disciple whom Jesus loved,"* who was sitting next to Jesus. Perhaps John whispered his question.

Contrary to Leonardo da Vinci's famous painting of the Last Supper, Jesus and his disciples did not sit on chairs, all on the same side of the table. Although people sat for everyday meals, reclining at table was reserved for special occasions. For the Passover dinner, the men reclined on large floor pillows or backless couches (see illustration below). They leaned on their left elbows, eating with one hand. The seats of honor were on either side of the host. Since John was sitting to the right of Jesus, he could lean his head back against Jesus' chest.

Reclining at Passover

Special meals, such as the Passover, may have been eaten on backless couches like these. Guests reclined on one elbow and used the other hand for eating.

> **John 13:26–27a** Jesus answered, "It is the one to whom I will give this piece of bread when I have dipped it in the dish." Then, dipping the piece of bread, he gave it to Judas Iscariot, son of Simon. As soon as Judas took the bread, Satan entered into him.

Bread For The Betrayer

Jesus evidently answered John in a quiet voice and chose a discreet method of identifying his betrayer. Jesus gave Judas a piece of bread dipped in herbs. This act was a sign of friendship and honor. The other disciples would not have thought it strange for Jesus to do this. Jesus showed his love for Judas. But Judas ignored the meaning. Judas chose to follow through with his plans, and at that moment Satan took control of him.

What Others are Saying:

David E. Garland: Table fellowship had more significance for Jews than simply a social gathering. Eating together was evidence of peace, trust, forgiveness, and brotherhood. To betray the one who had given you his bread was a horrendous act.[9]

John MacArthur Jr.: On the night he [Judas] betrayed Jesus, he was so prepared to do Satan's bidding that Satan was able to enter him and take complete control of him.[10]

CULTURE CLUE

The bread Jesus gave Judas was *matzah,* a flat bread baked without yeast that is used in the Passover meal. Most of the food on the table represented something associated with the time the Israelites were slaves in Egypt and God brought them out. The *matzah* represents the bread the Israelites didn't have time to let rise when they escaped. Jesus dipped it in bitter herbs—horseradish (see GWHN, pages 109–110), which reminded the diners of the misery of being slaves—and *charoset,* or *haroset,* a mixture of apples, wine, and nuts that represents the bricks the Israelites had to make.

> **John 13:27b–30** "What you are about to do, do quickly," Jesus told him, but no one at the meal understood why Jesus said this to him. Since Judas had charge of the money, some thought Jesus was telling him to buy what was needed for the Feast, or to give something to the poor. As soon as Judas had taken the bread, he went out. And it was night.

Into The Night

Now that Jesus had identified Judas as the betrayer, Jesus told him to do his job quickly. Jesus commanded Judas to do what he had planned. Jesus' words show that he was in control of the situation and willing to follow God's plan for him.

The rest of the disciples had no idea what Jesus was talking about. They thought Jesus was sending Judas to buy something for the Feast of Unleavened Bread, which began that night and would go on for seven days, or to give money to the poor. It was customary to make donations to the poor on Passover night. The temple gates were left open after midnight, and beggars gathered there. So the disciples assumed that Judas, the group's treasurer, was going to do some chore.

No doubt flustered by Jesus' earlier actions of love and his words now, Judas went out into the darkness of the night.

Leon Morris: "Night" is more than a time note. In view of the teaching of this Gospel as a whole it must . . . point us to the **strife** between light and darkness and to the night, black night, that was in the soul of Judas (*cf.* 11:10). He had cut himself off from the light of the world and accordingly shut himself up to night.[11]

> **What Others are Saying:**

strife: war

A COMMAND TO KEEP

> **John 13:31–32** When he was gone, Jesus said, "Now is the Son of Man glorified and God is glorified in him. If God is glorified in him, God will glorify the Son in himself, and will glorify him at once."

Turn On The Spotlight

If you knew that one of your closest friends was going to betray you and that his deeds would cost you your life, what would you do? Most of us would rebel. If you knew that your death would save millions, how would you feel? Most of us would be angry and say, "Why me?"

Not Jesus. Once Judas was gone, Jesus could get on with God's program for salvation. He knew what was coming and he was ready to get on with it. His death on the cross for our sins and resurrection would bring glory to, or spotlight attention on, both him and the Father. Jesus' act of obedience in telling Judas to do what he planned to do gave glory to Jesus now. And he would get even greater glory later.

> **John 13:33–35** "My children, I will be with you only a little longer. You will look for me, and just as I told the Jews, so I tell you now: Where I am going, you cannot come.
>
> "A new command I give you: Love one another. As I have loved you, so you must love one another. By this all men will know that you are my disciples, if you love one another."

Known By Your Love

The time of Jesus' death, of his return to heaven to be with the Father, was near. The disciples couldn't follow right away. They would go later when they died, however. At this time, Jesus began to prepare his disciples for being left behind without him. He started by giving them a new command to *"love one another."* It wasn't really new in the sense of having been just issued; they already had a command to <u>love</u> their neighbors. But Jesus made it new in quality by adding a new twist: to <u>love others as he loved them—unconditionally, humbly, and sacrificially.</u> Love would become the mark that identified them as his followers.

☞ **GO TO:**

Leviticus 19:18 (love)

What Others are Saying:

Bill Myers: Before He [Jesus] goes He gives His disciples a *new* commandment—a commandment to love one another. Not with the gushy, on-again-off-again, heart-flutter stuff we call love—but with a dedication and commitment so intense for our fellow brothers and sisters in Christ that, regardless of whether it makes us feel good or not, we would lay down our lives for them.[12]

Larry and Sue Richards: The night before he was crucified, Jesus issued a "new commandment" that his disciples love one another (John 13:34). The call to love others isn't new (Leviticus 19:18, 34). What then is "new" about this commandment?

- A new relationship—Christians are family, not just neighbors.
- A new standard—Christians love as Jesus loved.
- A new outcome—when Christians love each other, people who are not yet believers realize these are Jesus' followers.[13]

Warren W. Wiersbe: It is love that is the true evidence that we belong to Jesus Christ. The church leader Tertullian (A.D. 155–220) quoted the pagans as saying of the Christians, "See how they love one another?" And how do we evidence that love? By doing what Jesus did: laying down our lives for the brethren (1 John 3:16). And the way to start is by getting down and washing one another's feet in sacrificial service.[14]

When a man was dying or leaving for battle, he wrote out important teachings for his children, who, in turn, read them to their children, who passed them on to the next generation. Since Jesus knew he was dying, he left his disciples with final instructions, which John recorded in chapters 13–17.

> **John 13:36–38** Simon Peter asked him, "Lord, where are you going?"
>
> Jesus replied, "Where I am going, you cannot follow now, but you will follow later."
>
> Peter asked, "Lord, why can't I follow you now? I will lay down my life for you."
>
> Then Jesus answered, "Will you really lay down your life for me? I tell you the truth, before the rooster crows, you will disown me three times!"

Ready To Die

Once again Peter was the first to ask the question everyone else wanted to: *"Where are you going?"* Jesus repeated the fact that his disciples couldn't follow him; they would go later when they died. Peter was brave enough to volunteer to die for Jesus, but Jesus knew better. Peter was too cowardly to do that. Jesus predicted that Peter would deny knowing him three times before the <u>rooster crowed</u> at dawn.

☞ **GO TO:**

John 18:27
(rooster crowed)

elicits: draws out

W. E. Vine: Peter is occupied especially with the staggering fact that the Lord was going away. His answer **elicits** that disciple's impetuous but faithful assurance of the utmost loyalty.[15]

Jesus knew that Judas would betray him and that Peter would deny him. Yet he never stopped loving either one of them. Jesus went out of his way to reach them. That situation hasn't changed through the years. Jesus knows what we will do, but he keeps on loving us, too.

Study Questions

1. What role did Jesus take during the Passover dinner with his disciples? Why?
2. How did Jesus handle Peter's protest against getting his feet washed?
3. What did Jesus teach by washing his disciples' feet?
4. How did the disciples react to Jesus' announcement that one of them would betray him?
5. What did Jesus say would be the mark of his followers?
6. What did Jesus predict about Peter?

CHAPTER WRAP-UP

- Jesus gave his disciples an example of servanthood by washing their feet. (John 13:1–5)

- When Peter protested against the foot washing, Jesus taught him the importance of daily cleansing from sin. (John 13:6–11)

- Jesus taught that his disciples are to follow his example of serving others. (John 13:12–17)

- Jesus announced that Judas would betray him. (John 13:18–30)

- Jesus issued a new command to love one another. (John 13:31–35)

- Jesus predicted that Peter would deny him instead of laying down his life for him. (John 13:36–38)

JOHN 14: JESUS THE COMFORTER

Let's Get Started

It's hard to say good-bye to a close friend who's moving away. When that happens, we talk about the good times we had together, the tough times when we encouraged each other, and how lonely it'll be without that person around. We may cry, but even if we don't, we grieve the loss to some extent.

Jesus knows what it's like to say good-bye to friends. When he chose the disciples three years earlier, he knew he'd be saying good-bye at this point. It was hard for the disciples to deal with Jesus' leaving; they must have felt depressed and hopeless. So Jesus continued his final briefing by comforting them. He told them about their heavenly home to give them something to look forward to. He talked about the relationship they would have with a different person of the Godhead, the Holy Spirit, after he left them. And he promised them peace in spite of the turmoil that was coming with his arrest and crucifixion.

LOOKING FORWARD TO HEAVEN

John 14:1–4 "Do not let your hearts be troubled. Trust in God; trust also in me. In my Father's house are many rooms; if it were not so, I would have told you. I am going there to prepare a place for you. And if I go and prepare a place for you, I will come back and take you to be with me that you also may be where I am. You know the way to the place where I am going."

A Better Place Ahead

Troubled hearts were the order of the day. A few minutes before, Jesus had announced that Judas was a betrayer. He told the disciples he was going away and they couldn't come with him. Then he told Peter he would deny him three times before morning. That was enough news to trouble anybody, and there were more bad times ahead for the disciples. Jesus' death would try their faith in him far beyond anything they had experienced so far.

To help calm their troubled hearts, and in light of the near future, Jesus told the disciples to keep trusting him and keep looking to what's ahead. He wouldn't let them down. After his death, he was going back to heaven to prepare places for them in the Father's house. One day he will return to take them home, which is a place they already knew how to get to.

What Others are Saying:

James Montgomery Boice: Have you ever decorated a room for someone special? If you have, you know what it is like to make a room suit one particular personality. If it is a daughter, you make the room pretty. . . . If it is a son, the room might have airplanes or model cars. If it is for Grandma, the room might have her favorite books; and it might be far from the playroom or the children's bedrooms. We take care in such preparation. Are we to think that Jesus will take less care for those whom He loves, who are to spend eternity with Him?[1]

Remember This . . .

We all experience troubles, suffering, pain, anxiety, disappointment, and losses. These circumstances don't have to trouble us if we know Jesus. He is bigger than our needs and circumstances. So, when you're feeling anxious or disquieted, take your eyes off your troubles and put them on Jesus.

CULTURE CLUE

John's readers would have pictured a first-century house when they read these words. Homes were built around a central courtyard (see illustration, page 195) and designed for sons to bring their spouses to live there as well and raise their families there. Each household had its own room or apartment within the house that provided privacy. Members also had closeness to the father of the family by gathering in the courtyard.

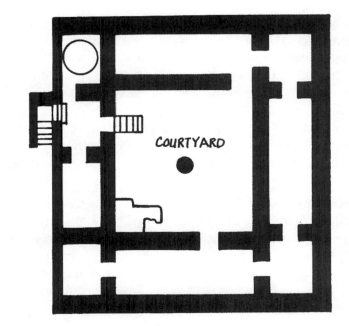

STREET

COURTYARD

First-Century House

This diagram shows how houses were built around an open courtyard. Ovens were usually located in the courtyard, which served as a kitchen.

Jesus is in heaven right now, preparing rooms for those who believe in him. We like to imagine what those rooms will be like, but that's not the important issue. What we need to be concerned about is whether or not we have a room. Do you know for sure that you have one waiting for you?

Something to Ponder

> **John 14:5–6** Thomas said to him, "Lord, we don't know where you are going, so how can we know the way?"
>
> Jesus answered, "I am the way and the truth and the life. No one comes to the Father except through me.

One Way Only

Jesus' leaving was a blow to his disciples. Their goal for the last three years was to follow him, and now he was going away and telling them they couldn't follow. Naturally, they'd have questions. Even though Jesus thought they knew where he was going, they didn't think so.

In answer to Thomas's question about getting to God's house, Jesus made his sixth "I am" statement: *"I am the way and the truth and the life."* He made it clear that not all religious roads lead to God and heaven. Only one does—Jesus himself. He bridges the gulf between sinful man and a holy God, with zero tolerance of other gods and religions.

Not only is Jesus the way to God; he is also the truth, the source of all our knowledge about God. Everything he said is true and trustworthy.

In addition, Jesus is the source of life as opposed to death. He gives eternal life to those who believe in him.

Karl Barth: God has not revealed himself in any religion, including Christianity. He has revealed himself in his Son. In Jesus Christ, God has spoken for himself, and we must hear that speech.[2]

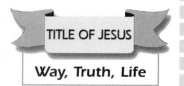

TITLE OF JESUS

Way, Truth, Life

Homer A. Kent Jr.: [Jesus] made it clear that the destination was the Father. He did not say that he came to show the way, but that he himself was the actual means for bringing men to God. An illustration might be a flowing river whose current actually conveys the boat to its destination, or the modern escalator which is not only the route but is also the conveyor from one level to another.[3]

C. S. Lewis: A man who was merely a man and said the sort of things Jesus said would not be a great moral teacher. He would either be a lunatic—on a level with the man who says he is a poached egg—or else he would be the Devil of Hell. You must make your choice. Either this man was, and is, the Son of God: or else a madman or something worse.[4]

Remember
This . . .

All roads don't lead to God. Attending church, doing good works, trying to be a good person, or following another religious leader won't get you to God. Jesus is the *only* way. It might seem like a narrow way, but thank God there *is* a way to eternal life.

Conversations with Christ

In preparation for his death, Jesus told the disciples he was going away to prepare places for them in heaven and that they already knew the way there. The disciples were confused, and Thomas spoke up. They didn't even know where he was going, much less how to get there. So Jesus explained that he is the only way to God and heaven. They may not have fully understood Jesus' teaching at that time, but after the Resurrection, they got it. A couple of months later, when Peter was preaching, he said, *"Salvation is found in no one else, for there is no other name under heaven given to men by which we must be saved"* (Acts 4:12).

> **John 14:7–9** "If you really knew me, you would know my Father as well. From now on, you do know him and have seen him."
>
> Philip said, "Lord, show us the Father and that will be enough for us."
>
> Jesus answered: "Don't you know me, Philip, even after I have been among you such a long time? Anyone who has seen me has seen the Father. How can you say, 'Show us the Father'?"

Show Us The Father

Because Jesus came to earth, we don't have to wait until we get to heaven to know what God is like. Jesus is God with flesh and bones. The disciples should have known God because they knew his Son; they already had a relationship with the Father through Jesus.

Philip had the right desire—to know God. But his request to see the Father must have disappointed Jesus. All those years, he had been showing his disciples the Father through his words and works. You'd think Lazarus's resurrection would have shown them plenty about God.

> **John 14:10–11** "Don't you believe that I am in the Father, and that the Father is in me? The words I say to you are not just my own. Rather, it is the Father, living in me, who is doing his work. Believe me when I say that I am in the Father and the Father is in me; or at least believe on the evidence of the miracles themselves."

Check Out My Record

In response to Philip's question, Jesus, in essence, told him, "If you are having a hard time believing me now, remember what I've said and done in the past. My words and works aren't mine; they came from the Father. We are **one**. If that's too hard to believe, don't forget the miracles. They prove I'm God."

one: *same God, but with different functions.*

THE FAITH FACTOR—Jesus taught and performed miracles so people would believe he is God. Even if they didn't believe his claims, the miracles prove what he said is true.

> **John 14:12–14** "I tell you the truth, anyone who has faith in me will do what I have been doing. He will do even greater things than these, because I am going to the Father. And I will do whatever you ask in my name, so that the Son may bring glory to the Father. You may ask me for anything in my name, and I will do it."

Is Jesus Handing Out Blank Checks?

It is astonishing that Jesus said the disciples would do greater works than he had done. He was God. In addition Jesus worked in the power of the Holy Spirit. How much better could the work get?

The description "greater" doesn't mean better; it means greater in numbers and extent. That's possible because God the Holy Spirit would be living and <u>working in</u> believers. With faith in Jesus, his disciples (and us) would do even greater works than Jesus had done. What's so amazing is that all-powerful God chose to work through us—flawed and sinful humans—and was able to accomplish so much.

From only eleven disciples, Christianity spread to worldwide influence. They would take the good news about Jesus beyond Israel to the whole world. The Book of Acts records some of these *"greater works"* in the first century.

Jesus' invitation to do what we ask in his name is not a blank check or magic formula to get what we want. Rather, he invites us to pray as he did—according to what God wants for us, for what will please him. When our requests are in line with his Word and will, Jesus will answer.

☞ **GO TO:**

Philippians 2:13
(working in)

What Others are Saying:

R. Kent Hughes: Because the Holy Spirit indwells us, we do the same works as Jesus—and they are greater than His works, simply because of the humble weakness of His instruments.[5]

apostles: disciples

Lawrence O. Richards: When Jesus encouraged the **apostles** to pray in his name . . . , he was not referring to an expression tacked on to the end of a prayer. To pray "in Jesus' name" means (1) to identify the content and the motivations of prayers with all that Jesus is and (2) to pray with full confidence in him as he has revealed himself. Jesus promised that prayer in his name would be answered.[6]

GETTING THE GODHEAD PERMANENTLY

> **John 14:15–17** "If you love me, you will obey what I command. And I will ask the Father, and he will give you another Counselor to be with you forever—the Spirit of truth. The world cannot accept him, because it neither sees him nor knows him. But you know him, for he lives with you and will be in you."

How Do You Love Me?

Jesus talked with his disciples quite a bit about loving. He even called <u>love</u> the mark of a believer. One way we can know we love Jesus is by whether or not we obey him. Notice the order: Love first, obey second. First we establish a relationship with him, then we do what he says.

To help us obey him, Jesus told his disciples that God would send a Counselor, the Holy Spirit. He's the third person of the Godhead. No one fully understands the Trinity. What we know for sure is that God is three persons in one, each distinct and each God.

As a man, Jesus couldn't be in more than one place at a time. His leaving the earth was actually better for his followers because he sent the Holy Spirit to live in them. Therefore, he is with every believer all the time, no matter where they are. The Spirit comforts us when we need it and shows us truth about God. He gives us the same sort of intimate relationship with the Father that Jesus had.

☞ **GO TO:**

John 13:35 (love)

The title "Counselor" for the Holy Spirit comes from a Greek word that means "one who is called alongside." It was used for a defense lawyer who stood alongside the accused person in court. A counselor is someone who encourages—not from a distance but while standing right beside a person.

The description of the Counselor as "another" uses the Greek word *allos,* which means another of the same kind—the same kind as Jesus. John did *not* use the word *heteros,* which means another of a different kind. The Holy Spirit is the same as God but with a distinct role. The Holy Spirit is a person—not an "it"—and a member of the Godhead.

CULTURE CLUE

Dig Deeper

To find out more about the Holy Spirit, check out these verses.

Characteristics	Names
Nehemiah 9:20	John 16:13
Psalm 139:7	Ephesians 1:13
Luke 1:35	Romans 8:2
Romans 15:30	Hebrews 10:29
1 Corinthians 2:10–11	1 Peter 4:14
1 Corinthians 12:11	
Ephesians 4:30	
Hebrews 9:14	

Remember This . . .

Keeping God's commandments is not a substitute for loving him. Anybody can look and act like a Christian to a certain degree. But God wants our love. When we love him, we'll want to obey him. It won't be a chore to do so.

What Others are Saying:

Henry Blackaby: When the Holy Spirit reveals Truth, He is not teaching you a concept to be thought about. He is leading you to a relationship with a Person.[7]

> **John 14:18–21** "I will not leave you as orphans; I will come to you. Before long, the world will not see me anymore, but you will see me. Because I live, you also will live. On that day you will realize that I am in my Father, and you are in me, and I am in you. Whoever has my commands and obeys them, he is the one who loves me. He who loves me will be loved by my Father, and I too will love him and show myself to him."

KEY POINT

Jesus told his disciples that after he died, he would send the Comforter, the Holy Spirit, to live in them.

Spiritual Survival Kit

Even though Jesus was going away, he wouldn't leave his disciples as orphans without families. He loved and cared for them as a father loves his children, so he would come back for them. After his death and resurrection, he met with the disciples and gave them the Holy Spirit to live in them when he returned to heaven. Because Jesus would live again after being crucified, his followers will also gain life after death—eternal life.

Then Jesus repeated himself. Whenever teachers repeat something, it must be important and they want their students to pay attention. So Jesus drove home the point that obeying his commands is proof that we love him. And when we love him, we receive his and the Father's love in return.

What Others are Saying:

John Calvin: Orphans [are] exposed to every kind of fraud and injustice, incapable of governing themselves, and in short unable of themselves to do anything. The only remedy for such a great weakness is for Christ to rule us by his Spirit, which he promises to do.[8]

Something to Ponder

It's easy to say we love Jesus, but can others see it in the way we obey him? Two people can say they love each other, but if they don't show it with actions and commitment, it's hard to believe their words. The same is true in our relationship with Jesus. He showed his love for us by dying for our sins. How do you show your love for him?

> **John 14:22–24** Then Judas (not Judas Iscariot) said, "But, Lord, why do you intend to show yourself to us and not to the world?"
>
> Jesus replied, "If anyone loves me, he will obey my teaching. My Father will love him, and we will come to him and make our home with him. He who does not love me will not obey my teaching. These words you hear are not my own; they belong to the Father who sent me."

Pay Attention

Jesus' teaching created questions in the disciples' minds. Some of it would have been hard to understand before his death and resurrection. So Judas asked for a clarification. John was careful to note that this wasn't the same Judas who would betray Jesus and who had already left the group. Judas wanted to know why Jesus was going to show himself to them and not to the world. It was a good question since Jesus had told them previously that he would appear to all nations.

Someday, when Jesus comes back to earth again, everyone will see him. But that's still in the future. In the meantime, Jesus' answer took the disciples back to their relationship with him. If they love and obey him, Jesus and the Father will abide with them (in the person of the Holy Spirit). But the Spirit only lives in those who believe in Jesus. This teaching isn't something Jesus made up; it came from the Father.

☞ GO TO:

Luke 6:16 (Judas)

Matthew 24:30 (appear)

> **John 14:25–26** "All this I have spoken while still with you. But the Counselor, the Holy Spirit, whom the Father will send in my name, will teach you all things and will remind you of everything I have said to you."

Spiritual Memory Jog

Most of us lament the fact that we can't remember everything. The disciples were probably the same way, especially since Jesus was giving them a lot of teaching in a short amount of time. No problem, according to Jesus. The Holy Spirit, whom he would send after his death and resurrection, would help them remember. Furthermore, the Spirit would continue Jesus' teaching ministry.

What Others are Saying:

Lawrence O. Richards: The Holy Spirit reminds us of what we have learned. The person who has made no effort to study and understand what Jesus has said will have nothing to be reminded of![9]

PEACE IN CHAOS

> **John 14:27** "Peace I leave with you; my peace I give you. I do not give to you as the world gives. Do not let your hearts be troubled and do not be afraid."

Peace Instead Of Fear

Jesus started this section by telling his disciples, *"Do not let your hearts be troubled."* Now he came full circle with this concept. They didn't have to be troubled and afraid, because he was leaving them his peace—peace that the world of unbelievers would never receive. It's peace that comes from inside, not from calm outward circumstances. It's a peace we can have in the midst of suffering, trials, or persecution because it comes from our relationship with Jesus and is totally independent of what's happening to us or around us.

The peace to which Jesus referred comes from the Hebrew word *shalom*. It is more than the absence of war or trouble. It includes the concepts of wholeness, harmony, soundness, health, fulfillment, and in some contexts, prosperity. The Old Testament, as well as Jesus, makes it clear that real peace comes from a relationship with God.

What Others are Saying:

R. Wade Paschal Jr.: The peace Jesus offers his disciples is not the peace of an easy life. It is the peace of the obedient servant who has the full confidence and support of his master, and carries out his commission effectively and joyfully.[10]

> **John 14:28–29** "You heard me say, 'I am going away and I am coming back to you.' If you loved me, you would be glad that I am going to the Father, for the Father is greater than I. I have told you now before it happens, so that when it does happen you will believe."

Rejoice With Me

Repeating what he had said earlier, Jesus reminded his disciples that he was <u>going away</u> (dying) and coming back (resurrecting). Knowing a friend is going to die makes us sad, but Jesus told those men it should make them happy. (You've probably noticed by now that often Jesus' teaching is the opposite of how we think or what we expect.) Jesus was glad to be going home to the Father. That's something to look forward to.

☞ **GO TO:**

John 13:3 (going away)

What Others are Saying:

John MacArthur Jr.: Before the **incarnation**, Jesus was in eternal glory. He experienced the Father's **infinite** love and fellowship in a way we cannot comprehend. But He left this glory to come to earth, not as a king to a magnificent palace but as a tiny baby to a stinking stable. He lived in poverty. He had no place even to lay His head. He suffered the hatred, abuse, and **jeers** of evil men. He was rejected by His own people and **vilified** even by the religious leaders. . . .

The hatred and abuse were almost over. Death would end them, and He would return to the glory He once had with the Father. He found joy as He approached the cross, because through His suffering there He would be restored to the full expression of deity. He looked forward to it. He rejoiced in anticipation of it. And He wanted His beloved friends to share His joy.[11]

incarnation: God becoming a man

infinite: unending

jeers: insults

vilified: spoke evil of

> **John 14:30–31** "I will not speak with you much longer, for the prince of this world is coming. He has no hold on me, but the world must learn that I love the Father and that I do exactly what my Father has commanded me.
>   "Come now; let us leave."

The End Is Near

It was time to leave the upper room. This intimate fellowship between Jesus and his disciples was almost over, and it was time for Jesus to die. Satan, *"the prince of this world,"* was God's instrument behind Jesus' crucifixion. But Jesus' death would not be permanent. In spite of the fact that Satan kept trying to defeat Jesus and take his place as God, he didn't have that kind of power. Jesus was going to die because that was God's will, not because Satan had a hold over him.

What Others are Saying:

John MacArthur Jr.: It was a supreme act of love to allow Satan to kill Him without legitimate reason, just because it was the Father's will that He die. Through His obedience, He showed the world how He loved the Father.[12]

Study Questions

1. What two things will Jesus do after he leaves this earth?
2. How did Jesus describe himself to Thomas?
3. In what ways will Jesus' followers do greater works than he did?
4. How do we prove that we love Jesus?
5. Who did Jesus say he would send when he went back to heaven?
6. What kind of peace does Jesus give his followers?

CHAPTER WRAP-UP

- Jesus claimed to be the only way to God. (John 14:1–6)
- Jesus reinforced the truth that he and the Father are one. His words and works prove that fact. (John 14:7–14)
- Jesus promised to send the Holy Spirit, who will live in believers. (John 14:8–21)
- Anyone who loves Jesus will obey him. (John 14:22–24)
- The Holy Spirit will remind Jesus' followers of what he said to them. (John 14:25–26)
- Jesus promised peace to his followers. (John 14:27–31)

JOHN 15: JESUS THE VINE

CHAPTER HIGHLIGHTS

- Through the Grapevine
- Life on the Vine
- Life beyond the Vine

Let's Get Started

Time was running out fast. Jesus was close to being arrested, tried, and crucified. And there was so much more to teach his disciples to prepare them for the time when he would no longer be with them. How do you cram a lot of information into tired minds? One way is to use pictures to help students remember. That's what Jesus did.

He and his disciples left the upper room in Jerusalem and walked through the Kidron Valley and up the Mount of Olives to the Garden of Gethsemane (see illustration, page 242). Along the way, they probably passed through at least one vineyard, which may have prompted Jesus to compare himself to a vine and his disciples to the branches.

After that lesson on fruitfulness, Jesus taught mini courses on love, friendship, persecution, and the Helper he'd send them after he left earth.

KEY POINT

Jesus taught that believers who abide in him will bear fruit, just like vine branches bear grapes.

THROUGH THE GRAPEVINE

> **John 15:1–2** "I am the true vine, and my Father is the gardener. He cuts off every branch in me that bears no fruit, while every branch that does bear fruit he prunes so that it will be even more fruitful."

Ouch, That Hurts

In the vineyard comparison, Jesus called himself the vine and called his Father the gardener. Believers are the branches, and the fruit they bear is character, such as the character qualities Paul called the fruit of the Spirit—*"love, joy, peace, patience, kindness, goodness, faithfulness, gentleness and self-control."*

Vines exist to bring forth fruit—large, sweet, juicy grapes. In order to get a crop like that, the gardener has to cut back the vines, getting rid of unproductive and dead branches. As the gardener, God knows what we need—and don't need—to develop Christlike character. In order to get that kind of fruit and to keep us depending on him, he allows hard times to "prune" us. No matter how painful the pruning is, God does it to produce something better from the process.

☞ **GO TO:**

Galatians 5:22–23
(fruit of the Spirit)

Merrill C. Tenney: The vine was . . . known as an emblem of their own nation, just as the eagle is the emblem of the United States. Over the temple of Herod which was then standing was the symbolic decoration of a great golden vine. Isaiah had used the same figure to point out how Israel had disappointed God by its unproductiveness (Isa. 5:1–7).[1]

TITLE OF JESUS

Vine

Lawrence O. Richards: The gardener who prunes his vine works with extreme care. There is no threat here in the picture of God as the gardener who prunes His vines. There is no warning to "produce, or else." Instead we're assured that God, the gardener, actively tending His vineyard, is fully committed to bring us to maximum fruitfulness.

God's pruning work benefits us; it doesn't threaten us.[2]

Vineyards were an important part of Jewish agriculture. Whether or not a family owned one to make a living, each family had at least one vine for grapes to eat and to make wine, as well as for shade in the summer. Grapevines were pruned way back for the first three years to keep them from bearing fruit, so that they would produce quality grapes later on. Each year after the third, they were pruned in late winter so they would yield larger harvests of fruit in August and September. Gardeners pruned with a hook that had a sharp, curved blade. They cut off fruitless and dead branches to make the sap flow to fruit-bearing branches. If a vineyard wasn't pruned, it was useless.

God prunes his children in a variety of ways. He may allow financial hardship, sickness, family members or friends who refuse to talk to them, or the loss of a loved one. Whatever it is, it's designed to drive us to God so we'll depend on him and grow to be more like Jesus.

Something to Ponder

> **John 15:3–4** "You are already clean because of the word I have spoken to you. Remain in me, and I will remain in you. No branch can bear fruit by itself; it must remain in the vine. Neither can you bear fruit unless you remain in me."

God's Green Thumb

God's Word had already cleaned, or pruned, the eleven men with Jesus. They were ready for bearing fruit. To do so, they needed to remain in Jesus. "Remain" means to stay with, be joined to, and spend time with someone. It's more than a casual relationship or a nodding acquaintance; it's an ongoing, deepening friendship.

R. Kent Hughes: When we abide, we set aside everything else from which we might derive strength and merit, to draw all from Christ. . . . Abiding involves a growing sense of our own weakness. . . . Those who learn well to abide will stay put for the pruning. We need the will to abide, the will to get into the Word, the will to associate with other believers, the will to put ourselves into places where we can grow.[3]

What Others are Saying:

Remaining in Jesus is not an automatic act. We have to work at the relationship through the following things:

- Praying
- Reading and studying the Bible
- Worshiping God alone and with other believers
- Being accountable to at least one other believer
- Serving others

Something to Ponder

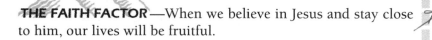

THE FAITH FACTOR—When we believe in Jesus and stay close to him, our lives will be fruitful.

Dig Deeper

The image of God as a gardener and his people as a vine was not new to the disciples. Check out some of the times it was used in the Old Testament Scriptures by reading these passages: Psalm 80; Isaiah 5:1–7; Jeremiah 2:21; Ezekiel 15:1–8.

> **John 15:5–6** "I am the vine; you are the branches. If a man remains in me and I in him, he will bear much fruit; apart from me you can do nothing. If anyone does not remain in me, he is like a branch that is thrown away and withers; such branches are picked up, thrown into the fire and burned."

The Vineyard Scene

Attachment to Jesus is the only way to produce fruit, since he is the source of our spiritual nourishment and strength. In the physical realm, the gardener cuts off dead branches and burns them like garbage. In the spiritual realm, God, the gardener, removes believers—sometimes through death—who don't bear fruit after he's pruned them.

Some Bible students believe the branches that are removed are believers who lost their salvation. Previously, Jesus taught that that isn't possible: *"I give them eternal life, and they shall never perish; no one can snatch them out of my hand. My Father, who has given them to me, is greater than all; no one can snatch them out of my Father's hand"* (John 10:28–29).

Others believe the dead branches are people who claim to be believers but were never saved, like Judas Iscariot. But dead branches on a grapevine started out being connected to the vine. People who have never believed in Jesus have never been connected to him. The subject of this passage is fruitfulness, not salvation.

What Others are Saying:

Wayne Jacobson: There is no fixed line that says the vine ends here and the branch begins there. That is why Jesus couldn't have chosen a better illustration of the intimate bond he seeks with his followers. He wants us to identify so closely with him that others cannot tell where he leaves off and where we begin.[4]

Lawrence O. Richards: Christ's observation here is not to be taken as a threat. We are not in danger of being lost if we fail to bear fruit. But we are in danger of living an essentially empty, useless life. God has chosen us to bear fruit. To do this we must stay close to Jesus, and respond obediently to His words. There is no use telling ourselves that any other goal to which we dedicate ourselves has lasting value. Christians are branches, and our only value to God is to be found in producing the fruit that He desires.[5]

> **John 15:7–8** "If you remain in me and my words remain in you, ask whatever you wish, and it will be given you. This is to my Father's glory, that you bear much fruit, showing yourselves to be my disciples."

A Bumper Crop

True followers of Jesus do more than believe in him. They remain in him and let Jesus' words change the way they live. When they're doing that, Jesus will answer their prayers that are in line with becoming more like Him and glorifying the Father. What draws attention to God is bearing much fruit, becoming more and more like Jesus.

What Others are Saying:

John MacArthur Jr.: In His **sovereign** wisdom, God sometimes answers the prayers of a non-Christian; but He does not obligate Himself to do so. If He does, it is His sovereign choice and for His purpose; but He does not have to. The promise of answered prayer is reserved only for those who abide in the true Vine.[6]

sovereign: supreme, excellent

Remember This . . .

For Jesus' words to change the way we live, we need to know what his words are. The primary way to know them is to read the Bible. We can also get to know his words by listening to sermons based on Scripture and studying the Bible with other believers.

> **John 15:9–11** "As the Father has loved me, so have I loved you. Now remain in my love. If you obey my commands, you will remain in my love, just as I have obeyed my Father's commands and remain in his love. I have told you this so that my joy may be in you and that your joy may be complete."

Love And Joy From The Vine

One of the advantages of being connected to Jesus is experiencing his love—the same kind of love the Father has for him. His love is unconditional, constant, and never ending. We remain in Jesus' love by obeying his commands, just like Jesus obeyed the Father. As a result, we'll be full of joy.

What Others are Saying:

Henry Blackaby: God is far more interested in a love relationship with you than He is in what you can do for Him.[7]

John Calvin: "Remain in my love." Some people explain this as meaning that Christ demands a return of love from his disciples. Others better understand it as Christ's love to us. He means for us to enjoy continually the love he had for us, and so he warns us to be careful not to deprive ourselves of it.[8]

R. V. G. Tasker: They are apostles of Him who was sent from God, and chosen servants of One whose destiny it was to lay down His life for His friends. Their love for others must therefore be a sacrificial love. But the practice of that love would never be a joyless duty. Jesus endured the cross for the joy that was set before Him, and part of that joy lay in the knowledge that His disciples, in obeying the commands He had given them, would find in their obedience the fullness of their own joy.[9]

LIFE ON THE VINE

> **John 15:12–13** "My command is this: Love each other as I have loved you. Greater love has no one than this, that he lay down his life for his friends."

Loving The Branches

Loving other believers must be important since Jesus repeated this command several times. It's the first fruit of the Spirit that Paul listed in Galatians. It's also the mark of believers. The ultimate expression of love is dying for someone else like Jesus did, although our death could never save a person the way Jesus saved us. The kind of love that Jesus wants his followers to show toward others is a selfless love—one that always does what is best for others rather than for oneself.

☞ **GO TO:**

Galatians 5:22–23
(first fruit)

John 13:35
(mark of believers)

We don't get many calls to be a hero and die for someone else. But we can lay down our lives for our friends in other ways: listening to someone who needs to talk, giving away money and other possessions, spending time with friends who are lonely, and helping out in a variety of ways.

Something to Ponder

> **John 15:14–15** "You are my friends if you do what I command. I no longer call you servants, because a servant does not know his master's business. Instead, I have called you friends, for everything that I learned from my Father I have made known to you."

Befriending The Branches

So often Jesus operated in a way that was opposite to the way of everybody else. In his day, a teacher's followers were servants. But Jesus called his followers friends. The master doesn't tell his servants about his business or share what he knows; he tells his friends. That's what Jesus did. He told his disciples what the Father told him.

Only two people who lived before Jesus are called friends of God: Abraham and Moses (see GWMB, pages 13–28 and 71–90, respectively). Jesus widened the friendship circle to include everyone who believes in him.

☞ **GO TO:**

2 Chronicles 20:7 (Abraham)

Exodus 33:11 (Moses)

William Barclay: Jesus called us to be his friends and the friends of God. That is a tremendous offer. It means that no longer do we need to gaze longingly at God from afar off; we are not like slaves who have no right whatever to enter into the presence of the master; we are not like a crowd whose only glimpse of the king is in the passing on some state occasion. Jesus gave us this intimacy with God, so that he is no longer a distant stranger, but our close friend.[10]

What Others are Saying:

Today we use the term "friend" in a much more casual way than Jesus and his disciples understood that word. For them, friendship included loyalty, equality, the sharing of possessions, and the intimacy of sharing secrets. The Greek word for "friend" means a friend in the court, someone who is part of the king's inner circle. To the Greeks of that time, the greatest expression of friendship was to die for a friend.

CULTURE CLUE

> **John 15:16–17** "You did not choose me, but I chose you and appointed you to go and bear fruit—fruit that will last. Then the Father will give you whatever you ask in my name. This is my command: Love each other."

Fruit Attraction

Jesus' disciples were his friends because he chose them. That left no room for them to be proud just because they were attached to Jesus. He chose them to be with him for three years and also to go out into the world and produce lasting fruit. As they became more like Jesus, they would attract people to put their faith in him, thus growing the fruit of more disciples. As they obeyed Jesus, God would answer their prayers.

Remember the principle of repetition indicating importance? Here it is again. Jesus commanded his disciples to love each other. It's the fruit that will make them most attractive to unbelievers.

What Others are Saying:

Wayne Jacobson: Anyone who has ever waited in line only to be the last chosen for a team knows the terrifying humiliation of not being wanted. When we are grafted into Christ, we never have to know that humiliation again. There is no greater assurance than knowing that Jesus has chosen you and me to be grafted into him. Yet his choosing does not exclude anyone else. On this Vine there is room for everyone.[11]

Remember This . . .

Loving other believers doesn't depend on our feelings for them. We can love a person we don't even like. That's because love is an action, not a feeling. When we show love, the feelings generally follow the action.

LIFE BEYOND THE VINE

> **John 15:18–19** "If the world hates you, keep in mind that it hated me first. If you belonged to the world, it would love you as its own. As it is, you do not belong to the world, but I have chosen you out of the world. That is why the world hates you."

This Is Good News?

Most of us would try to encourage our friends if we knew we were dying, but what Jesus told his friends was enough to depress any group. He had startling news: The world of unbelievers hated Jesus enough to kill him, and they could expect the same treatment because he had chosen them out of that group. Definitely *not* a selling point for following Jesus. (But he offers plenty of benefits to offset this drawback.) Jesus made it clear that we can't be a <u>friend</u> of both him and the world; they are mutually exclusive.

Unsaved people hated Jesus and his disciples almost two thousand years ago. They have hated Christians through the years since then and still hate them today. The reasons may change, but the reality of that relationship has not. God's values and absolutes always run counter to the world.

> **John 15:20–21** "Remember the words I spoke to you: 'No servant is greater than his master.' If they persecuted me, they will persecute you also. If they obeyed my teaching, they will obey yours also. They will treat you this way because of my name, for they do not know the One who sent me."

Persecution Prophecy

Because believers are connected to Jesus, they will get the same treatment Jesus did. All his life, Jesus was hated—from King Herod's attempt to <u>kill</u> <u>him</u> as a young child (see GWLC, pages 37–38) to the religious leaders' convincing the ruling Romans to crucify him within twenty-four hours. So believers can expect persecution too.

John MacArthur Jr.: The Jews of Jesus' day prided themselves on what they thought was an in-depth knowledge of God. When Jesus said that they did not know God, the religious leaders were infuriated. But in rejecting Christ they themselves proved that He was right. They claimed to know God, yet they hated Christ, who was God in human flesh. Their love for God was a **facade**.[12]

☞ **GO TO:**

James 4:4 (friend)

Remember This . . .

☞ **GO TO:**

Matthew 2:13–16 (kill him)

What Others are Saying:

facade: *pretense*

> **John 15:22–25** "If I had not come and spoken to them, they would not be guilty of sin. Now, however, they have no excuse for their sin. He who hates me hates my Father as well. If I had not done among them what no one else did, they would not be guilty of sin. But now they have seen these miracles, and yet they have hated both me and my Father. But this is to fulfill what is written in their Law: 'They hated me without reason.' "

No Excuse For The World

☞ **GO TO:**

Psalm 69:4 (predicted)

Jesus had given the people enough evidence to prove he is God. They heard his teaching and saw his miracles, but they rejected him anyway. Therefore, they were guilty of rejecting God and were without an excuse for that sin. Their unfounded hatred and rejection didn't surprise Jesus, though. God had already <u>predicted</u> it in the Scriptures.

What Others are Saying:

Herschel H. Hobbs: Why did the world hate Jesus? Because in His ministry He had revealed to them their sin (v. 22). Under the searching gaze of His perfect life and teaching, they no longer could hide under cloaks of self-righteousness.[13]

> **John 15:26–27** "When the Counselor comes, whom I will send to you from the Father, the Spirit of truth who goes out from the Father, he will testify about me. And you also must testify, for you have been with me from the beginning."

Time For Testimonies

Jesus was big on repetition, especially in those last hours before his death. In repeating the fact that the Holy Spirit would be coming, he added that he would be the one sending him, not the Father. It's a subtle way of saying again that he's God. Jesus also used a new name, *"Spirit of truth."* The Spirit will teach people God's truth and point to Jesus, *the* truth. The Spirit isn't the only one who will witness about Jesus; his followers will too.

This whole chapter is part of a conversation Jesus had with his disciples before his death. In this portion, he did all the talking without questions or comments from the men. We know from the Book of Acts that they practiced what he said to them about remaining in him: *"When they saw the courage of Peter and John and realized that they were unschooled, ordinary men, they were astonished and they took note that these men had been with Jesus"* (Acts 4:13).

Conversations with Christ

Study Questions

1. What natural object did Jesus use to describe his relationship with his disciples?
2. When we remain in Jesus, what do we produce?
3. What does God do to be sure we are productive?
4. Why did Jesus call his disciples friends?
5. What did Jesus tell his disciples to expect after he was gone?

CHAPTER WRAP-UP

- Jesus expects his disciples to remain in him, like branches on a vine, in order to be fruitful spiritually. (John 15:1–8)

- Jesus commanded his disciples to love one another, even to the point of dying. (John 15:9–14)

- Jesus called his disciples friends instead of servants and shared God's words with them. (John 15:15–17)

- Because the world hated Jesus, it would also hate his disciples. (John 15:18–25)

- When Jesus sent the Holy Spirit, he would tell people about Jesus, along with his disciples. (John 15:26–27)

JOHN 16: JESUS THE TEACHER

CHAPTER HIGHLIGHTS

- Mission of Conviction
- Guide into Truth
- Joy for the Pain

Let's Get Started

Most of us like to know what's going to happen in the future, no matter how bad it is. At least that way we can prepare for it. The night before Jesus was crucified, he tried to prepare his disciples for the near future—some of which was going to be bad.

One more time, to be sure they understood before he went back to heaven, Jesus revisited several truths: he was going away; the disciples would be persecuted; he was sending the Holy Spirit in his place; they could pray in his name; he'd give them peace in the midst of trouble. Jesus fortified and encouraged those eleven men for the days ahead when they'd need his teaching most.

MISSION OF CONVICTION

> **John 16:1–3** "All this I have told you so that you will not go astray. They will put you out of the synagogue; in fact, a time is coming when anyone who kills you will think he is offering a service to God. They will do such things because they have not known the Father or me."

Coming Attractions

Jesus' preview of coming attractions was not a pleasant one. He wanted to prepare his disciples for what was ahead so they wouldn't be taken by surprise and go AWOL. What was ahead was persecution. Unbelieving Jewish people would think they were doing God a favor by kicking them out of the synagogues and even killing them. When John wrote this book, Jesus' warning had already come true.

CULTURE CLUE

The Greek word for *"go astray"* paints a picture of stumbling over unexpected objects. It's like walking through a dark room with toys strewn on the floor and not being able to see where they are. No matter how careful you are, you end up tripping over at least one.

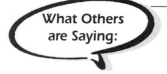

What Others are Saying:

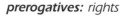

prerogatives: rights

William Hendriksen: The followers of the Nazarene would be excommunicated from the religious and social life of Israel. They would be cut off from the hopes and **prerogatives** of the Jews. They would be viewed by their former friends as worse than pagans. They would lose their jobs, would be exiled by their families, and would even lose the privilege of honorable burial. Worse than this even, they would actually be killed.[1]

Something to Ponder

Believers today are not immune to persecution for their faith. Christians are still persecuted physically around the world. Others are persecuted verbally. No matter what form persecution takes, it's a compliment to be persecuted for our faith. It puts us in the same company with Jesus, and that's the best place to be.

> **John 16:4–6** "I have told you this, so that when the time comes you will remember that I warned you. I did not tell you this at first because I was with you.
>
> "Now I am going to him who sent me, yet none of you asks me, 'Where are you going?' Because I have said these things, you are filled with grief."

Forewarning For The Future

It must have been confusing and discouraging for Jesus to keep telling his disciples that he was going away, especially since he had just told them to remain in him. Even though they couldn't sort it all out that night, they would remember what he said when the events happened. So he repeated that he was going back to the Father, who had sent him. His departure would certainly cause the disciples grief. After all, they were about to lose their best friend.

Matthew Henry: Christ dealt faithfully with his disciples when he sent them forth on his errands, for he told them the worst of it, that they might sit down and count the cost.[2]

> **John 16:7** "But I tell you the truth: It is for your good that I am going away. Unless I go away, the Counselor will not come to you; but if I go, I will send him to you."

I'm Doing This For Your Own Good

How many times did your parents tell you they were doing something for your own good when it hurt you? This was the same kind of situation for the disciples. When Jesus went away, he would send the Counselor, the Holy Spirit. The Holy Spirit can be everywhere at once; Jesus was limited to wherever his body was; so the disciples really were getting something better.

When John wrote *"It is for your good,"* he used the Greek word *sumphero,* which means good in the sense of beneficial or profitable. He did not use the word *kalos,* which means good in the sense of beautiful or pleasant. It wasn't pleasant for the disciples to have Jesus leave, but it was beneficial.

> **John 16:8–11** "When he comes, he will convict the world of guilt in regard to sin and righteousness and judgment: in regard to sin, because men do not believe in me; in regard to righteousness, because I am going to the Father, where you can see me no longer; and in regard to judgment, because the prince of this world now stands condemned."

Conviction Report

The Spirit not only ministers to believers, but also has a mission *world.* He is the prosecuting attorney in God's courtroom, charged with showing unsaved human beings their lost condition.

To "convict" means to show, to expose, to unmask. The Spirit's special ministry to the world is to convict of sin in three specific areas.

First, the Spirit convicts of sin *"because men do not believe in me."* The issue is not the specific sins that human beings com-

☞ **GO TO:**

Romans 3:23 (sin)

mit, but the one condemning <u>sin</u> of unbelief. No wonder we need to keep the focus on Jesus as we witness to unsaved friends.

Second, the Spirit convicts *"in regard to righteousness, because I am going to the Father."* Christ's return to heaven established a new standard of righteousness. No longer can righteousness be considered a matter of do's and don'ts. The issue is no longer one of keeping rules, but of living as perfect a life as Jesus did. Our friends might argue that "I kept that commandment." But no one can claim to have led as perfect a life as Jesus Christ.

Third, the Spirit convicts in regard to judgment, *"because the prince of this world now stands condemned."* Satan is the prince of this world, and at times it may look as if he is getting away with evil. The cross is God's announcement that he does and will punish sins—Satan's and everyone else's. No longer can anyone scoff at the idea that those who do evil are doomed. God revealed his commitment to judge sin by sending his own innocent Son to a cross for our sakes.

Each convicting ministry of the Holy Spirit is focused on Jesus Christ. And he should be our focus as we cooperate with the Spirit in telling others the good news.

What Others are Saying:

Everett F. Harrison: Sin is man's central problem. Even as Christ came to deal with it objectively at the Cross (Rom. 8:3), so the Spirit is promised to press home to sinful hearts the reality of sin and the awfulness of adding to all other offenses this crowning one of refusing the Saviour.[3]

David H. Stern: The world is wrong . . . about sin, in that people don't put their trust in me [Jesus]. Instead, they have other theories about sin, theories which downgrade the horribleness of sin and upgrade their own holiness. Thus they find no need to accept for themselves **Yeshua**'s atoning death.[4]

Yeshua: Jesus

Remember This . . .

Sometimes those of us who believe in Jesus try to guilt-trip people into believing too. Jesus said it's the Spirit's job to convict people of their sin, not ours. He's the only one who can change their hearts permanently.

THE FAITH FACTOR—One of the Holy Spirit's jobs is to convict people of the sin of not believing in Jesus so they will put their faith in him.

GUIDE INTO TRUTH

> **John 16:12–13** "I have much more to say to you, more than you can now bear. But when he, the Spirit of truth, comes, he will guide you into all truth. He will not speak on his own; he will speak only what he hears, and he will tell you what is yet to come."

You've Got Spirit

Not only will the Spirit convict unbelievers of their sin; he will also guide believers into knowledge of the truth. Like a guide leads a stranger into an unknown place, the Spirit will guide Jesus' followers into an understanding of Jesus' death and resurrection. He works in tandem with the Son to tell them what Jesus didn't have time to teach, including what we now have as the New Testament.

KEY POINT

In preparation for his dying, Jesus taught his disciples about the Holy Spirit and that he would rise from the dead.

> **John 16:14–15** "He will bring glory to me by taking from what is mine and making it known to you. All that belongs to the Father is mine. That is why I said the Spirit will take from what is mine and make it known to you."

Passing Along Jesus' Words

While people in the world are busy rejecting Christ and persecuting Christians, the Holy Spirit is working in believers to glorify Christ. The harder the world works against Christians, the more God will pour into them his wisdom. But it won't happen to us painlessly while we sleep. We have to go through the hard times and be diligent to study the Bible.

Studying Scripture is not an exercise in filling our minds with information or stockpiling facts to win religious arguments. We study God's Word to get to know Jesus. That's what the Holy Spirit helps us do. He shines the spotlight on Jesus while helping us understand what he said and how to live victoriously.

JOY FOR THE PAIN

> **John 16:16–18** "In a little while you will see me no more, and then after a little while you will see me."
>
> Some of his disciples said to one another, "What does he mean by saying, 'In a little while you will see me no more, and then after a little while you will see me,' and 'Because I am going to the Father'?" They kept asking, "What does he mean by 'a little while'? We don't understand what he is saying."

A Short Leave

Yes, the Holy Spirit was coming. But first Jesus had to die and rise again. This news was not something the disciples could process. Although Jesus had raised people, like Lazarus, from the dead, no one had risen by his own power before. They talked among themselves, trying to figure out what Jesus meant.

What Others are Saying:

D. A. Carson: It is true that the Counselor, the blessed Spirit of truth, will be sent to the disciples; but first, the cross. It is true that the disciples will learn to serve as witnesses in a hostile world; but first, the cross. They will, of course, enter into deep, spiritual intimacy with the exalted Lord; but first, the cross. More revelation will be given by the coming Holy Spirit; but first, the cross. And so it is to the cross, this crucial saving appointment, that Jesus now turns his attention.[5]

> **John 16:19–20** Jesus saw that they wanted to ask him about this, so he said to them, "Are you asking one another what I meant when I said, 'In a little while you will see me no more, and then after a little while you will see me'? I tell you the truth, you will weep and mourn while the world rejoices. You will grieve, but your grief will turn to joy."

Grieving Isn't Forever

Nothing escaped Jesus. He knew the disciples wanted to question him but were probably afraid or embarrassed to. So he voiced their question—but didn't answer it directly. Instead, he talked about the emotions they would experience after his death. They would mourn his death, while unbelievers would rejoice that Jesus was no longer around to challenge them. The disciples' grief wouldn't last, however. It would *"turn to joy"* when they understood why Jesus died and when they saw him alive again.

D. A. Carson: Jesus replies to their need, rather than to their question. Their question is phrased in terms of understanding what Jesus has said; but Jesus discerns that their deepest concern is his departure, not the meaning of a phrase. They are upset, confused; but above all they are still ill-prepared for the acute grief that will be theirs.[6]

> **John 16:21–22** "A woman giving birth to a child has pain because her time has come; but when her baby is born she forgets the anguish because of her joy that a child is born into the world. So with you: Now is your time of grief, but I will see you again and you will rejoice, and no one will take away your joy."

Birth Pangs

When a woman is about to give birth, she experiences great pain. Then when she hears the baby cry, her pain becomes joy. The cross would affect Jesus' disciples in a similar way. Watching their friend and teacher die would bring great pain, but his resurrection would change their grief into everlasting joy.

Philip Yancey: Although childbirth may involve great pain, the pain is not a dead end, like pain caused by cancer. The effort of giving birth produces something—new life!—and results in joy. In the same way, the great sorrow he and the disciples are about to undergo will not be a dead end. His pain will bring about the salvation of the world; their grief will turn to joy.[7]

It was common for women to die in childbirth in Jesus' day. In the Old Testament Scriptures, suffering was often described as birth pains, especially when it was the result of God's judgment on his people Israel. Hebrew words for mental and physical agony were used to explain that the spiritual birth pains were intense and that God's coming judgment was serious.

Dig Deeper

The Bible has much to say about the lasting joy believers can experience. For a quick overview, read these verses: Psalm 16:11; 43:4; Proverbs 10:28; Acts 13:52; Romans 15:13; Philippians 1:4; Philemon 7; James 1:2.

> **John 16:23–24** "In that day you will no longer ask me anything. I tell you the truth, my Father will give you whatever you ask in my name. Until now you have not asked for anything in my name. Ask and you will receive, and your joy will be complete."

Direct Line To God

After Jesus' resurrection, the disciples would have answers to all their questions about Jesus' leaving. His death would make sense. Then they could go directly to God in prayer and ask him for anything in Jesus' name. They wouldn't need a human priest as a go-between. To ask in Jesus' name does not mean bringing a shopping list of requests and expecting home delivery of everything. It does mean asking for the things Jesus desires, like more people believing in him and a Christlike character. Not only will God answer requests like that; he will also give great joy when the answers are received.

What Others are Saying:

Larry and Sue Richards: Jesus' promise means that when you want to glorify God as he did and serve others as he served them, God will answer those prayers with a glad "Yes!"[8]

Leon Morris: God is interested in the wellbeing and the happiness of His people. They will go through trials . . . , but when their trust is in Him He puts a joy into their hearts that can never be removed. Notice that this is connected with prayer. They are to pray in order that their joy may be made complete.[9]

Something to Ponder

Although believers have a direct prayer line to God, we don't always use it. Sometimes we talk to everyone else but God about a situation or need. Sometimes we ignore him when he's the only one who can help. Sometimes we're too busy to talk to God. But he's waiting to hear from us.

> **John 16:25–26** "Though I have been speaking figuratively, a time is coming when I will no longer use this kind of language but will tell you plainly about my Father. In that day you will ask in my name. I am not saying that I will ask the Father on your behalf."

The Situations Are Changing

The Resurrection changed religion and history. It also changed the way Jesus would talk to his disciples. Afterward, he could talk plainly and they would understand. He wouldn't have to demonstrate truth by washing feet or explain relationships by comparing them to a vine and branches. At that time Jesus wouldn't have to be the go-between for the disciples and God. They could talk directly to the Father.

> **John 16:27–28** "No, the Father himself loves you because you have loved me and have believed that I came from God. I came from the Father and entered the world; now I am leaving the world and going back to the Father."

Father Love

Even though Jesus was going away, his disciples would not go unloved. The Father loved them because they loved Jesus and believed in him. Then, in one sentence, Jesus clearly summarized his life and mission:

- *"came from the Father"*: He left heaven.
- *"entered the world"*: He became a man.
- *"leaving the world"*: He would die—for our sins.
- *"going back to the Father"*: He would rise from the dead and return to heaven.

☞ **GO TO:**

Philippians 2:5 (from the Father)

Philippians 2:6–7 (became a man)

Philippians 2:8 (die)

Philippians 2:9; Acts 1:11 (return to heaven)

Ruth Myers: Why is our love so important to God? Why does He care so much whether or not we love Him? I think it's because He has always been a relational God. He was never a lonely, solitary, figure somewhere out in eternity, all alone in the empty reaches of space. He has always been a **triune** God in intimate relationship—the Father, Son, and Holy Spirit in loving communion. And before time began God decided He wanted to include many others in that circle of love.[10]

What Others are Saying:

triune: three parts or aspects in one

> **John 16:29–30** Then Jesus' disciples said, "Now you are speaking clearly and without figures of speech. Now we can see that you know all things and that you do not even need to have anyone ask you questions. This makes us believe that you came from God."

Now We Get It

It took them a while, but the disciples finally got what Jesus had been saying—that he was going to die, rise again, and go back to heaven. Once they understood that, they didn't have to ask any more questions (at least for the time being). Jesus' knowledge and prediction of the future persuaded them that Jesus knew everything and is truly God. You could almost see the lightbulbs going on in everyone's mind.

> **John 16:31–32** "You believe at last!" Jesus answered. "But a time is coming, and has come, when you will be scattered, each to his own home. You will leave me all alone. Yet I am not alone, for my Father is with me."

Watch Out For The Curve Ball

Once the disciples understood what was going to happen to Jesus, he threw them a curve ball. Not only was he leaving them but in addition they would all <u>scatter</u>, leaving him alone. In only a couple of hours, that prediction would come true when Jesus was arrested. Even though Jesus would be alone physically, the Father would still be with him.

☞ **GO TO:**

Zechariah 13:7 (scatter)

Conversations with Christ

Jesus repeatedly told his disciples that he was going away, meaning he would die and rise again. Finally, it became a two-way conversation when the disciples acknowledged that they understood what he was saying. That understanding led to their declaration of Jesus' deity.

> **John 16:33** "I have told you these things, so that in me you may have peace. In this world you will have trouble. But take heart! I have overcome the world."

Defeating Deity

Wrapping up his teaching, Jesus left the disciples with a word of encouragement. He promised them peace in times of trouble—and there would be plenty of troubled times ahead. But Jesus' death would break Satan's choke hold on the world system that causes trouble for believers. It was a sure thing, even though his death was still hours away.

J. Vernon McGee: He closes with peace. The child of God can have peace in this life because peace is found in Christ and in no other place. You won't find peace in the church. You won't find peace in Christian service. Peace is found in the person of Jesus Christ.[11]

W. E. Vine: "Be of good cheer" *["take heart"]* suggests that naturally there would be cause for depression of heart. But against this He is Himself the antidote. He had been through it all, and defeated the influences of the world.[12]

Dana Gould: The **verb** John used here means to "conquer," "overcome." The force of this verb indicates a continuing victory. Jesus' words, "I have overcome the world," were not so much a promise as a statement of fact. His victory also applies to us today.[13]

verb: *overcome*

All that Jesus promised his disciples that night—peace, a direct line to God, the power of God, the Holy Spirit living in them, spiritual fruit, a room in heaven, and his constant presence—is available to believers today.

Remember This . . .

Study Questions

1. Why can people who believe in Jesus expect to be persecuted?
2. What will the Counselor do for unbelievers?
3. What will the Spirit of truth do for believers after Jesus goes back to heaven?
4. How did the disciples react to Jesus' teaching about his going away?
5. What does it mean to ask in Jesus' name?
6. Why can Jesus' followers be sure of having peace?

- Jesus predicted the persecution of his disciples, including their deaths, which the Jewish people considered a favor to God. (John 16:1–4)

- Jesus repeated that when he went back to heaven, he would send the Counselor, or Holy Spirit, in his place. (John 16:5–11)

- After Jesus left earth, the Spirit would teach believers further truth about him. (John 16:12–15)

- The disciples did not understand what Jesus meant when he said he was going away. (John 16:16–19)

- Jesus explained that the disciples' grief at his departure would turn to joy. (John 16:20–22)

- After Jesus' death, his followers could pray directly to God the Father. (John 16:23–28)

- The disciples finally understood what Jesus was saying about his death and resurrection. (John 16:29–33)

JOHN 17: JESUS THE PRAY-ER

Let's Get Started

The clock was counting down to Jesus' crucifixion. Before he was arrested, however, Jesus prayed. This was not an unusual occurrence, since prayer was a priority in his life. The other Gospel writers noted that Jesus often got up early in the morning to pray before his day was crowded with people and crises.

Earlier in his ministry, Jesus taught his disciples to pray. That prayer, which begins with *"Our Father in heaven"* and is repeated often in worship services, is called the Lord's Prayer. That one was a model to follow. This one is the real Lord's prayer.

In this chapter, we get to eavesdrop on Jesus talking to his Father. We don't know if he prayed in the presence of all eleven disciples or if only John overheard him, enabling him to record Jesus' words for us. In this prayer, we get a brief glimpse into a conversation between members of the Godhead. We learn that Jesus prayed for himself, for his disciples, and for future believers.

EAVESDROPPING ON JESUS

> **John 17:1–2** After Jesus said this, he looked toward heaven and prayed:
> "Father, the time has come. Glorify your Son, that your Son may glorify you. For you granted him authority over all people that he might give eternal life to all those you have given him."

TITLE OF JESUS

Son

Glory Be

"I have overcome the world," Jesus declared to his disciples (John 16:33), and this prayer illustrates that fact. As he prayed for himself, Jesus focused on glorifying the Father—turning the spotlight of attention on him. It was time for Jesus to die. His whole ministry on earth had led to this point in time. He left heaven to become a man for the sole purpose of dying for our sins, so we can have eternal life with God. Jesus' request was not a selfish one like many of our prayers for ourselves. Instead, he asked God to draw attention to the supreme sacrifice of himself so that he, in turn, could focus people's attention on the Father.

Martin Luther: This is truly beyond measure a warm and hearty prayer. He opens the depths of His heart, both in reference to us and to His Father, and He pours them all out. It sounds so honest, so simple. It is so deep, so rich, so wide. No one can fathom it.[1]

Everett F. Harrison: God is not someone afar off whose attention must be won by frantic appeal. He is addressed as naturally as a bosom friend who is at one's side.[2]

Arthur W. Pink: It was the hour for fulfilling and accomplishing many prophecies, types and symbols which for hundreds and thousands of years had pointed forward to it. It was the hour when events took place which the history of the entire universe can supply no parallel: when the **Serpent** was permitted to bruise the heel of the **woman's Seed**.[3]

Serpent: *Satan*

woman's Seed: *Jesus*

CULTURE CLUE

The Bible speaks of several prayer postures, none of which match what we usually do today—sit with our heads bowed, eyes closed, and perhaps hands clasped. Jewish people generally stood or knelt with their hands and eyes lifted to heaven. Or they laid on the floor or ground with their faces touching the ground.

Something to Ponder

What people pray in private reveals what is uppermost on their minds and hearts. If someone could listen in on your private conversations with God for a week or two, what would they learn about you?

> **John 17:3–5** "Now this is eternal life: that they may know you, the only true God, and Jesus Christ, whom you have sent. I have brought you glory on earth by completing the work you gave me to do. And now, Father, glorify me in your presence with the glory I had with you before the world began."

Giving God Glory

The concept of eternal life is hard for many people to grasp. Here Jesus makes it clear and easy to understand: Eternal life is personally knowing the one true God and Jesus Christ, his Son. Eternal life is not only what we can have after death; it's a quality of life we can enjoy now.

Jesus reported to his Father that he had brought God glory by finishing his work—dying on the cross. He spoke of it as though it had already happened, leaving no doubt he would follow through. Then he asked that God would return the **glory** he had before he created the world and before he came to earth. That glory is a glow or light so brilliant no human being could look at it. It would be like standing in front of the sun instead of looking at it from 93 million miles away.

☞ **GO TO:**

John 1:1, 18;
 Philippians 2:5–11
 (glory)

glory: display of God's nature

R. Kent Hughes: What is involved in knowing Christ? And what is involved in gaining a deeper knowledge of him? First, knowing Christ involves *knowing something about him. . . .* Second, knowing Christ involves *intimacy of relationship. . . .* Third, knowing Christ means *a growing knowledge.*[4]

What Others are Saying:

W. E. Vine: He finished the work, not simply bringing it to an end, but perfectly fulfilling it and achieving its object.[5]

At the end of his earthly life, Jesus was able to say he had completed the work God gave him to do. The apostle Paul said the same thing: *"I have fought the good fight, I have finished the race, I have kept the faith"* (2 Timothy 4:7). Will you be able to say the same thing when you get to the end of your life?

Something to Ponder

God doesn't leave us in the dark when it comes to knowing the work he wants us to do. Read the following verses to find out what to do. Micah 6:8; Matthew 28:19–20; Hebrews 13:15–16; James 1:27.

Dig Deeper

BESEECHING FOR BELIEVERS

> **John 17:6–8** "I have revealed you to those whom you gave me out of the world. They were yours; you gave them to me and they have obeyed your word. Now they know that everything you have given me comes from you. For I gave them the words you gave me and they accepted them. They knew with certainty that I came from you, and they believed that you sent me."

Know-It-Alls

After praying for himself, Jesus prayed for his disciples. He had revealed to the eleven men with him (plus Judas, who left) who God is and what he is like through the way he lived, what he taught, and the miracles he did. As a result, they believed in Jesus and obeyed God's Word. They accepted what Jesus said as being the words of God, thus believing that Jesus *is* God.

What Others are Saying:

Paul N. Tassell: Once again the towering truth of God's message comes to the forefront. Too many people are looking for a miracle when God is concerned about giving them a message.[6]

THE FAITH FACTOR—Faith comes from listening to what Jesus said, watching how he lived, and seeing what he did. Even though he is no longer here in person to be observed, we can know his words, character, and actions by reading the Gospels.

CULTURE CLUE

The Greek word translated "revealed" in verse 6, when used with a person, means to show that person's character, to make him or her visible and clear. It also means to uncover or to lay bare. Often it was used in conjunction with the personal appearance of deity.

Something to Ponder

Before Jesus came to earth, God revealed himself through his names. Each name pictured an aspect of his character. Here are a few of them:

- *Elohim*—Creator
- *Jehovah*—Self-existent One, I Am
- *El Shaddai*—Almighty God

- *Adonai*—Lord, Master
- *Jehovah-Jireh*—God provides
- *Jehovah-Rophe*—God heals
- *Jehovah-Shalom*—God is peace
- *Jehovah-Rohi*—God my shepherd

> **John 17:9–10** "I pray for them. I am not praying for the world, but for those you have given me, for they are yours. All I have is yours, and all you have is mine. And glory has come to me through them."

Community Property People

As Jesus prayed, he focused on the disciples whom God had given him. Those men belonged to both Jesus and the Father, since they shared everything. They were the men whose lives brought glory to Jesus and would continue to do so after his resurrection from the dead.

> **John 17:11–12** "I will remain in the world no longer, but they are still in the world, and I am coming to you. Holy Father, protect them by the power of your name— the name you gave me—so that they may be one as we are one. While I was with them, I protected them and kept them safe by that name you gave me. None has been lost except the one doomed to destruction so that Scripture would be fulfilled."

The Name That Protects

Jesus was going back to the Father, but he would leave the disciples behind in the world to tell people about him and salvation through believing in him. While Jesus was on earth, he was able to keep them safe. True, he did lose Judas Iscariot. However, it was Judas's decision to reject Jesus' protection. God had already predicted this action.

Jesus' leaving prompted the first of four prayer requests for his disciples: protection. When the disciples would start preaching about Jesus, they would need protection from Satan, God's enemy, who still controls this world system. Satan does everything he can to get people to turn away from God, so it was a sure thing

☞ **GO TO:**

Psalm 41:9 (predicted)

that the disciples would be persecuted. When Jesus asked the Father to protect them in his name, he asked God to keep them with his power and authority. That's the ultimate protection; nobody is more powerful than God!

Jesus' second request for his disciples was for their oneness with him, like the Father and Son are one. The members of the Trinity live in harmony with one another and have a oneness of purpose—to do the Father's will. Jesus wants his followers to have that same relationship with him. That includes showing what Jesus is like by the way we live and what we say, even as he showed us what the Father is like by his life and teachings.

Jesus did not pray that all people who call themselves Christians would come together in one organization, regardless of what they believe. He never asked us to give up our biblical beliefs and tolerate false teachings for the sake of oneness with one another.

What Others are Saying:

Leon Morris: The reference to the fulfilling of Scripture brings out the thought of divine purpose. This does not mean that Judas was an automaton. He was a responsible person and acted freely. But God used his evil act to bring about His purpose.[7]

> **John 17:13** "I am coming to you now, but I say these things while I am still in the world, so that they may have the full measure of my joy within them."

Bring On The Joy

☞ **GO TO:**

Nehemiah 8:10 (joy)

In light of going back to the Father, Jesus made his third request for the disciples: joy. No matter how much they would mourn his death or be persecuted after his resurrection, they could be filled with joy. Remember, joy comes from a relationship with Jesus, not from outward circumstances. He is the source of joy.

> **John 17:14–16** "I have given them your word and the world has hated them, for they are not of the world any more than I am of the world. My prayer is not that you take them out of the world but that you protect them from the evil one. They are not of the world, even as I am not of it."

Not Of This World

Because believers love God, live by different standards, teach that Jesus is the only way to God and that absolute truth exists, and expose sin, they will get plenty of hatred and persecution from the world of unbelievers and Satan. Jesus' disciples <u>don't belong</u> to the world, because he doesn't. Knowing this, Jesus repeated the request for protection, this time specifically from the evil one, Satan. Notice that he didn't pray that God would take his followers out of the world. He was leaving them behind to spread the good news of salvation.

☞ **GO TO:**

Colossians 1:13
(don't belong)

D. A. Carson: The spiritual dimensions to this prayer of Jesus are consistent and overwhelming. By contrast, we spend much more time today praying about our health, our projects, our decisions, our finances, our family, and even our games than we do praying about the danger of the evil one. Materialists at heart, we often discern only very, very dimly the spiritual struggle of which Paul (for instance) was so deeply aware (Eph. 6:10ff.).[8]

What Others are Saying:

Charles U. Wagner: Clearly, our Savior was praying that His followers be kept from evil. That is, we are to be *insulated* from the world rather than *isolated* from it. When you insulate a wire, you wrap it so that when it touches other wires, the power or current of the wire won't be affected. Anything that drains our power lessens and endangers our testimony. It is possible to live in the world without taking part in its activities and values.[9]

> **John 17:17–19** "Sanctify them by the truth; your word is truth. As you sent me into the world, I have sent them into the world. For them I sanctify myself, that they too may be truly sanctified."

Called Into The World

Jesus' final request for his disciples was for God to sanctify them, to set them apart for him, to make them holy. There are two stages to sanctification. At the same moment we believe in Jesus, we are also set apart for God, once and for all. The disciples had already completed stage one, so there was no use praying for that. The second stage is day-by-day walking with God, separated from sin and becoming more like him. This is the process that Jesus prayed for. Daily holiness comes from knowing and obeying the truth.

Truth comes from three sources:

- God's Word—*"your word is truth"* (John 17:17)
- Jesus—*"I am . . . the truth"* (John 14:6)
- the Holy Spirit—*"the Spirit is the truth"* (1 John 5:6)

Just like God <u>sent his Son</u> into the world, so Jesus has sent his followers into the world. Their mission was the same as Jesus'—to tell people about God. Jesus had set himself apart for God to do his work. He, in turn, set apart his disciples for the same purpose.

☞ **GO TO:**

John 3:16–17
(sent his Son)

What Others are Saying:

Homer A. Kent Jr.: As the disciples lived for God day by day, the application of God's truth to their lives would have a purifying effect as it would call sin to their attention, and cause confession and restoration to follow. By this means they would be set apart from sin and consecrated to the ministry to which Christ had called them.[10]

INCLUDING US IN HIS PRAYERS

> **John 17:20–21** "My prayer is not for them alone. I pray also for those who will believe in me through their message, that all of them may be one, Father, just as you are in me and I am in you. May they also be in us so that the world may believe that you have sent me."

For Those To Come

Jesus prayed for himself and his disciples. Then he prayed for all the people through all the ages who would become believers through his disciples' message. That includes us and others we tell about Jesus. Those eleven men spread the good news about Jesus, and some of them, like John, wrote books of the New Testament. The rest of the New Testament was written by men who became believers as a result of this original group's message.

Many people think this passage refers to Jesus' desire for Christians to have unity among themselves. Some use this passage to support their claim that Christians should not be divided into denominations or other organizations. But that is not the meaning here.

In John 10:30 when Jesus said, *"I and the father are one"* he meant that he and the Father had a oneness. So we are to under-

KEY POINT

Jesus prayed for himself that he would glorify the Father, for his disciples that they would build up one another, and for those who would become his disciples later.

stand this as a prayer that believers might experience the same oneness with God that Jesus experienced. In the passages in John when Jesus spoke of his oneness with the Father, he talked about their unity of purpose and action. Jesus always did the Father's will and reflected his character.

Jesus did not, despite the common mischaracterization of this passage, ask that Christians experience oneness with each other—whether organizational or in a common commitment to key biblical teachings. What Jesus did pray was that Christians might experience the relationship he had with the Father. It is a oneness preserved by always seeking and doing God's will. As believers do God's will, they will be united in mutual love for God. Part of doing God's will involves spreading the word about Christ to others.

David Jeremiah: Jesus asked His Father that the church might be unified. . . . The Father had sent Jesus from heaven to earth to redeem a people for His very own. Jesus was now about to go to the cross to achieve that purpose. Just a few days after His resurrection, He would return to heaven, yet His mission to redeem the world would go on. The necessary sacrifice, Himself, already would have been made—but word about that sacrifice needed to be spread. How would that happen? Through the disciples. . . .

Jesus' heartbeat was evangelism and missionary outreach. He had a passion that all men and women might be saved. That's what He prayed about in this remarkable prayer.[11]

What Others are Saying:

When people believe in Jesus, they automatically become part of God's family, called the Body of Christ. Paul described this body as a unit with many parts, having unity with diversity. Although we don't all have the same gifts or abilities, we are all united in Christ.

Remember This . . .

> **John 17:22–24** "I have given them the glory that you gave me, that they may be one as we are one: I in them and you in me. May they be brought to complete unity to let the world know that you sent me and have loved them even as you have loved me. Father, I want those you have given me to be with me where I am, and to see my glory, the glory you have given me because you loved me before the creation of the world."

☞ **GO TO:**

1 Corinthians 12:12–30 (body)

Passing On The Glory

Even future believers will receive the glory God the Father gave his Son. Through his death, the whole world would see God's character and nature. That glory will become real to those who believe in Jesus, and they will enjoy unity with God and with one another. When believers get along, their unity makes an impact on unbelievers who see God's love in them.

The Son of God *wants* to be with his followers. Isn't that great? For the disciples who overheard this prayer, being with Jesus meant being in the same place—for a little while anyway. For the followers to come, being with Jesus means spending time reading the Bible and praying. That situation will change when we get to heaven and see him face-to-face; then we'll be with him in the same location. Jesus prayed that our relationship with him would include seeing his character, the glory God gave him because he loved him from eternity past.

> **John 17:25–26** "Righteous Father, though the world does not know you, I know you, and they know that you have sent me. I have made you known to them, and will continue to make you known in order that the love you have for me may be in them and that I myself may be in them."

It's Who You Know

Jesus wrapped up his prayer time with the Father not with another request but with a final report before his death. By addressing God as *"Righteous Father,"* he called attention to the fact that God is sinless. Jesus affirmed that the world didn't know God, but he did and so did his eleven disciples. Jesus had done his job of communicating God to them and would continue to do so in order that they would know God's love.

Since Jesus would not always be with believers in physical form, he would continue the work through the Holy Spirit. Jesus wanted his followers to know the love God had for him by experiencing that love within them. As his followers experienced his love they would become more loving people. They would be changed from inside out by the work of the Holy Spirit.

This whole chapter is Jesus' conversation with his Father. Prayer is a dialogue, not a monologue, but we don't get to read the Father's side of it. We do know some of the results, though. For example, God did indeed glorify Jesus through his resurrection, and vice versa. The disciples knew great joy in spreading the news about Jesus' death and resurrection even in the midst of persecution.

Conversations with Christ

Study Questions

1. What was Jesus' primary request for himself?
2. How did Jesus define eternal life?
3. What were Jesus' main requests for his disciples?
4. What did Jesus ask for future believers?
5. Why did Jesus call God *"righteous Father"*?

CHAPTER WRAP-UP

- Jesus asked God to glorify him and for his death to glorify the Father. (John 17:1–5)

- Jesus reported that he had revealed the Father to his disciples. (John 17:6–8)

- Jesus prayed that the Father would protect the disciples whom he had given to Jesus. (John 17:9–12)

- Jesus asked that God would keep his disciples safe from Satan while they were still in the world, not that he would take them out of the world. (John 17:13–19)

- Jesus also prayed for those who would believe in him in the future. (John 17:20–24)

- Jesus reported that he had made the Father known to the disciples and would continue doing so. (John 17:25–26)

JOHN 18: JESUS THE PRISONER

Let's Get Started

"It was the best of times, it was the worst of times." Although Charles Dickens didn't begin *A Tale of Two Cities* by describing Jesus' death, that sentence could apply to the night Jesus was arrested and to the next day, when he died on the cross.

That was the dark night of the soul for Jesus and his disciples. Emotions raged on all sides as Jesus was falsely arrested, then tried in a **kangaroo court** before the religious leaders and Pilate, the Roman governor.

Even though it appeared on the surface that Jesus' fate was in the hands of unbelieving men, at no time did Jesus lose control. From the moment the temple priests arrived to arrest him in the garden, through a number of trials and Peter's denial, to the people's insistence that Jesus was not the prisoner they wanted released, God's plan for the salvation of the world was unfolding. Jesus could have prevented all these events or escaped at any moment. But he didn't. He voluntarily chose to go to the cross to die for our sins.

kangaroo court: a corrupt or biased court

LEADERS ARREST JESUS

> **John 18:1** When he had finished praying, Jesus left with his disciples and crossed the Kidron Valley. On the other side there was an olive grove, and he and his disciples went into it.

Walking To The Grove

Jesus had just spent time talking with the Father about himself, his disciples, and his future followers. The time for prayer with the disciples was over. The time for death was near, and Jesus knew it. He had prepared himself and his disciples as much as he could. So they walked across the Kidron Valley (see illustration below), a ravine north of Jerusalem, to a familiar olive grove. The other Gospel writers called it the Garden of Gethsemane.

John didn't record all the events of that evening, however. Between this verse and the next one, Jesus told Peter again that he would deny Jesus three times. Then he prayed privately, during which he wrestled with God over the enormity of the suffering before him and submitted to the Father's will to go through with the Crucifixion.

☞ **GO TO:**

Matthew 26:36
(Gethsemane)

Matthew 26:37–46
(prayed)

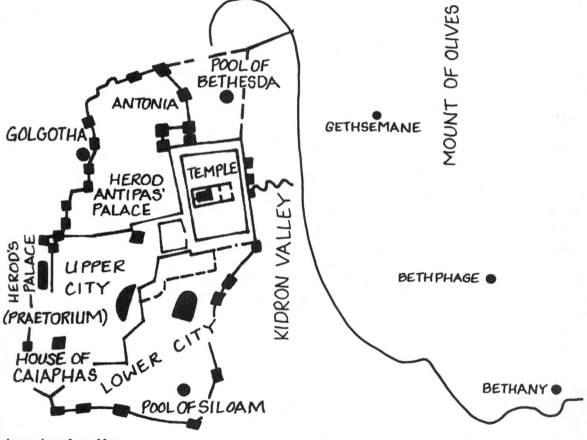

Jerusalem Area Map

This map shows the location of Gethsemane outside Jerusalem, although only the road to Bethany is shown. Before his arrest Jesus walked from Jerusalem across the Kidron Valley.

R. Kent Hughes: There is a strong poetic imagery even in the physical surroundings of moving toward the Garden of Gethsemane. . . . A drain ran from the temple altar down to the Kidron ravine to take away the blood of sacrifice. Since it was the Passover, more than 200,000 lambs would be slain in the next day. When Jesus and His band crossed the Kidron, it was red with the blood of the lambs prepared for sacrifice. Within a few hours, the blood of the Lamb of God would flow.[1]

> **John 18:2–3** Now Judas, who betrayed him, knew the place, because Jesus had often met there with his disciples. So Judas came to the grove, guiding a detachment of soldiers and some officials from the chief priests and Pharisees. They were carrying torches, lanterns and weapons.

Secret Arrest For Public Messiah

From the beginning, Jesus' arrest and trial resembled mayhem more than justice. That was no accident.

Jesus had been highly visible for three years, teaching and working miracles in public. If the temple priests and guards wanted to arrest him, they could have done it openly at any time. So where did they do it? In a private garden. And who turned him in? One of his own disciples who had been with him for those three years. Sure, it makes no sense. But it's what God had predicted hundreds of years earlier. Score one more for the reliability of God's Word.

Judas knew where Jesus likely would be. He and the disciples had spent a lot of time in that garden to escape the crowds. Judas led the "soldiers" and officials right to where Jesus was. It was nighttime, so the band led by the high priests and followed by a mob of excitement seekers had to search the dark garden using torches and lanterns. The knowledge that Judas had of the special places Jesus liked would have helped in finding him.

Commentators disagree on whether there were any actual Roman soldiers involved. Possibly the hysterical chief priests had asked for aid from Pilate, and he had released a detachment from the barracks in Jerusalem to tag along for the arrest. Other Bible scholars believe the translation of the word "soldiers" is unfortunate because the temple priests had no authority over or access to Roman soldiers. Roman soldiers would not have wanted to get involved in an internal affair. These commentators believe the "soldiers" were temple guards, Levites who served as civil guards in the temple under the authority of the high priests. They kept order in the temple area.

In either case, the power behind the arrest came from the Jewish leaders. Well, no, it didn't. The *real* power came from Jesus. Even if hundreds of soldiers had turned up, Jesus could have escaped if he wanted. But he didn't. He allowed the priests to find and arrest him because it was God's will.

What Others are Saying:

Edwin A. Blum: Judas was not an unusual monster but a common man caught in a common sin (greed) which Satan used to accomplish his purpose. Judas knew the habits of Jesus, and his deed stands out in black contrast with Jesus' unselfish love.[2]

> **John 18:4–6** Jesus, knowing all that was going to happen to him, went out and asked them, "Who is it you want?"
>
> "Jesus of Nazareth," they replied.
>
> "I am he," Jesus said. (And Judas the traitor was standing there with them.) When Jesus said, "I am he," they drew back and fell to the ground.

Never Out Of Control

In spite of the fact that he was one unarmed teacher against a batch of movers and shakers, Jesus still had power and authority as the Son of God. To let them know who was in charge, Jesus went out to meet them. He opened the conversation by asking them who they were after.

When they identified the man, Jesus answered literally, "I am." It is the same statement he had used a number of times in his teaching. It is God's name and a declaration that he is God. His using God's name affected the men who were there in an unusual way. We don't know for sure why they fell to the ground. Maybe it was the way Jesus took control. They were startled by Jesus' admission; they had expected him to run. Or maybe he used his power to give them a glimpse of who he is. No matter why, they knew Jesus was no ordinary man.

☞ **GO TO:**

Exodus 3:14
(God's name)

What Others are Saying:

J. Vernon McGee: Even in this dark hour when He was yielding Himself as the Lamb of God that taketh away the sin of the world, He revealed His deity—and they fell backwards! He revealed to these men that He was absolutely in charge, and they could not arrest Him without His permission. They didn't fall forward to worship Him. They fell backward in fear and in absolute dismay.[3]

> **John 18:7–9** Again he asked them, "Who is it you want?"
> And they said, "Jesus of Nazareth."
> "I told you that I am he," Jesus answered. "If you are looking for me, then let these men go." This happened so that the words he had spoken would be fulfilled: "I have not lost one of those you gave me."

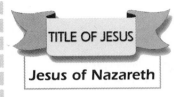

TITLE OF JESUS

Jesus of Nazareth

One More Time

Jesus repeated his question to make sure the temple guards understood they came for him, not the eleven disciples with him. He wanted to protect his men, asking that they be let go. John saw this concern as a fulfillment of Jesus' <u>prayer</u> for his disciples.

Just in case the guard didn't believe Jesus was who he said he was, Judas <u>kissed</u> him as a friend or family member would. A kiss was a sign of devotion or affection, neither of which Judas meant. This is another detail that John omitted.

☞ **GO TO:**

John 17:12 (prayer)

Matthew 26:48–50 (kissed)

> **John 18:10–11** Then Simon Peter, who had a sword, drew it and struck the high priest's servant, cutting off his right ear. (The servant's name was Malchus.)
> Jesus commanded Peter, "Put your sword away! Shall I not drink the cup the Father has given me?"

Wild Sword Bearer

Peter had a reputation for impulsiveness and brashness. Even in this serious situation, he wasn't shy. He had guts—but not many smarts. Peter had enough courage to take on the temple police and the whole crowd with one dagger. Either Peter's aim was lousy or the guy ducked just in time! Instead of killing the servant, Peter only cut off his ear. The Greek word for "sword" and "knife" is the same. Since Peter was a fisherman it is more likely that he had a fishing knife and not a military sword.

Luke the physician recorded that Jesus <u>healed</u> Malchus's ear, saving Peter from the consequences of his action. Then Jesus rebuked Peter for what he had done. Jesus had told his disciples

☞ **GO TO:**

Luke 22:50–51 (healed)

☞ **GO TO:**

Isaiah 51:17
(cup of judgment)

Remember
This . . .

What Others
are Saying:

☞ **GO TO:**

Matthew 26:39–45
(example)

plenty of times that dying was part of the plan. That's why he came to earth. He didn't need Peter to stop something he was doing willingly. The cup the Father gave him was the cross, the <u>cup of judgment</u> for the sins of humankind, which Jesus would "drink."

God rarely calls believers to be crucified today. But he does allow hard times and suffering to mold us into the kind of people he wants us to be. No matter what "cup" he gives us, we don't have to be afraid of it. Nor should we run away from it. Jesus gave us the <u>example</u> to follow by accepting God's will, even if that means being jailed and executed for our faith.

D. Edmond Hiebert: The aggressive action of Peter reflected self-confidence as well as love for Jesus. It also revealed his rashness; he intended to make good on his claim that he would not fail Jesus, but he did not stop to consider the risk to himself or the futility of his single-handed action.[4]

Alexander MacLaren: The whole story of the Gospels is constructed upon the principle, and illustrates the fact, that our Lord's life, as our Lord's death, was a voluntary surrender of Himself for man's sin, and that nothing led Him to, and fastened Him on, the Cross but His own will.[5]

PRIESTS PASS JUDGMENT ON JESUS

> **John 18:12–14** Then the detachment of soldiers with its commander and the Jewish officials arrested Jesus. They bound him and brought him first to Annas, who was the father-in-law of Caiaphas, the high priest that year. Caiaphas was the one who had advised the Jews that it would be good if one man died for the people.

Let The Games Begin

With no doubt about who they were arresting, the Jewish police seized and tied up Jesus. The first stop that night was Annas's house. Annas was the high priest until Pilate replaced him, but his influence continued long after his stint in office. Several of his sons and a son-in-law, Caiaphas (the current high priest), succeeded him. According to Jewish law, the high priest was appointed for life. However, under Roman rule, the governors deposed and appointed high priests at will. Even though Annas didn't officially hold the office, the people still treated him as high priest.

Annas may have requested the first crack at Jesus. He was probably still mad that Jesus had <u>cleansed the Temple</u> of the merchants who sold animals for sacrifices to God at exorbitant prices. Annas had a good little racket going with the temple merchants. He got rent from the merchants, set their prices, and may have taken a percentage of the profits as well.

To be sure his readers remembered <u>Caiaphas</u>, John added a footnote that he was the one who was willing to sacrifice one man, Jesus, to keep the peace with the Romans. That was now happening.

☞ **GO TO:**

John 2:13–16
(cleansed the Temple)

John 11:49–51
(Caiaphas)

Revell Bible Dictionary: [Annas] was deposed in A.D. 15 by Valerius Gratus. Yet he carried such clout that he placed five sons, one son-in-law, and a grandson in the high priesthood. This high priestly family was noted for vast wealth, materialism, and greed. . . . The reputation of the family was so **odious** that the Jewish **Talmud** contains the curse, "Woe to the family of Annas!"[6]

What Others are Saying:

odious: deserving of hatred

Talmud: official body of Jewish instruction

> **John 18:15–16** Simon Peter and another disciple were following Jesus. Because this disciple was known to the high priest, he went with Jesus into the high priest's courtyard, but Peter had to wait outside at the door. The other disciple, who was known to the high priest, came back, spoke to the girl on duty there and brought Peter in.

Follow The Leader

Like a good writer or movie director, John switched scenes to keep his readers in suspense. He cut away from inside the house to the courtyard surrounding the house. There Peter and another disciple tried to find out what was happening to their leader. Many Bible students believe the second man was John. Others think he was Nicodemus or Joseph of Arimathea, who helped bury Jesus, since it wasn't likely that fisherman John would know the high priest. These other two possibilities did.

Since the yard was walled and had a guarded entrance, they couldn't just walk in on the proceedings. The unnamed disciple gained entrance because he knew the high priest. Then he got permission for Peter to enter as well and went back to fetch him.

> **John 18:17–18** "You are not one of his disciples, are you?" the girl at the door asked Peter.
>
> He replied, "I am not."
>
> It was cold, and the servants and officials stood around a fire they had made to keep warm. Peter also was standing with them, warming himself.

Lying By The Fire

The girl who gave permission for Peter to enter the courtyard wanted to know if he was one of Jesus' disciples. Without hesitating, Peter said no. It's hard to believe this was the same man who wasn't afraid to defend Jesus by taking out his knife and trying to kill a servant in the garden minutes before. Peter had turned into a coward who was afraid to be known as one of Jesus' disciples. He stood there with his enemies, warming himself at their fire.

> **John 18:19–21** Meanwhile, the high priest questioned Jesus about his disciples and his teaching.
>
> "I have spoken openly to the world," Jesus replied. "I always taught in synagogues or at the temple, where all the Jews come together. I said nothing in secret. Why question me? Ask those who heard me. Surely they know what I said."

No Secret Teaching

KEY POINT

The religious leaders falsely arrested Jesus, tried him in a kangaroo court, and turned him over to Pilate for the death sentence.

When selecting details, John didn't mention that the religious leaders huddled behind closed doors all night, questioning Jesus and discussing how to get rid of him permanently. Alternating scenes again, he switched back to the illegal hearing in the house.

Trying to gather enough evidence for the death sentence, Annas questioned Jesus. How many disciples did he have? Who was following him? What had he taught? He was trying to figure out how big a threat Jesus really was.

Jesus had spent three years teaching publicly. Annas could have heard him in person if he'd chosen to do so. But he hadn't. Jesus had not been holding secret meetings to overthrow the leaders or the Romans. He had not formed a secret cult. If Annas wanted to know his teaching, he could ask the people who heard him; there were plenty to ask. Jesus had nothing to hide. However, he protected his disciples by leaving them out of the conversation.

> **John 18:22–24** When Jesus said this, one of the officials nearby struck him in the face. "Is this the way you answer the high priest?" he demanded.
>
> "If I said something wrong," Jesus replied, "testify as to what is wrong. But if I spoke the truth, why did you strike me?" Then Annas sent him, still bound, to Caiaphas the high priest.

Angered At His Answer

Jesus' answer wasn't what this group wanted to hear. In fact, one of the officers was so angry that he hit Jesus across the face. It was against the law to strike a prisoner, but by this time, Annas didn't care about the law. He'd already broken it by questioning Jesus without outside witnesses and by asking incriminating questions. Jesus' answer pointed Annas back to the law, thus condemning the one who accused him of wrongdoing. Jesus didn't deserve the treatment he was getting. He only told the truth.

Annas sidestepped the issue by sending Jesus to Caiaphas, the high priest. That trial was another detail John skipped.

Lawrence O. Richards: Called before an illegally convened court, Jesus was questioned behind closed doors, beaten, and then sent away to the Roman authorities, who alone had the power to condemn a person to death. The other Gospels described this scene in more detail than John did. He seemed to turn from the final revelation of the dark hearts of those religious leaders who were the keepers of the written Word, but now were struggling to suppress its light.[7]

What Others are Saying:

Annas had already made up his mind about Jesus before he talked with him. He knew he had to help get rid of him permanently. To do so, he and the rest of the religious leaders had to convict Jesus of blasphemy, a Jewish crime punishable by death. They needed to establish a legal basis within Judaism for Jesus' execution even though under Roman rule Jews could not carry out that sentence. Jesus refused to answer Annas's questions, however, which angered one of the officers. The result of this conversation was total rejection of Jesus.

Conversations with Christ

> **John 18:25–27** As Simon Peter stood warming himself, he was asked, "You are not one of his disciples, are you?"
>
> He denied it, saying, "I am not."
>
> One of the high priest's servants, a relative of the man whose ear Peter had cut off, challenged him, "Didn't I see you with him in the olive grove?" Again Peter denied it, and at that moment a rooster began to crow.

The Cock Crows On Time

Jumping back to the courtyard scene, John picked up the conversation around the fire. Someone else asked Peter if he was one of Jesus' disciples. For the second time, Peter forcefully denied it. One of Annas's servants recognized him from the garden, however. He may have been standing near Malchus when Peter cut off his relative's ear. For the third time, Peter denied he knew Jesus. Immediately, the rooster crowed to announce daybreak—and fulfill Jesus' <u>prediction</u>. Luke recorded that <u>Jesus looked</u> at him on his way out of Annas's house, and Peter repented.

☞ **GO TO:**

John 13:38 (prediction)

Luke 22:60–62 (Jesus looked)

Something to Ponder

If you haven't discovered already, it's always easier to take a stand for Jesus when there's a crowd around to back you up. But when it's just you and no friends around to encourage and support you, it's easier to keep your mouth shut or deny the Lord, like Peter did.

Unlike Judas, who walked away from Jesus and never came back, Peter was sorry he had denied his Lord. Jesus forgave him and restored their relationship. He is willing to forgive you, too, if you've done the same thing.

PILATE CUTS A PASSOVER DEAL WITH JESUS

> **John 18:28–29** Then the Jews led Jesus from Caiaphas to the palace of the Roman governor. By now it was early morning, and to avoid ceremonial uncleanness the Jews did not enter the palace; they wanted to be able to eat the Passover. So Pilate came out to them and asked, "What charges are you bringing against this man?"

Hypocrisy In Action

The all-night trials with the religious leaders ended. They had gone as far as they could with Jesus, so they took him over to Pilate for sentencing. Pilate would have wanted to talk with Jesus and the leaders anyway to avoid a riot. He especially wanted to keep the peace during Passover, since the city was flooded with Jewish pilgrims.

Pilate didn't live in Jerusalem. He was there because of Passover. That was convenient since he was the only one around who could order a death sentence.

Those religious leaders were unbelievable. They had arrested an innocent man and had already broken a number of their own laws. But they refused to enter Pilate's palace because they didn't want to defile themselves. Entering a Gentile's house would make them religiously unclean and unable to worship in the Temple or participate in the Feast of Unleavened Bread, commonly called Passover. They obeyed the letter of God's law while plotting the death of God's Son. They wanted to stay clean for Passover while seeking to kill the Son who fulfilled the Passover rituals. What a bunch of hypocrites!

To accommodate the Jewish leaders, Pilate came out to them. The first thing he wanted to know was what Jesus was charged with.

Although the Romans allowed the Jewish people to practice their religion, they did not allow them to order anyone's execution. Rome was tolerant in many ways and permitted a great degree of self-government, including the right of **subject authorities** to have their own courts. Disputes between members of a subject people were handled in people's courts. If the dispute was between a Roman citizen and a subject person, the trial was in a Roman court. You can guess which side won such disputes!

Romans couldn't be bothered with religious disputes. To execute Jesus, the Jewish leaders fabricated new charges by accusing Jesus before Pilate not of blasphemy, but of inciting rebellion and calling himself a "king." That got the Romans' attention. They executed traitors.

CULTURE CLUE

subject authorities:
leaders of nationalities living under Roman rule

> **John 18:30–32** "If he were not a criminal," they replied, "we would not have handed him over to you."
>
> Pilate said, "Take him yourselves and judge him by your own law."
>
> "But we have no right to execute anyone," the Jews objected. This happened so that the words Jesus had spoken indicating the kind of death he was going to die would be fulfilled.

Pass-the-Buck Sentencing

Pilate could not have cared less about the blasphemy charge against Jesus. That was not punishable by Roman law. If he was going to do anything about Jesus, there had to be a criminal reason, and he wanted to know what it was. Not only were those leaders hypocrites but also they got high marks for avoiding questions.

Pilate was known for taking bribes, insulting the Jews, robbing the temple treasury to pay for a building project, and executing men without a trial. It was no secret that Pilate and the Jews shared a mutual hatred and contempt for one another. He clearly did not want to get involved in a religious matter, so he told the leaders to deal with Jesus under their law.

Normally the Jewish leaders would have stayed clear of Pilate, but he was their only hope of carrying out the death penalty on Jesus. Moreover, he was God's means of fulfilling Scripture as to how Jesus would die. Based on Pilate's past actions, the Jewish leaders expected him to order execution without much deliberation on the matter.

What Others are Saying:

Thomas Whitelaw: If Christ had only been a minor offender they could have punished Him themselves: the fact that they had delivered Him up into Pilate's hand was in their estimation proof sufficient that he was an extraordinary criminal.[8]

> **John 18:33–34** Pilate then went back inside the palace, summoned Jesus and asked him, "Are you the king of the Jews?"
>
> "Is that your own idea," Jesus asked, "or did others talk to you about me?"

One Too Many Kings

Although John didn't mention the criminal <u>charge</u> against Jesus, the Jewish leaders registered Jesus' claim to be king. That was a red flag for Pilate. Such a claim was treason against the Roman emperor and sufficient reason for the death penalty. Pilate went inside to check out the claim with Jesus.

Notice how slickly Jesus turned the conversation around. He challenged Pilate to figure out for himself what kind of king he was. The Jewish leaders used the title as referring to a religious ruler, the Messiah who would usher in God's kingdom. Pilate associated a king with a political ruler who would be a threat to his rule. Pilate thought he was trying Jesus. Little did he know Jesus put Pilate on trial.

☞ **GO TO:**

Luke 23:1–2 (charge)

> **John 18:35–36** "Am I a Jew?" Pilate replied. "It was your people and your chief priests who handed you over to me. What is it you have done?"
>
> Jesus said, "My kingdom is not of this world. If it were, my servants would fight to prevent my arrest by the Jews. But now my kingdom is from another place."

King Of Another World

Since Pilate despised the Jews, his question to Jesus most likely dripped with sarcasm. Pilate was involved in this mess only because the Jewish leaders had pressured him into it. Since they had brought Jesus to him, there had to be some basis for the charge, and Pilate wanted to know what it was.

This time Jesus answered Pilate clearly. Yes, he was a king. But not in the way Pilate used that title. Jesus wasn't interested in taking over Pilate's rule. If he had been, his followers would have fought to keep him from being arrested. His kingship was in the spiritual realm. He would rule God's kingdom, which will one day be set up on earth.

The Life and Times Historical Reference Bible: The concept of "kingdom" in Jesus' time was rooted in the Old Testament: "kingdom" most often referred to the reign or royal authority of a king. Jewish people prayed daily for the coming of God's reign. When they prayed for His kingdom, they did not doubt that God reigned over His creation in the present. Yet they longed for the day when God would rule unchallenged and all peoples would acknowledge Him. . . .

What Others are Saying:

The Romans, however, guarded the title "king." Anyone who, without the emperor's permission, claimed to be even a client king was committing the offense of high treason.[9]

> **John 18:37** "You are a king, then!" said Pilate.
> Jesus answered, "You are right in saying I am a king. In fact, for this reason I was born, and for this I came into the world, to testify to the truth. Everyone on the side of truth listens to me."

The Truth, The Whole Truth, And Nothing But The Truth

Pilate had trouble sorting out what Jesus said. He didn't understand the concept of God's kingdom. In his mind, Jesus was either a political king who threatened his rule or he wasn't. There wasn't a third option. Pilate's exclamation, *"You are a king, then!"* is sometimes translated as a question. Question or not, the fact that Jesus answered him tells us Pilate wanted an explanation.

Jesus agreed he was a king. That much is clear. But he was king of a spiritual kingdom of truth. He was born a man, but he was also God who *"came into the world."* His mission was to tell people the truth about God. Those whom God had chosen to be part of his kingdom would listen to Jesus and believe in him.

When Jesus mentioned truth, Pilate might have thought he was a philosopher. It was not a crime to seek and teach about truth. Pilate must have been relieved; he could let Jesus go and get on with his life.

What Others are Saying:

Merrill C. Tenney: From the standpoint of Jesus, Pilate was a person in need; and Jesus gave him the opportunity of receiving truth if he would have it. Jesus made a greater effort to penetrate Pilate's mind than to defend himself. When Pilate asked, "What is truth?" (18:38), he was near to the kingdom of God because incarnate truth was standing before him. Pilate sacrificed truth for what he thought was security and lost both.[10]

THE FAITH FACTOR—One reason Jesus came to earth was to tell people the truth about God. Faith in him starts with reading and listening to the truth he taught.

> **John 18:38–40** "What is truth?" Pilate asked. With this he went out again to the Jews and said, "I find no basis for a charge against him. But it is your custom for me to release to you one prisoner at the time of the Passover. Do you want me to release 'the king of the Jews'?"
>
> They shouted back, "No, not him! Give us Barabbas!" Now Barabbas had taken part in a rebellion.

Free Barabbas

Pilate's question about truth was a cynical one. The Romans, like many people today, did not believe in absolute truth. Officials like Pilate decided what was true based on the majority vote or what was practical at the time. The sad thing is, he looked at <u>truth</u> embodied in a man and didn't even see him.

☞ **GO TO:**

John 14:6 (truth)

It didn't take Pilate long to figure out that Jesus wasn't a political threat, so he didn't want to have anything more to do with him. Under Roman law, he didn't have a charge to level against him. He could have released Jesus and been done with this matter. However, he was afraid that action would start a riot, his superiors in Rome would investigate, and he'd lose his job.

The other Gospel writers record details John left out that help to explain the events he included. While Pilate was questioning Jesus, the religious leaders outside kept up a storm of accusations. Jesus didn't defend himself, which amazed Pilate. When Pilate announced that he couldn't find a reason to convict Jesus, the religious leaders insisted Jesus was guilty of a crime, saying he had stirred up people all over the country, including Galilee.

The mention of Galilee gave Pilate a way to escape dealing with Jesus. Galilee was in Herod's jurisdiction. Between verses 38 and 39, Pilate sent Jesus to <u>Herod</u>, who was in town for the holiday. Herod, however, decided to play a game of Hot Potato and passed Jesus back to Pilate.

☞ **GO TO:**

Luke 23:6–12 (Herod)

Mark 15:7 (overthrow)

So Pilate devised a compromise. He offered to let a prisoner go, which was a Passover custom to make the Jews happy. The man in custody was Barabbas, a true criminal. Barabbas had acted to <u>overthrow</u> the Roman government and had committed murder. Since the religious leadership worked hard to get along with the Roman ruler, Pilate figured they would want Barabbas killed for sure.

That was a mistake. Pilate must have been shocked to hear the Jewish people clamoring for him to release Barabbas instead of Jesus. So Pilate was still stuck with a man he wanted nothing to do with and who was a political bomb.

Louis Barbieri: Pilate's motives were not completely dictated by the ideals of justice and humanity. He had seen through . . . the ruse of the chief priests. He knew perfectly well that they had delivered up Jesus Christ not because of true charges but because of envy in their hearts. . . .

Pilate, however, did not count on the ability of the chief priests to stir up . . . the multitudes.[11]

David E. Garland: The crowd chooses the one who takes the lives of others to achieve his own selfish ends and condemns the one who gives his life for others in obedience to God. They want a king who will be comfortable with murder and mayhem, not one who refuses to resist evil with violence. It is a fatal preference.[12]

☞ **GO TO:**

Luke 23:19 (Barabbas)

Barabbas was a first-century terrorist. He may have been one of the "dagger men," a group of assassins who targeted Roman officials with the hope of driving Rome out of Palestine. More likely he was a vicious criminal who preyed more on his own people than on Rome. He had been arrested for murder and revolt against the government—two actions that guaranteed a sentence of crucifixion.

Laws Broken At Jesus' Trial

Laws about the Trial	What Happened
No arrests or trials after sundown.	Jesus was arrested and tried at night.
No trials on holidays.	Jesus tried on first day of the Feast of Unleavened Bread.
Capital offense trials to be held in the Temple.	Jesus was tried in high priest's house.
Trials to be scheduled after morning prayers and sacrifices.	Jesus' trial was right after sunrise.
Governors could not try cases outside their jurisdiction.	Herod, governor of Galilee, tried Jesus in Judea.

Laws about Witnesses and Charges	What Happened
Formal charges must be stated.	Jesus was not charged during his arrest or trials.
Witnesses who testify against a person must be people of integrity.	Judas was a traitor and informer. False witnesses were sought.
Charges were to be read at the beginning of a trial.	No such charges were read.
Witnesses had to agree on the answers to seven questions about the event.	The questions were not asked, and the witnesses did not agree.

Laws about Witnesses and Charges (continued)	What Happened (continued)
False witnesses were to be put to death.	None were.
High priests could not file charges.	Caiaphas acted as a witness with accusations.
Written charges were to be given to the governor.	None were. Plus, the Jewish leaders changed the charges from blasphemy to treason before Pilate.
Governors could not sit in judgment by themselves.	Pilate tried Jesus by himself.

Laws about the Accused	What Happened
Judges served as counsel for the accused.	Annas judged Jesus by himself as an accuser.
Prisoners were not to be abused.	Jesus was hit and beaten.

Laws about the Verdict	What Happened
Voting in the Sanhedrin was to be done one person at a time, from the youngest to the oldest.	Caiaphas asked for an oral vote.
A unanimous vote equaled an acquittal. (If the vote was unanimous, the Jews felt they had not done a good job defending the accused. The accused was released.)	Jesus was not let go when the Sanhedrin all voted guilty.
A verdict of condemnation had to be made at least one day after the trial.	Jesus was condemned on the same day he was tried.
Innocent people were to be released.	Pilate declared Jesus was innocent but did not release him.

Study Questions

1. What happened when Jesus and his disciples went to the olive grove?
2. How did Jesus show he was in control of his arrest?
3. How did Peter respond to questions about his association with Jesus?
4. What did Jesus tell Annas about his teaching?
5. Why did the religious leaders take Jesus to Pilate?
6. What did Pilate learn about Jesus from questioning him privately?
7. When Pilate offered to release a prisoner, who did the Jewish people choose?

CHAPTER WRAP-UP

- Judas led a group of priests and temple guards to Jesus so they could arrest him. (John 18:1–3)

- Jesus took control of the situation and voluntarily surrendered to the mob's leaders. (John 18:4–9)

- Peter tried to defend Jesus but ended up cutting off a servant's ear, which Jesus healed. (John 18:10–11)
- While Annas was questioning Jesus in preparation for sentencing, Peter was in the courtyard denying he was one of Jesus' disciples. (John 18:12–27)
- The religious leaders took Jesus to Pilate to pronounce the death sentence, but Pilate couldn't find that Jesus was guilty of a crime that deserved crucifixion. (John 18:28–38)
- Pilate offered to release a prisoner, hoping the Jewish people would choose Jesus. Instead, they chose Barabbas. (John 18:39–40)

Part Three

JESUS' DEATH AND RESURRECTION

"It's getting so you can't trust anyone these days!"

JOHN 19: JESUS THE CORPSE

CHAPTER HIGHLIGHTS

- Mock to the King
- Trial and Error
- Love on a Cross
- No Tomb to Call His Own

Let's Get Started

If you lived in Jesus' day and were voting for the worst way to die, you'd pick crucifixion. You wouldn't even have to think about it for a few seconds. The cross was *the* most painful way to die. Nothing else came close. Amazingly, it was the way God chose for Jesus to make the final payment for our sins.

Jesus came to earth to die, to pay the penalty for our sins, so we don't have to spend an eternity separated from the God who loves us. (That's what sin does to us.) Since our sins are so monstrous in God's eyes, it took something as horrible as Jesus' crucifixion to pay the price to bring us back to God.

Mercifully, John chose not to describe all the gory details of Jesus' death on the cross. If he had, most people would quit reading at this point. It's worse than a marathon of horror movies. Instead, he gave us enough details to understand that the price for our sins was high.

In this chapter, John continued Jesus' trial before Pilate (remember, there were no chapter divisions in the original book). Then he described Jesus' death and burial.

MOCK TO THE KING

> **John 19:1–3** Then Pilate took Jesus and had him flogged. The soldiers twisted together a crown of thorns and put it on his head. They clothed him in a purple robe and went up to him again and again, saying, "Hail, king of the Jews!" And they struck him in the face.

True Grit

Still not wanting to pronounce the death sentence on Jesus, Pilate had him beaten, hoping it would be enough for the Jewish people. During flogging, the victim was stripped and tied to a post. The flogger used a whip, which consisted of several pieces of leather strips fastened to a wooden handle. Each strip had butterfly-shaped metal pieces attached to the end (see illustration below).

That flogging would have turned Jesus' back into one giant, open wound. The most amazing fact about it is that Jesus just stood there and took it. Anyone who could raise a dead man could zap Pilate and his soldiers in an instant. Or escape. Or at least dazzle them with an argument in his own defense. He did none of these. He took the torture.

After the flogging, the soldiers ridiculed Jesus' claim to be king by pressing a crown of thorns on his head and dressing him up in a robe. Both a crown and a purple robe were symbols of royalty. Now that he looked like a king, the soldiers repeatedly mocked him as one, using a sarcastic form of the normal greeting for the Roman emperor, "Hail, Caesar." And they beat him.

James M. Stalker: To us it is incomprehensible how the whole band should have been called together merely to gloat over the sufferings of a fellow-creature and to turn His pain and shame into brutal mockery. This, however, was their purpose; and they

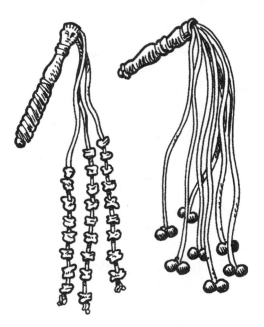

Roman Whips

Jesus was beaten with whips such as these composed of leather strips with sharp pieces of metal on the ends.

enjoyed it as schoolboys enjoy the terror of a tortured animal. It must be remembered that these were men who on the field of battle were **inured** to bloodshed and at Rome found their chief delight in watching the sport of the arena, where **gladiators** butchered one another to make a Roman holiday.[1]

inured: accustomed

gladiators: trained fighters

The whip the soldiers used on Jesus literally shredded a person's back and was an instrument of death. Few people lived through a flogging, which saved the trouble and expense of crucifying them. Jewish law permitted a maximum of forty lashes. Roman law had no limit.

The thorns in Jesus' crown were the giant variety, an inch long and sharp as needles.

Purple was the color of royalty since purple dye was so expensive that only rich people owned purple garments. It was as valuable as gold.

> **John 19:4–5** Once more Pilate came out and said to the Jews, "Look, I am bringing him out to you to let you know that I find no basis for a charge against him." When Jesus came out wearing the crown of thorns and the purple robe, Pilate said to them, "Here is the man!"

Beaten And Battered King

For the third time, Pilate went out to talk with the Jewish people. This time he brought out Jesus, who would have been unrecognizable (or close to it) from the beatings. For the second time, Pilate declared Jesus' innocence. When Pilate said, *"Here is the man!"* he wasn't politely introducing Jesus to the crowd. He was mocking them. "Look at this poor man. How can you believe he is a king? Have mercy and drop the charges."

> **John 19:6–7** As soon as the chief priests and their officials saw him, they shouted, "Crucify! Crucify!"
>
> But Pilate answered, "You take him and crucify him. As for me, I find no basis for a charge against him."
>
> The Jews insisted, "We have a law, and according to that law he must die, because he claimed to be the Son of God."

Kill The King

The religious leaders were not about to back down. They hated Jesus with a vengeance and would not quit until they saw him dead. The courtyard scene may have been similar to a ball game today. Just like the crowds in the stadium chant for their team, the religious leaders began to shout repeatedly, "Crucify him!"

By this time, Pilate was fed up with the Jews. He dared them to crucify Jesus even though they had no authority to do so. For the third time, Pilate pronounced him innocent.

Finally, the religious leaders clearly stated the real reason they wanted to kill Jesus: *"He claimed to be the Son of God."* That claim carried the <u>death penalty</u>, but they couldn't execute it. Jesus didn't deserve the charge; he really was the Son of God.

☞ **GO TO:**

Leviticus 24:16
(death penalty)

> **John 19:8–10** When Pilate heard this, he was even more afraid, and he went back inside the palace. "Where do you come from?" he asked Jesus, but Jesus gave him no answer. "Do you refuse to speak to me?" Pilate said. "Don't you realize I have power either to free you or to crucify you?"

Don't You Know Who I Am?

Undoubtedly, this was the worst day of Pilate's life. Hearing that Jesus claimed to be the Son of God sent his fear temperature up another twenty degrees. Romans believed that gods came to earth, and maybe Jesus was one of them. If that were the case, it was not in Pilate's best interests to kill him. Earlier his wife had had a dream about Jesus and had sent him a <u>message</u> to have nothing to do with this innocent man. He must have been thinking about her words. Now, with the crowd chanting for crucifixion, he could sense a riot coming.

☞ **GO TO:**

Matthew 27:19
(message)

John 18:36–37
(told him)

Unable to make a firm decision, Pilate went back into the house to talk to Jesus. Jesus wouldn't tell him where he was from so that Pilate would know if he were a god or not. Jesus had already <u>told him</u>. What was the point in repeating truth Pilate didn't want to know or act on?

Frustrated, Pilate changed tactics. If Jesus wasn't going to talk with him, he'd remind him of who was in charge. Pilate thought he had the power to decide Jesus' future, but the real director was God. If Pilate had all that power, why didn't he let Jesus go like he wanted to? It was a hollow boast.

What Others are Saying:

John MacArthur Jr.: Pilate was by now beginning to see the enormity of his wrongdoing from Jesus' perspective. Perhaps it was merely a superstitious fear on Pilate's part, but he was clearly shaken by Jesus' claim of deity (for Pilate would have correctly understood the implications of the expression "Son of God"). And he wanted no part of the guilt he knew he would bear if such a claim were true, because he had already wrongfully abused Jesus merely by having Him flogged. And even though Pilate was not a believer in the Hebrew God, his Roman **polytheistic** world-view was laden with superstition about offending the gods and the heavy price one could pay for such an offense.[2]

polytheistic: belief in many gods

> **John 19:11** Jesus answered, "You would have no power over me if it were not given to you from above. Therefore the one who handed me over to you is guilty of a greater sin."

Enough Guilt To Go Around

The last thing Jesus said to Pilate was a reminder that his power came from God, not from himself or the Roman government. It was useless to pull a power play with Jesus; he always wins. Pilate wasn't the only loser in this game. Caiaphas, the high priest who had handed Jesus over to Pilate for execution, committed a greater sin than Pilate was about to.

Jesus' conversation with Pilate, which began in the last chapter, focused on the charges the Jewish religious leaders leveled against him. Jesus clearly stated that he is a king but not an earthly one. He also told Pilate that God is in charge of giving out power; a political office and authority are not necessarily the same. As a result, Pilate compromised his belief about Jesus' innocence by giving in to the pressure from the Jewish religious leaders.

Conversations with Christ

TRIAL AND ERROR

> **John 19:12** From then on, Pilate tried to set Jesus free, but the Jews kept shouting, "If you let this man go, you are no friend of Caesar. Anyone who claims to be a king opposes Caesar."

Choose Your Side

Some days it doesn't pay to get out of bed. This was one of those days for Pilate. The situation just kept getting worse. The more he tried to free Jesus, the more the Jewish people argued against that action. Finally, the Jews hurled a threat that hit the target. They accused Pilate of being Caesar's enemy instead of his friend if he let Jesus go. That was a statement that would terrify any Roman governor. If word got back to Rome that Pilate had released a man whose claim to be king was a threat to Caesar's rule, he would lose his job and maybe his life. The threat was effective even though it came from hypocrites who had no allegiance to Roman rule.

CULTURE CLUE

Pilate ruled Israel from A.D. 26 to 35. As governor, he controlled the military and justice system and supervised the collection of taxes for Rome. Once a year, he visited all the provinces to hear legal cases and complaints. He was paid by Rome and forbidden to take bribes and presents. His subjects, however, could report him to the Roman emperor if he went beyond his stated duties. Since the Jewish people hated the many gods of Rome and served only God, Israel was a problem area.

Pilate made several huge errors before Jesus was brought to him for crucifixion. The first time he visited Jerusalem, Pilate brought soldiers who carried standards with busts of the Roman emperor. Since the emperor was considered a god, the Jewish people viewed those busts as <u>idols</u>, strictly forbidden in Scripture. Previous governors had had those images removed before entering the city in respect for the Jews' religious beliefs. Pilate refused to do so.

Then Pilate decided to build a new aqueduct to improve the water supply for Jerusalem. He financed it by taking money from the temple treasury. The Jewish people rioted and could have reported him to Rome.

Another time when Pilate was in Jerusalem, he had special shields made with the name of the emperor engraved on them. They were displayed in honor of the emperor, a god to the Romans. The Jewish people were enraged, but Pilate refused to remove them. That time the Jews reported him to Rome, and the emperor ordered Pilate to remove the shields.

Pilate was in danger of losing his job as governor. Consequently, he gave in to the Jewish leaders' blackmail and crucified Jesus.

☞ **GO TO:**

Exodus 20:4 (idols)

> **John 19:13–14** When Pilate heard this, he brought Jesus out and sat down on the judge's seat at a place known as the Stone Pavement (which in Aramaic is Gabbatha). It was the day of Preparation of Passover Week, about the sixth hour.
>
> "Here is your king," Pilate said to the Jews.

Presenting His Royal Highness

Pilate finally made a decision. He moved Jesus to the Fortress of Antonia, where he sat on the judgment seat in the paved courtyard and sentenced Jesus indirectly. John noted that it was about 6:00 A.M. on the day of preparation, the day the Passover lamb was killed to be eaten that night. In a mocking voice, Pilate presented Jesus to the Jewish people as their king. By then, Jesus looked like a walking dead man, not a king.

> **John 19:15–16** But they shouted, "Take him away! Take him away! Crucify him!"
>
> "Shall I crucify your king?" Pilate asked.
>
> "We have no king but Caesar," the chief priests answered.
>
> Finally Pilate handed him over to them to be crucified. So the soldiers took charge of Jesus.

Choosing The Wrong King

The Jewish people, however, didn't want *that* king. They wanted him crucified. Instead, the leaders swore their allegiance to Caesar, rejecting God as their king. According to Matthew, Pilate washed his hands of Jesus' blood, declaring Jesus to be innocent of a political crime. But he buckled under the pressure and sold Jesus out to the religious leaders. He was more interested in keeping peace than in doing what was right. He turned Jesus over to the soldiers for crucifixion.

☞ **GO TO:**

Matthew 27:24 (washed his hands)

Manford George Gutzke: Heaven must have looked down on this scene with anguish and horror. It must have hurt the heart of God the Father to see His Son suffer. And yet salvation was being wrought out in the plan of God, as the Son was carrying out the will of the Father. Not only was the Son of God put to a shameful death by men not worthy to tie His shoelaces, but God had allowed this to come to pass.[3]

What Others are Saying:

Remember This . . .

Pilate knew Jesus was innocent, but he refused to buck the crowd. Standing up for what is right isn't always easy. More often than not, it's just plain hard. But God always honors us when we take a stand for him.

LOVE ON A CROSS

> **John 19:17–18** Carrying his own cross, he went out to the place of the Skull (which in Aramaic is called Golgotha). Here they crucified him, and with him two others—one on each side and Jesus in the middle.

The Darkest Day In History

In two sentences, John summarized the worst—and best—time in history. Until he collapsed under the weight, Jesus was forced to carry his own cross from the judgment hall (Antonia) to the execution hill (Golgotha) outside the city of Jerusalem (see illustration, page 242). There the Roman soldiers crucified him between two other <u>criminals</u>—an act that God had predicted hundreds of years before. Although it was a horrible time, it was also the best time. Jesus died on that cross so we can have eternal life.

☞ GO TO:

Isaiah 53:12 (criminals)

What Others are Saying:

ignominy: shame

J. W. Shepherd: The cross was the most disgraceful and one of the cruelest instruments of death ever invented. The Romans . . . would not allow a Roman citizen to be crucified; but reserved crucifixion for slaves and foreigners or provincials. The Jews customarily used stoning and never crucifixion. It was not only the death of greatest **ignominy** but of the most extreme anguish and suffering.[4]

B.C.E.: before the common era, B.C.

Louis Goldberg: In Psalm 22:16 we read, ". . . they pierced my hands, and my feet." This is a Messianic psalm (it has always been regarded as such), and there is an amazing accuracy in what is proclaimed here. David wrote this Psalm about 1000 B.C.E., and in that day stoning was the method of capital punishment. David spoke of Messiah's hands and feet being pierced. Under the influence of the Spirit of God, he described a manner of execution that was foreign to the people of his day. The period in which crucifixion was the common mode of execution was hundreds of years future, in the time of the Romans, who used this peculiar method. Not only was the death described, but the rest of Psalm 22 relates the suffering accompanying His death.[5]

C. Marvin Pate: The crucifixion of Jesus was truly a divine drama. It was, in effect, a **parody** on kingship. Jesus, the king of the Jews . . . , was enthroned on the cross, with the two highest seats of honor, the one on the right and the one on the left, occupied by criminals. . . . The subjects of the king—the leaders, the soldiers, and the people—taunted their royal ruler. . . . Jesus' regal **regalia**, a tattered garment, was taken from Him. . . . His kingly drink was sour wine . . . , and His **ensign** was a placard attached to the cross, an instrument of capital punishment. . . . His kingdom was invisible and without apparent clout.[6]

What Others are Saying:

parody: mockery

regalia: royal dress

ensign: banner

> In Jesus' day, condemned criminals carried their own crosses to the site of crucifixion. Although Jesus is normally pictured with an entire cross on his back, he would have toted only the horizontal crossbeam. Several stakes already in the ground at Golgotha were reused for crucifixions. The victim was nailed to the crossbeam on the ground. Then it was lifted up and set in a groove near the top of the stake. His feet would have been only two to four feet above the ground.

CULTURE CLUE

John 19:19–22 Pilate had a notice prepared and fastened to the cross. It read: JESUS OF NAZARETH, THE KING OF THE JEWS. Many of the Jews read this sign, for the place where Jesus was crucified was near the city, and the sign was written in Aramaic, Latin and Greek. The chief priests of the Jews protested to Pilate, "Do not write 'The King of the Jews,' but that this man claimed to be king of the Jews."

Pilate answered, "What I have written, I have written."

TITLE OF JESUS

King of the Jews

King In Any Language

Jesus hung in a public place outside the city where thousands of Passover pilgrims could see him. As revenge for his political defeat, Pilate posted a notice in three languages to call attention to Jesus' humiliating crime. He made sure everyone could read it. Jewish people spoke Aramaic, Romans spoke Latin, and Greek was the common language. Labeling that beaten, crucified man as King of the Jews would embarrass and insult the Jewish people.

Of course, the chief priests took issue with the sign and asked Pilate to edit it to say Jesus *claimed* to be king of the Jews. They weren't going to claim him as king, so why advertise that fact? For once Pilate refused to give in to them and left it as written.

> **John 19:23–24** When the soldiers crucified Jesus, they took his clothes, dividing them into four shares, one for each of them, with the undergarment remaining. This garment was seamless, woven in one piece from top to bottom.
>
> "Let's not tear it," they said to one another. "Let's decide by lot who will get it."
>
> This happened that the scripture might be fulfilled which said,
>
> "They divided my garments among them
> and cast lots for my clothing."
> So this is what the soldiers did.

Used Clothing Division

Unlike pictures we see of Jesus hanging on the cross while wearing a loincloth, he was naked, as was customary for crucifixions. Part of the soldiers' pay was the victims' belongings, so they divided up Jesus' clothes, which were all he had. Each of them got one piece—sandals, turban, robe, and sash. Since the tunic worn under the robe was seamless, they decided to throw dice for it instead of tearing it in four pieces. Little did they know that they were fulfilling <u>prophecy</u>.

☞ **GO TO:**

Psalm 22:18 (prophecy)

> **John 19:25–27** Near the cross of Jesus stood his mother, his mother's sister, Mary the wife of Clopas, and Mary Magdalene. When Jesus saw his mother there, and the disciple whom he loved standing nearby, he said to his mother, "Dear woman, here is your son," and to the disciple, "Here is your mother." From that time on, this disciple took her into his home.

☞ **GO TO:**

Matthew 27:55–56 (wife of Zebedee)

Women Around The Cross

Few of Jesus' followers stuck around for the Crucifixion. John mentioned only five: Jesus' mother, Mary; his aunt Salome, the <u>wife of Zebedee</u> and the mother of John (the writer of this book) and James; Mary, the wife of Clopas who was the <u>mother</u> of James the younger and Joses; Mary Magdalene; and John, the author. (To learn more about the feelings of Jesus' mother, Mary, see WBFM, pages 285–288.)

In the midst of his pain and agony, Jesus thought about his mother. Part of <u>honoring</u> one's mother and father was providing for them when they got old. Since Jesus wouldn't be around that long, he asked John to take care of her.

☞ **GO TO:**

Mark 15:40 (mother)

Exodus 20:12 (honoring)

John MacArthur Jr.: This was a beautiful gesture, and it says a lot about the personal nature of Jesus' love. Although he was dying under the most excruciating kind of anguish, Jesus, the King of love, selflessly turned aside to care for the earthly needs of those who stood by His side. Although He was occupied with the most important event in the history of redemption, He remembered to make provision for the needs of one woman, His mother.[7]

What Others are Saying:

If you had lived in Jesus' day and had been one of his followers, would you have been with Judas, who betrayed him; with Peter, who denied him; with the other disciples, who scattered when he was arrested; or with the women and John, who stayed with Jesus until he died?

Something to Ponder

While hanging on the cross, Jesus spoke seven statements, only three of which John recorded:

Dig Deeper

1. *"Father, forgive them, for they do not know what they are doing"* (Luke 23:34). Jesus forgave all those who were killing him, including the Roman soldiers who nailed him to the cross, the Jewish leaders who had him arrested, and Pilate who gave the order for crucifixion.

2. *"Today you will be with me in paradise"* (Luke 23:43). One of the two thieves who was crucified next to Jesus believed in him as Savior from his sins while he was on the cross. As a result, Jesus told him he would go to paradise, or heaven.

3. *"Dear woman, here is your son. . . . Here is your mother"* (John 19:26–27). While he was dying, Jesus took care of his mother by committing her to John to make sure she would be taken care of.

4. *"My God, my God, why have you forsaken me?"* (Matthew 27:46). On the cross, Jesus took on himself all of our sins. Because God is holy, he cannot look at sin. So

Jesus was separated spiritually from the Father during that time. This question was a fulfillment of prophecy in Psalm 22:1.

5. *"I am thirsty"* (John 19:28). After three hours of hanging in the sun, Jesus' mouth would have been so parched he could barely talk. Although he didn't need the pain-deadening wine, he uttered this statement to fulfill prophecy in Psalm 69:21.

6. *"It is finished"* (John 19:30). This was a cry of victory. Jesus had completed the payment for our sins.

7. *"Father, into you hands I commit my spirit"* (Luke 23:46). As he breathed his last breath, Jesus committed himself to his Father. No one forced Jesus to die; he did it voluntarily for us.

> **John 19:28–30** Later, knowing that all was now completed, and so that the Scripture would be fulfilled, Jesus said, "I am thirsty." A jar of wine vinegar was there, so they soaked a sponge in it, put the sponge on a stalk of the hyssop plant, and lifted it to Jesus' lips. When he had received the drink, Jesus said, "It is finished." With that, he bowed his head and gave up his spirit.

Final Payment

GO TO:

Matthew 27:34 (drink wine)

Psalm 69:21 (thirsty)

Matthew 27:45–50 (3:00 P.M.)

hyssop: *tall cornlike plant*

Previously, Jesus had refused to <u>drink wine</u> mixed with a pain-killer that was given to victims before crucifixion. He endured all the excruciating agony of hanging on that stake. Nearing the end of his mission, and to fulfill what God had predicted earlier, he cried out, *"I am <u>thirsty</u>."* The soldiers soaked a sponge with sour wine, fastened it to the end of a **hyssop** branch (see illustration, page 273), and let Jesus sip the liquid from it.

That wasn't enough wine to quench his thirst after hanging on the cross for three hours. But it was enough to permit him to shout a victory cry, *"It is finished,"* at <u>3:00 P.M.</u> The Greek word for this phrase means a debt is paid in full, something is accomplished, and assigned work is completed. Nothing else needed to be done for our salvation from sin. Jesus' death on the cross fulfilled all the predictions about his death and completed the payment for our sins. Then he voluntarily gave up his life. Jesus was in control of his death to his final breath.

Edwin A. Blum: The wording in John 19:28 indicated that Jesus was fully conscious and was aware of fulfilling the details of prophecies (Pss. 42:1–2; 63:1). The paradox of the One who is the Water of life (John 4:14; 7:38–39) dying in thirst is striking.[8]

Philip Yancey: Why does Jesus have to die? Theologians who ponder such things have debated various theories of "the Atonement" for centuries, with little agreement. Somehow it requires love, sacrificial love, to win what cannot be won by force.[9]

What Others are Saying:

Old Testament Prophecies Fulfilled In Jesus' Death

Passage	Prophecy	Fulfillment
Isaiah 50:6	Beaten and spit on	John 19:1; Matthew 27:30
Psalm 69:19	Shame	Matthew 27:28
Psalm 22:18	Clothing divided among the soldiers	John 19:24
Isaiah 53:7	Silent at the trial	Matthew 27:13–14
Isaiah 53:5–6, 10	Death by crucifixion	John 19:16
Psalm 69:3	Thirst	John 19:28
Psalm 69:21	Wine vinegar to drink	John 19:29
Psalm 22:17	Stared at	Matthew 27:36
Psalm 22:16	Hands and feet pierced	John 19:18
Zechariah 12:10	Side pierced	John 19:34
Psalm 22:14	Broken heart/blood and water	John 19:34
Psalm 22:8	Mocked	Matthew 27:43
Isaiah 53:12	Prayed for others	Luke 23:34
Psalm 22:1	Cry to God	Matthew 27:46
Psalm 22:31	Victory cry	John 19:30
Exodus 12:46	No broken bones	John 19:33, 36
Isaiah 53:12	Numbered with law breakers	Luke 23:33
Genesis 3:15	Bruised heel	John 19:18
Isaiah 53:9	Place of burial	Matthew 27:57–60

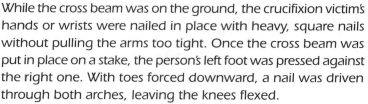

While the cross beam was on the ground, the crucifixion victim's hands or wrists were nailed in place with heavy, square nails without pulling the arms too tight. Once the cross beam was put in place on a stake, the person's left foot was pressed against the right one. With toes forced downward, a nail was driven through both arches, leaving the knees flexed.

As the victim hung there, he sagged, causing pressure on the nerves and excruciating pain shooting through his fingers and arms. It was like a fire exploding in the brain. To relieve this pain, he pushed himself up. The extra weight on the nail in his feet tore the nerves in his feet, causing more exploding pain.

His tired arms cramped, producing throbbing muscle pain and preventing him from pushing himself up. He could barely breathe and tried to raise himself again to draw air, taking some in but not being able to exhale. So carbon dioxide built up in his lungs and blood stream, temporarily relieving the arm cramps and allowing him to pull himself up to breathe.

The victim could endure hours of this cycle of pain, tearing the tissue from his back each time he moved up and down on the rough wood. Slowly the sac around the heart filled with fluid, compressing his heart and causing crushing chest pain. Finally, he reached the critical stage and died.

Dig Deeper

Jesus died to pay for our sins. Read what some of the other scripture writers said about his death and what it accomplished: Isaiah 53; Romans 6:23; Ephesians 1:7; 2:8–9; Colossians 1:19–22; 1 Timothy 1:15–16; Hebrews 2:14–17; 9:27–28.

> **John 19:31–34** Now it was the day of Preparation, and the next day was to be a special Sabbath. Because the Jews did not want the bodies left on the crosses during the Sabbath, they asked Pilate to have the legs broken and the bodies taken down. The soldiers therefore came and broke the legs of the first man who had been crucified with Jesus, and then those of the other. But when they came to Jesus and found that he was already dead, they did not break his legs. Instead, one of the soldiers pierced Jesus' side with a spear, bringing a sudden flow of blood and water.

Whole Bones, Not Broken Pieces

Part of the horror of crucifixion was a long, drawn-out death. Since it was disrespectful for the Jewish people to leave a dead <u>body</u> hanging on the Sabbath, something had to be done to make sure the three men died before sundown when the Sabbath began. The holiday made it even more urgent to clear the crosses. So the Jewish leaders asked Pilate to hasten death by having soldiers break the victims' legs. That was normal procedure to keep them from pushing up and breathing longer. With broken legs, they would suffocate in their own body fluids.

The soldiers obeyed with the two thieves. When they saw that Jesus was already dead, they didn't bother with him. Just to be sure, one of them stuck a spear in Jesus' side. The fact that blood and water had separated confirmed his death and that Jesus was a man with a human body.

☞ **GO TO:**

Deuteronomy 21:22–23 (body)

Mark Bailey and Tom Constable: The flow of blood and water from His pierced side affirmed the physical reality of Jesus' death. Affirming the truth of what he wrote about Jesus' death, John then encouraged the faith of his readers by quoting Old Testament passages he saw fulfilled in the events of the Cross (Exod. 12:46; Num. 9:12; Ps. 34:20; Zech. 12:10).[10]

What Others are Saying:

> **John 19:35–37** The man who saw it has given testimony, and his testimony is true. He knows that he tells the truth, and he testifies so that you also may believe. These things happened so that the scripture would be fulfilled: "Not one of his bones will be broken," and, as another scripture says, "They will look on the one they have pierced."

Scripture Clues

John was an eyewitness to Jesus' death and the soldiers' actions to hasten death for the trio on the crosses. What he wrote was not secondhand knowledge or something he made up. It was true, and John included this information so readers would believe in Jesus. (To read about others who witnessed Jesus' death, see GWLC2, page 248.) As with other events of the past two days, these also fulfilled Scripture. The absence of <u>broken bones</u> referred to the Passover lamb, which pictured Jesus as *"the Lamb of God, who takes away the sin of the world"* (John 1:29). The prophet Zechariah predicted that the Messiah would be <u>pierced</u>.

☞ **GO TO:**

Exodus 12:46 (broken bones)

Zechariah 12:10 (pierced)

THE FAITH FACTOR—We have John's report about Jesus' death, including how the final details fulfilled God's Word, so those who read it will recognize him as the Son of God and Savior of the world and believe in him.

NO TOMB TO CALL HIS OWN

> **John 19:38–40** Later, Joseph of Arimathea asked Pilate for the body of Jesus. Now Joseph was a disciple of Jesus, but secretly because he feared the Jews. With Pilate's permission, he came and took the body away. He was accompanied by Nicodemus, the man who earlier had visited Jesus at night. Nicodemus brought a mixture of myrrh and aloes, about seventy-five pounds. Taking Jesus' body, the two of them wrapped it, with the spices, in strips of linen. This was in accordance with Jewish burial customs.

No More Secret Believers

Crucified criminals were thrown into a common grave unless someone in the family had enough clout to request the body for proper burial. Since Jesus' arrest and sentencing happened quickly, his family didn't have time to purchase a burial tomb or make funeral arrangements. Other than John, his disciples were not around. So Joseph of Arimathea and Nicodemus quit hiding their belief in Jesus and took care of his body.

Joseph asked Pilate for permission to take Jesus' body away, and Pilate granted it. He and Nicodemus—the same man who met Jesus at night three years earlier—picked up the body and prepared it for burial. Since shops would be closed for Passover, Nicodemus must have had the spices on hand, ready for this moment. There wasn't time to wash and anoint the body as was customary, but they wrapped it in linen strips with an enormous amount of **myrrh** and **aloes**, both expensive spices.

Ed Glasscock: Joseph came and asked for the body of Christ "when it was evening," that is, some time after 3:00 P.M. on Friday but before 6:00 P.M., which would begin the high Sabbath of Pass-

---

☞ **GO TO:**

Mark 15:43; Luke 23:50–51
(Joseph of Arimathea)

John 3:1–21
(Nicodemus)

myrrh: *fragrant spice*

aloes: *thick leaves with a bitter liquid inside*

What Others are Saying:

---

over (Luke 23:54). According to Deuteronomy 21:22–23, a criminal executed and hanged on a tree was not to be left hanging overnight. Since the coming day was a Sabbath, and a special Sabbath at that, the Jews would not allow removal of the body after sunset.[11]

> **John 19:41–42** At the place where Jesus was crucified, there was a garden, and in the garden a new tomb, in which no one had ever been laid. Because it was the Jewish day of Preparation and since the tomb was nearby, they laid Jesus there.

Buried In A Borrowed Tomb

Jesus had not bought a tomb before he died, but Joseph had one ready for him. Since Joseph was rich, he would not have bought a tomb for himself that close to Golgotha. After all, his relatives would not have wanted to pay their respects while listening to criminals dying. And he could have afforded a better location within Jerusalem. There he and Nicodemus buried Jesus.

Jesus died and was buried. For other people, that would be the end of the story. But not for Jesus. His story is to be continued.

Study Questions

1. How did the soldiers mock Jesus?
2. What arguments did the Jewish leaders use to convince Pilate that Jesus should die?
3. Where did Pilate's power come from?
4. How did Pilate identify Jesus when he was on the cross?
5. What did Jesus do for his mother before he died?
6. Who took care of Jesus' burial, and what did they do with his body?

CHAPTER WRAP-UP

- Pilate had Jesus beaten, and he and the soldiers mocked him as a king. (John 19:1–5)
- The Jewish leaders continued to demand that Pilate crucify Jesus. (John 19:6–7)
- Pilate tried to pull a power play on Jesus, but Jesus reminded him that his power came from God. (John 19:8–11)
- Pilate tried to set Jesus free but bowed to the pressure of the Jewish leaders to crucify him. (John 19:12–16)

KEY POINT

Pilate sentenced Jesus to death by crucifixion, and two of his secret disciples buried him.

- Jesus was crucified between two thieves. (John 19:17–24)
- Before he died, Jesus arranged for John to take care of his mother. (John 19:25–27)
- Jesus voluntarily died and did not have to have his bones broken to hasten death. (John 19:28–37)
- Joseph of Arimathea and Nicodemus claimed Jesus' body and buried him. (John 19:38–42)

JOHN 20: JESUS THE RISEN LORD

CHAPTER HIGHLIGHTS

- Can't Keep a Good Man Down
- Appearing behind Closed Doors
- Signposts to Belief

Let's Get Started

Anybody can claim to be God. There are a lot of people in mental hospitals who make that claim, but proving it is another story. That's exactly what Jesus did when he rose from the dead. His resurrection was the final proof that he is the Son of God.

Jesus' bodily resurrection is historical fact, not a myth. There is more evidence for the Resurrection than for any other event from the same time period. One of my Bible professors used to say, "If you cannot believe the Resurrection based on historical records, you cannot believe any other fact of history."

As John recorded some of Jesus' postresurrection appearances, we learn that the Resurrection gave Mary Magdalene joy, gave the disciples courage, and gave Thomas assurance of his faith. John wrapped up this chapter with his purpose statement: *that you may believe that Jesus is the Christ, the Son of God, and that by believing you may have life in his name."*

CAN'T KEEP A GOOD MAN DOWN

> **John 20:1–2** Early on the first day of the week, while it was still dark, Mary Magdalene went to the tomb and saw that the stone had been removed from the entrance. So she came running to Simon Peter and the other disciple, the one Jesus loved, and said, "They have taken the Lord out of the tomb, and we don't know where they have put him!"

The Case Of The Missing Body

After Joseph and Nicodemus buried Jesus, the religious leaders went back to Pilate. They asked him to <u>seal</u> and <u>guard</u> Jesus' tomb so no one could steal the body. They had acted stupidly in crucifying Jesus, but they weren't stupid. They knew Jesus had claimed he would <u>rise</u> on the third day, and they wanted to be sure no one stole the body and claimed Jesus was alive. They also wanted to be sure Jesus didn't get out of the tomb.

Since Jesus had been buried hastily, Mary Magdalene showed up at the tomb early Sunday morning. She arrived shortly before <u>Mary</u> the mother of James <u>and Salome</u> to anoint Jesus' body for burial. They were concerned about getting someone to <u>roll away</u> the heavy stone so they could get into the tomb. But God was way ahead of them. The tomb was already open, the stone having been rolled away earlier by an <u>angel</u>.

Mary Magdalene peered into the tomb, expecting a dead body. Instead, her eyes took in a lot of emptiness. Shocked, Mary ran to Peter and John to tell them someone had taken Jesus' body. The women didn't even know where to look for it.

☞ **GO TO:**

Matthew 27:66 (seal)

Matthew 27:62–65 (guard)

Matthew 16:21 (rise)

Mark 16:1 (Mary and Salome)

Mark 16:3 (roll away)

Matthew 28:2 (angel)

Theories Of Jesus' Missing Body

To explain away Jesus' missing body, people have made up several theories.

Theory	Description	Evidence against It
Fraud Theory	Someone stole it.	Roman guards were posted, so no one could steal it.
		Disciples didn't believe Jesus was going to rise.
		If Jesus' enemies had taken it, they would have produced the body to show he didn't rise.
		Disciples wouldn't have died for a fraud.
Swoon Theory	Jesus didn't really die; he passed out.	Jesus' wounds (hands and feet pierced with nails, side pierced with sword) were so bad he couldn't have gotten up and walked away.
		Soldiers didn't break his legs because he was dead.
		After hanging on the cross, he wouldn't have had enough strength to roll away a rock that weighed two tons and fight the guards to escape.
Ghost Theory	Disciples only thought they saw Jesus alive.	Disciples didn't expect to see Jesus alive.
		Jesus had a real body after the Resurrection.

Bruce Milne: The fact that the women were the first to discover the empty tomb is certainly authentic, as this alone would have discredited the story with the Jewish public (in Jesus' society, sadly, women were not even thought fit witnesses in court).[1]

Josh McDowell: After more than seven hundred hours of studying this subject and thoroughly investigating its foundation, I have come to the conclusion that the resurrection of Jesus Christ is one of the *most wicked, vicious, heartless hoaxes ever foisted upon the minds of men,* OR it is the most fantastic fact of history. . . .

The resurrection of Jesus Christ and Christianity stand or fall together. A student at the University of Uruguay once said to me: "Professor McDowell, why can't you refute Christianity?" I answered: "For a very simple reason: I am not able to explain away an event in history—the resurrection of Jesus."[2]

Something to Ponder

Mary and the other women didn't have a lot to offer Jesus. Nor could they do much for him, given the restrictions of their society. But they stayed by him when he was crucified and most of his other disciples disappeared. Also, they brought ointments to anoint Jesus' body for burial after the Sabbath was over. (For ideas about how you can help those in crisis, see WBFW, page 216.) As a result, Jesus appeared to Mary first after he rose from the dead.

You may not have much to give Jesus either. You may not have the opportunity or ability to do great things for him. But you can give him your love and devotion like these women did.

> **John 20:3–7** So Peter and the other disciple started for the tomb. Both were running, but the other disciple outran Peter and reached the tomb first. He bent over and looked in at the strips of linen lying there but did not go in. Then Simon Peter, who was behind him, arrived and went into the tomb. He saw the strips of linen lying there, as well as the burial cloth that had been around Jesus' head. The cloth was folded up by itself, separate from the linen.

Race For The Tomb

When Peter and John heard the news about Jesus' missing body, they took off for the tomb to see for themselves. John won the race, but he didn't enter the cave. He glanced in and saw the linen strips but no body.

When Peter arrived, he walked past John and entered the tomb. Sure enough, Mary was right. The body was missing, but evidence showed that it had been there. The grave clothes—linen strips—lay in the shape of a body as though someone had energized Jesus to another location. The napkin that had covered his head was neatly folded.

What Others are Saying:

J. Carl Laney: Whereas grave-robbers would have taken the body with the wrappings, or ripped and scattered them, John records Peter's observation that the burial cloth used on Jesus' head remained rolled or had been folded and set carefully aside.[3]

Remember This . . .

Without the Resurrection, there would be no Christianity: *"If Christ has not been raised, your faith is futile; you are still in your sins"* (1 Corinthians 15:17). People in every other religion worship or look to a dead leader. Muhammad is dead. Buddha is dead. Joseph Smith (founder of Mormonism) is dead. Mary Baker Eddy (founder of Christian Science) is dead. Only Jesus is alive. Christianity is a relationship with the living God and his Son, Jesus.

> **John 20:8–9** Finally the other disciple, who had reached the tomb first, also went inside. He saw and believed. (They still did not understand from Scripture that Jesus had to rise from the dead.)

Seeing Is Believing

When John entered the tomb, he also saw the grave clothes in the shape of a body. Like the other disciples, he wasn't expecting a missing body. But the fact that it was gone made him believe that Jesus rose from the dead. He saw and understood the evidence firsthand, making him a trustworthy witness to write this book. The empty tomb brought to mind what <u>Jesus</u> had <u>told</u> the disciples about his resurrection. However, John still didn't get the connection with the <u>prophecies</u> in the Old Testament Scriptures. His belief wasn't fully developed yet.

☞ **GO TO:**

John 2:19 (Jesus told)

Psalm 16:10; Isaiah 53:10 (prophecies)

> **John 20:10–12** Then the disciples went back to their homes, but Mary stood outside the tomb crying. As she wept, she bent over to look into the tomb and saw two angels in white, seated where Jesus' body had been, one at the head and the other at the foot.

Angel Encounter

Not knowing what else to do, the disciples went home. Mary Magdalene probably returned to the tomb after they left. She stood alone, crying loudly with grief and wondering where the body was. Maybe, when she looked inside, she hoped it would be there. Instead, two angels, wearing white, sat where the body had been. We can assume from Mary's reaction that these angels looked like humans and weren't wearing wings and halos.

John Calvin: Although the apostles and the women were suffering the same disease, the apostles' stupidity was less excusable because they had profited so little by their thorough and careful teaching.[4]

What Others are Saying:

> **John 20:13–14** They asked her, "Woman, why are you crying?"
> "They have taken my Lord away," she said, "and I don't know where they have put him." At this, she turned around and saw Jesus standing there, but she did not realize that it was Jesus.

Missing Body Shows Up

Skipping introductions and small talk, the angels asked Mary why she was crying. In one sense, it was a stupid question. What else would they expect from someone who loved the dead man and was standing at his tomb? In another sense, it was an obvious question to remind Mary that she had no reason to cry because Jesus was alive. It was a joyous occasion! She told the angels what was on her mind: Jesus' body was gone, and she didn't know where to look for it.

Then she heard something or someone behind her. She turned around to see who or what it was. Standing there was Jesus, whom she didn't recognize. Maybe she couldn't tell who he was because her eyes were blurred with tears. Or maybe Jesus temporarily blinded her. We don't know for sure.

KEY POINT

Jesus rose from the dead and appeared to Mary and his disciples.

> **John 20:15–16** "Woman," he said, "why are you crying? Who is it you are looking for?"
>
> Thinking he was the gardener, she said, "Sir, if you have carried him away, tell me where you have put him, and I will get him."
>
> Jesus said to her, "Mary."
>
> She turned toward him and cried out in Aramaic, "Rabboni!" (which means Teacher).

Jesus In The Flesh

"Why are you crying?" must have been the question of the day. Jesus followed it with another one, asking Mary who she was looking for. Not knowing the man was Jesus, she figured he must be the gardener. Who else would be hanging around a tomb? So she asked him where he had taken Jesus' body. She was desperate to find him even though she could not have carried two hundred fifty pounds (or whatever he weighed plus seventy-five pounds of spices) of dead weight back to the tomb. And what would she say if someone saw her lugging a corpse? Obviously, she was grief-stricken and wasn't thinking.

In response, Jesus spoke her name. That was enough for her to recognize him. Perhaps it was the sound of his voice. Perhaps Jesus removed her blindness toward him. Whatever it was, Mary looked at him and called him "Rabboni," the personal, informal form of "rabbi," which means teacher.

What Others are Saying:

Merrill C. Tenney: One of the strange commonplaces of life is that the most penetrating utterance one can understand, no matter by whom spoken, is one's personal name. Furthermore, the way it is spoken often identifies the speaker.[5]

> **John 20:17–18** Jesus said, "Do not hold on to me, for I have not yet returned to the Father. Go instead to my brothers and tell them, 'I am returning to my Father and your Father, to my God and your God.' "
>
> Mary Magdalene went to the disciples with the news: "I have seen the Lord!" And she told them that he had said these things to her.

Jesus Is Alive!

Overcome with emotion, Mary grasped Jesus. She'd lost him once; she wasn't going to lose him again. Jesus had other plans, however. He couldn't hang around the tomb. He had other people to see, and he would see her again. Besides, he had a job for her to do. Jesus told Mary to stop clinging to him and tell his disciples, whom he now called brothers, that he was alive and would ascend to his Father and God and their Father and God. He was careful to keep his relationship with God distinct from theirs.

Imagine how happy the disciples must have been when Mary delivered her news. They had spent three years with Jesus and had grown to love him. He had changed their lives. They had just been through the worst three days of their lives and thought Jesus was dead. Now they heard that he was alive. What great news!

What Others are Saying:

Warren W. Wiersbe: Mary not only shared the fact of His resurrection and that she had seen Him personally, but she also reported the words that He had spoken to her. Again, we see the importance of the Word of God. Mary could not transfer her experience over to them, but she could share the Word; and it is the Word that generates faith (Rom. 10:17).[6]

Conversations with Christ

Jesus appeared to Mary Magdalene at the tomb, but she didn't recognize him until he spoke her name. She wanted to know where Jesus' body was; he wanted to show her he was alive. He gave her a message to take to his disciples, and she was overjoyed with the news she had to report.

APPEARING BEHIND CLOSED DOORS

> **John 20:19–20** On the evening of that first day of the week, when the disciples were together, with the doors locked for fear of the Jews, Jesus came and stood among them and said, "Peace be with you!" After he said this, he showed them his hands and side. The disciples were overjoyed when they saw the Lord.

Peace In The Midst Of Fear

Mary had brought good news of Jesus' resurrection, but the disciples didn't fully believe it. If they had, they would not have huddled behind locked doors Sunday night, afraid of the religious leaders. Instead, they would have been out shouting the news to everyone they met. Since Jesus rose from the dead, he certainly was more powerful than the men responsible for his death and could therefore keep his followers safe.

Jesus' followers who were present—a larger group than his ten disciples with Thomas missing—had a lot to talk about together. They had Mary's report of Jesus' appearance to her, and Peter and <u>two others</u> had seen him that afternoon. Undoubtedly, they had also received reports from others who had seen Jesus. Now he appeared in their midst, as though he had beamed into the room. Or perhaps he walked through a wall or the locked door. However he got there, his resurrection body came in a different form than before his death and was no longer limited by the laws of nature.

Standing in the midst of his frightened disciples, Jesus spoke the customary greeting: *"Peace be with you!"* He had spoken these familiar words the night of his arrest to prepare the men for the ordeal they would face. Now Jesus showed them his hands and feet with the nail holes, since they thought they saw a <u>ghost</u>. That was enough evidence to convince the men that he was the same Jesus who had died three days earlier and to fill them with joy.

For forty days after his resurrection, Jesus made a number of appearances besides the ones recorded in this chapter. Check them out in the passages listed below.

☞ **GO TO:**

Luke 24:13–32 (two others)

John 14:27 (peace)

Luke 24:37 (ghost)

Dig Deeper

Passage	People	Place
Matthew 28:9–10	Mary the mother of James	Empty tomb
Luke 24:34	Simon Peter	Jerusalem
Luke 24:13–32	Cleopas and other disciple	On Emmaus road
John 21:1–24	Seven disciples	Sea of Galilee
Matthew 28:16–20	Eleven disciples	Mountain in Galilee
1 Corinthians 15:6	More than five hundred	Galilee
1 Corinthians 15:7	Brother James	Unknown
Acts 1:4–12	Eleven disciples and others	Mount of Olives

What Others are Saying:

Charles U. Wagner: Christ's first words to His disciples that Sunday evening were, "Peace be unto you." He could have chosen any greeting, but he recognized their need for peace. The source of peace is the Lord, and the basis of that peace is His death and resurrection.[7]

W. E. Vine: Whatever other scars there had been were **obliterated** at His resurrection, but not these marks of His crucifixion and the significant wound in the side.[8]

> **John 20:21–23** Again Jesus said, "Peace be with you! As the Father has sent me, I am sending you." And with that he breathed on them and said, "Receive the Holy Spirit. If you forgive anyone his sins, they are forgiven; if you do not forgive them, they are not forgiven."

Sent To The World

Once more Jesus pronounced peace on the gathered disciples. Then he commissioned his followers to go into the world and tell people about his death and resurrection like the Father had sent him. They had deserted him after his arrest, let him die almost alone, and allowed the Jewish leaders to frighten them. Nevertheless, Jesus forgave them and gave them a job to do.

In order for them to have power to do that job, he breathed the Holy Spirit on them. This action is similar to when God breathed life into Adam when he created the first man. After Jesus went back to heaven and the Spirit came on the day of Pentecost, the Spirit would automatically come to live in people at the time of their salvation. But this was still a transition time.

Jesus did not give his followers the right to forgive sins. Only God can do that. What he did give his followers was the right to announce forgiveness based on a person's response to the message of salvation through Jesus.

☞ **GO TO:**

Genesis 2:7 (God breathed)

Mark 2:7 (only God)

> **John 20:24–25** Now Thomas (called Didymus), one of the Twelve, was not with the disciples when Jesus came. So the other disciples told him, "We have seen the Lord!"
>
> But he said to them, "Unless I see the nail marks in his hands and put my finger where the nails were, and put my hand into his side, I will not believe it."

Show Me The Evidence

For whatever reason, Thomas the twin missed the meeting when Jesus appeared to a group of his disciples in an upper room. When the other disciples kept telling him they had seen Jesus, he didn't believe them. He wanted to see physical evidence that Jesus really was alive and to put his hands in the nail holes and the side wound. Thomas insisted that he had to see the proof before he would believe in Jesus' resurrection. Actually, he wasn't any different than the other people who had been in that room. They had seen Jesus in the flesh, which is what Thomas wanted to do.

SIGNPOSTS TO BELIEF

> **John 20:26–27** A week later his disciples were in the house again, and Thomas was with them. Though the doors were locked, Jesus came and stood among them and said, "Peace be with you!" Then he said to Thomas, "Put your finger here; see my hands. Reach out your hand and put it into my side. Stop doubting and believe."

Repeat Appearance

A week later, the disciples were locked behind closed doors again, but this time Thomas was with them. Jesus appeared like he had the week before, suddenly standing in their midst without walking through the door like a normal person. His greeting was the same too: *"Peace be with you!"* Then he showed Thomas the evidence he wanted—the nail holes in his hand and the wound in his side. The Lord invited his disciple to touch him in those spots. Jesus wanted Thomas to believe instead of doubting his resurrection.

What Others are Saying:

Lawrence O. Richards: What a blessing Thomas is to Christians everywhere. He reminds us that the skeptic is not rejected by God—that doubts and uncertainty do not lose us a place in God's kingdom. He reminds us too that Jesus willingly comes to us, to show us His hands and side, that we might believe.[9]

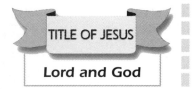

TITLE OF JESUS

Lord and God

> **John 20:28–29** Thomas said to him, "My Lord and my God!"
> Then Jesus told him, "Because you have seen me, you have believed; blessed are those who have not seen and yet have believed."

Made A Believer Out Of Me

Thomas didn't need to touch the evidence of Jesus' scars that proved he was the same man who had died. Seeing Jesus was enough for him to blurt out, *"My Lord and my God!"* Thomas finally believed Jesus was who he said he was—God the Messiah who rose from the dead. He first had to see for himself, though.

In another month, no one else would be able to see Jesus face-to-face before believing in him. Faith is not dependent on sight, however. In fact, those who believe without seeing (that's us) are "blessed," or made happy.

☞ **GO TO:**

Romans 10:17 (faith)

Earl F. Palmer: John does not record that Thomas actually placed his hands upon the hand of Jesus. Instead, Thomas speaks the greatest affirmation in this gospel: "My Lord and my God!" Thomas does not need as many signs as he thought at first he did.[10]

What Others are Saying:

Erwin W. Lutzer: A Buddhist in Africa who was converted to Christianity was asked why he changed religions. He replied, "It's like this. If you were walking along and came to a fork in the road and two men were there and one was dead and the other alive, which man's directions would you follow?"[11]

Jesus didn't scold Thomas for doubting that he was alive and for wanting tangible proof of his resurrection. (For more about Thomas and different personality types, see WBFW, pages 106–108.) Instead, he met Thomas where he was at spiritually and provided the evidence Thomas thought he needed. Doubts from a searching heart, not a hard heart, are not sinful. We can take those doubts to Jesus in prayer and Bible reading and get answers.

Remember This . . .

> **John 20:30–31** Jesus did many other miraculous signs in the presence of his disciples, which are not recorded in this book. But these are written that you may believe that Jesus is the Christ, the Son of God, and that by believing you may have life in his name.

Purpose Statement

Remember writing term papers and essays in high school or college? English teachers taught us to start a paper with a thesis or theme statement—a purpose statement. John had a clear purpose statement, although he stated it near the end of the book instead of at the beginning. These verses are the key verses for the book. They explain why John wrote this Gospel: so people who read it will believe that Jesus is God's Son and gain eternal life. John didn't record every miracle Jesus did. Instead, he selected the ones that clearly point to Jesus' deity. He told us all we need to know about Jesus so we can have eternal life.

F. L. Godet: He [John] aims, not at knowledge, but at faith, and through faith at life. He is not a philosopher, but a witness; his work as a historian forms a part of his apostolic ministry. In all times, those who *have not seen* will be able through his testimony to reach the same faith and the same life as himself.[12]

THE FAITH FACTOR—John wrote this book for the sole purpose of leading readers to believe that Jesus is God's Son and to put their faith in him to gain eternal life.

Study Questions

1. What did Mary expect when she went to Jesus' tomb on Sunday morning?
2. What did Peter and John see in the tomb?
3. What message did Jesus give Mary to take to his disciples?
4. How did Jesus convince the group of disciples gathered in the locked room that he was alive?
5. What did Jesus do for his disciples to give them power to tell others about him?
6. What did it take for Thomas to believe Jesus was risen from the dead?
7. What is John's purpose statement for this book?

CHAPTER WRAP-UP

- Mary Magdalene, Peter, and John discovered that Jesus was not in his tomb. (John 20:1–9)
- Mary talked with two angels in Jesus' tomb. (John 20:10–13)
- Jesus appeared to Mary at the tomb and told her to tell his disciples that he was alive. (John 20:14–18)
- Jesus appeared to a group of disciples locked in an upper room and commissioned them to tell others about himself. (John 20:19–23)

- Thomas refused to believe Jesus was alive until he touched his wounds. Jesus appeared to him and showed him his hands and side. As a result, Thomas believed. (John 20:24–29)
- John recorded selected miracles to prove Jesus is the Son of God so people who read this book will believe in Jesus. (John 20:30–31)

JOHN 21: JESUS THE COMMISSIONER

CHAPTER HIGHLIGHTS

- Back in Business
- Beach Breakfast
- Assignment to Feed Sheep
- Mind Your Own Business

Let's Get Started

Undoubtedly you've heard or read them: speakers who say they are concluding, then go on for another fifteen to thirty minutes; friends who wrap up with "just one more thing" and talk about another half an hour; letter writers who add postscripts that are a page or two long.

As a writer, John fits that category of speakers and writers who don't know when to quit. Technically, his Gospel ended with chapter 20. John recorded enough of Jesus' appearances after his resurrection to let the world know he didn't stay dead. Then he wrapped up the book with his <u>purpose statement</u>.

Sometime later, John added an epilogue, a concluding section, which we have as chapter 21. He had several reasons for doing so. John hadn't mentioned Jesus' appearance to Peter, although Luke did. Without this epilogue, readers are left hanging as to Peter's relationship with Jesus after denying him three times the night of his arrest and trials. John filled in the details of Jesus' forgiveness of Peter and assignment to feed his sheep. John also recorded Jesus' prediction of Peter's death by crucifixion, which happened about twenty years before John wrote this book. Also, there was a rumor going around that John would not die before Jesus returned, so John wanted to refute it.

☞ **GO TO:**

John 20:30–31
(purpose statement)

BACK IN BUSINESS

> **John 21:1–3** Afterward Jesus appeared again to his disciples, by the Sea of Tiberias. It happened this way: Simon Peter, Thomas (called Didymus), Nathanael from Cana in Galilee, the sons of Zebedee, and two other disciples were together. "I'm going out to fish," Simon Peter told them, and they said, "We'll go with you." So they went out and got into the boat, but that night they caught nothing.

Follow The Fisherman

Jesus had risen from the dead and was appearing to his followers before returning to heaven. One of those appearances was to seven disciples—Peter, Thomas, Nathanael, brothers James and John (whose father was Zebedee), and two others—by the **Sea of Tiberias** (see appendix A).

The disciples must have felt lost as to what to do next. Jesus had told them he would meet with them in <u>Galilee</u>, although he hadn't specified a date. They returned there and waited for him while he was out talking to others. With nothing on the agenda, Peter took the lead and announced he was going fishing. The others followed right behind him. Although night fishing generally was profitable, they caught nothing.

Sea of Tiberias: Sea of Galilee

☞ **GO TO:**

Matthew 28:10 (Galilee)

What Others are Saying:

Anne Graham Lotz: Peter and the other disciples obeyed the Lord's instructions and went to Galilee where they waited for Jesus to join them. And they waited. And they waited. And they *waited* . . . Finally, impulsive, compulsive Peter had had enough! He was not the type to sit idly around, reading magazines, completing crossword puzzles, clipping coupons, watching ESPN, and just chilling out. He hated to wait. So he announced to the others, "I'm going out to fish." . . .

I wonder if Jesus delayed joining His disciples in Galilee on purpose in order to test their patience and obedient commitment to His call in their lives. If so, Peter failed the test. Because he returned to his old lifestyle.[1]

The Sea of Galilee was the prime fishing spot in Israel. Since the disciples were close to shore, they would have been fishing with a cast net. It was circular, about fifteen feet in diameter, with weights along the edges and a long rope attached to the center. When the men saw a school of fish in the shallow water near shore, they dropped the net over them, trapping the fish. Pulling on the rope tightened the net, and the fishermen could then draw the catch into the boat.

CULTURE CLUE

> **John 21:4–6** Early in the morning, Jesus stood on the shore, but the disciples did not realize that it was Jesus.
>
> He called out to them, "Friends, haven't you any fish?"
>
> "No," they answered.
>
> He said, "Throw your net on the right side of the boat and you will find some." When they did, they were unable to haul the net in because of the large number of fish.

Full Of Fish

After a wasted night of fishing, the disciples headed for shore. Standing there was a man they didn't recognize. Perhaps it was their tiredness, the early morning haze, the lack of light, or the fact that their minds were on fishing and they weren't expecting Jesus. (Also remember, people didn't always recognize him after the Resurrection. Mary Magdalene, for example, didn't.)

When they were about a hundred yards away, Jesus asked if they had caught any fish. They hadn't. So Jesus told them to throw the net over the starboard side. When they obeyed, the net filled up with so many fish they couldn't haul it in. This was not the first time this kind of miracle had happened to some of the disciples. In fact, it was a close rerun from the beginning of Jesus' ministry with the twelve disciples.

☞ **GO TO:**

John 20:14 (Mary Magdalene)

Luke 5:1–11 (miracle)

Lawrence O. Richards: The net filled with fish was a promise. It was Jesus' way of saying, "Don't worry. I can and will continue to meet every material need." The disciples would soon set out on the most insecure of all lives: they would be traveling **evangelists**, dependent on others for their food and lodging. Though these skilled fishermen had practiced their trade all night, they had caught nothing. But a single word from Jesus filled their nets.[2]

What Others are Saying:

evangelists: *people who tell others about Jesus*

Remember
This . . .

Too often we're like these disciples, trying to do things in our own strength, making decisions without praying about them. It wasn't until Jesus told the disciples where to fish that they caught any. When we reach the end of our own resources, he is standing by to share his. (For more about how God can help during difficult times, especially raising children, see WBFM, pages 216–227.)

BEACH BREAKFAST

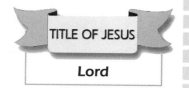

TITLE OF JESUS

Lord

> **John 21:7** Then the disciple whom Jesus loved said to Peter, "It is the Lord!" As soon as Simon Peter heard him say, "It is the Lord," he wrapped his outer garment around him (for he had taken it off) and jumped into the water.

Lightbulb Moment

John was the first to recognize Jesus. It may have been the repeat catch of fish that did it. Or perhaps it was Jesus' voice. Whatever the reason, he turned to Peter and identified the man on shore as their Lord, or Master. When Peter heard that, he was so excited that he put on his robe and dove in to swim to shore. (If he'd been thinking clearly, he would have left the robe behind.)

> **John 21:8–9** The other disciples followed in the boat, towing the net full of fish, for they were not far from shore, about a hundred yards. When they landed, they saw a fire of burning coals there with fish on it, and some bread.

Breakfast Is Ready

Peter stepped out of the water, weighed down with dripping clothes. Although Jesus had already <u>appeared</u> privately to Peter and no doubt Peter had confessed his sin of denial and received forgiveness, the two of them may not have spent much time together. Maybe this was an awkward moment for Peter. Maybe he was embarrassed by the fact that he had gone fishing instead of waiting. Maybe he was just overjoyed to see his Lord and friend. We can only speculate.

☞ **GO TO:**

Luke 24:34;
   1 Corinthians 15:5
   (appeared)

While Peter stood there, the rest of the crew rowed or sailed in, dragging a net stuffed with fish. When they hit the beach, they noticed Jesus had built a campfire and was charbroiling fish for breakfast.

What Others are Saying:

Max Lucado: Peter plunges into the water, swims to the shore, and stumbles out wet and shivering and stands in front of the friend he betrayed. . . . For one of the few times in his life, Peter is silent. What words would **suffice**? The moment is too holy for words. . . . What do *you* say at a moment such as this? It's just you and God. You and God both know what you did. And neither of you is proud of it. What do you do? You might consider doing what Peter did. Stand in God's presence. Stand in his sight. Stand still and wait. Sometimes that's all a soul can do.[3]

suffice: do

Mark Bailey and Tom Constable: The second mention of the charcoal fire (see 18:18) is appropriate for the scene when Jesus restored Peter. Peter had denied Him three times at the first fire and then affirmed his love for the Lord three times now at the second fire.[4]

KEY POINT

After Peter denied knowing him, Jesus restored Peter to service by commissioning him to take care of God's people.

> **John 21:10–11** Jesus said to them, "Bring some of the fish you have just caught."
>
> Simon Peter climbed aboard and dragged the net ashore. It was full of large fish, 153, but even with so many the net was not torn.

Dragging The Net Behind

When Jesus asked for some of the freshly caught fish, Peter was the first one to volunteer to bring the miraculous catch ashore. John was careful to record the exact number of fish and to mention that they were large—truly an overabundance. The catch was so big that it should have torn the net, but it didn't. Only a fisherman would have been so impressed as to note those kinds of details. If Peter hauled that catch ashore, he wasn't a wimpy lightweight. That many fish, plus a wet net, weighed about three hundred pounds.

Earl F. Palmer: These men are fishermen, and when the fish are big you count them, especially if you are poor. The fact is that John likes to note details which other narrators would ignore.[5]

What Others are Saying:

> **John 21:12–14** Jesus said to them, "Come and have breakfast." None of the disciples dared ask him, "Who are you?" They knew it was the Lord. Jesus came, took the bread and gave it to them, and did the same with the fish. This was now the third time Jesus appeared to his disciples after he was raised from the dead.

Breakfast Is Served

Before talking with Peter, Jesus met his physical needs. He gave him breakfast, time to dry off from his swim, a chance to warm up by the fire, and time to relax with a friend. Jesus was still caring for his disciples.

By this time, the disciples had all figured out the man on the beach was Jesus. As if to confirm his identity, he offered them bread and fish. They couldn't help but recall the feeding of the <u>five thousand</u> when Jesus multiplied bread and fish and used his disciples to pass the food out to the crowd.

John noted that this was the third time Jesus appeared to the disciples. The first <u>two times</u> were in the upper room.

☞ **GO TO:**

John 6:1–13
(five thousand)

John 20:19–23, 26–29
(two times)

What Others are Saying:

Merrill C. Tenney: Doubtless they had eaten in this fashion many times beside the lake. His return to them would renew the continuity of their life with Him; and the fact that He ate with them would strengthen the conviction that He was really before them.[6]

Brenda Quinn: Peter has recently failed Jesus by denying him three times. Now Jesus gives him another chance, coming to meet with him, share a meal, and express concern three times over their relationship. Jesus' care for Peter sends the message that God's grace extends to believers even when we fail God in a big way. He forgives those who are sorry and genuinely love him.[7]

ASSIGNMENT TO FEED SHEEP

> **John 21:15–17** When they had finished eating, Jesus said to Simon Peter, "Simon son of John, do you truly love me more than these?"
>
> "Yes, Lord," he said, "you know that I love you."
>
> Jesus said, "Feed my lambs."
>
> Again Jesus said, "Simon son of John, do you truly love me?"

> He answered, "Yes, Lord, you know that I love you."
> Jesus said, "Take care of my sheep."
>
> The third time he said to him, "Simon son of John, do you love me?"
>
> Peter was hurt because Jesus asked him the third time, "Do you love me?" He said, "Lord, you know all things; you know that I love you."
>
> Jesus said, "Feed my sheep."

Singled Out

After breakfast, Jesus revisited the subject of Peter's love for him. Peter had denied Jesus publicly. Now Jesus restored him to service publicly. (For more about God's forgiveness, see WBFT, page 185.)

Before Jesus was crucified, Peter had boasted of his love for the Lord: *"I will lay down my life for you"* (John 13:37). Although he meant those words at the time, he didn't fully understand what he was saying. Nor did he live them under the pressure of Jesus' arrest. Instead, he <u>denied</u> he ever knew Jesus but later <u>repented</u> of his sin.

When Jesus had first called Peter to follow him, he had addressed him as *"Simon son of John"* (John 1:42). Coming full circle, Jesus used the same name.

Peter had denied Jesus three times. It was no coincidence that Jesus asked Peter three times if he loved him and commissioned Peter three times to take care of God's people. Peter would have quickly made the association.

Jesus asked Peter if he loved him more than the other disciples did. Before Jesus was arrested, Peter had said he did: *"Even if all fall away on account of you, I never will"* (Matthew 26:33). He had not been shy then about declaring his love for Jesus; he wasn't shy now. In a straightforward manner, with no comparisons with the other disciples, he readily affirmed his love for Jesus. By the third time, he was hurt that Jesus asked him again, but he got the message. So Jesus assigned him to feed—supply with the spiritual food of God's Word—and take care of his sheep. Peter's ministry would be feeding and shepherding God's children like Jesus had. His fishing career was over.

Many Bible students have emphasized the different Greek words Jesus and Peter used for the word *love*, one meaning sacrificial love and the other, friendship love. Since John used both words as synonyms throughout the book, it's better not to make fine distinctions.

☞ **GO TO:**

John 18:17, 25, 27 (denied)

Matthew 26:75 (repented)

Something to Ponder

What Others are Saying:

stave off: drive away

THE FAITH FACTOR—Although the word "believe" is not used in this passage, the concept is. Jesus commanded those who believe in and love him to keep on following him.

Suppose you had been in Peter's sandals that morning on the beach after Jesus' resurrection. You're sitting around the fire, talking with Jesus, when he asks you, *"Do you love me?"* How would you answer him?

Anne Graham Lotz: Jesus reached into Peter's heart and put His finger on Peter's motivation for service. Peter's motivation to live for Jesus and to serve Jesus was not to be . . .

an attempt to **stave off** guilt,

an attempt to earn forgiveness,

an attempt to avoid criticism,

an attempt to measure up to the opinions of others,

an attempt to prove something to someone,

an attempt to gain approval or recognition,

an attempt to accumulate more good works than bad works.

Peter's sole motivation in service was to be his love for Jesus, pure and simple. If he did love Jesus, even a little, his mission was to do something about it. He was to get involved in the lives of others.[8]

> **John 21:18–19** "I tell you the truth, when you were younger you dressed yourself and went where you wanted; but when you are old you will stretch out your hands, and someone else will dress you and lead you where you do not want to go." Jesus said this to indicate the kind of death by which Peter would glorify God. Then he said to him, "Follow me!"

Following Jesus To The Death

Peter had just gotten his life straightened out when Jesus leaped to the topic of his death. He indicated how serious and important it was by beginning with the statement *"I tell you the truth."* In a picturesque way, he contrasted the end of Peter's ministry with the beginning of it and went a step further to say how he would die. *"Stretch out your hands"* refers to being fastened to the horizontal beam of a cross.

Peter had already died when John wrote this book. According to Jerome, one of the early church fathers, Peter was crucified upside down because he thought he was unworthy to die the same way as Jesus.

Jesus ended his **commission** for Peter with the same words with which he had called him three years earlier: *"Follow me!"* The form of the command in the Greek means to keep on following. It's not a onetime step but a lifetime walk. A lot had happened to Peter between those two commands, some of which John recorded in this book. But the command didn't change, and Peter still had the rest of his life to obey it.

Jesus still commands believers to follow him. There are no conditions attached to this command. He didn't say, "Follow me if it's convenient for you." Or "Follow me if you feel like it." Or "Follow me if you don't get a better offer." Or "Follow me if you don't have anything else to do." Following Jesus is a way of life for the rest of our lives—no matter what.

commission: assignment

☞ **GO TO:**

Matthew 4:18–19 (follow me)

Something to Ponder

MIND YOUR OWN BUSINESS

> **John 21:20–21** Peter turned and saw that the disciple whom Jesus loved was following them. (This was the one who had leaned back against Jesus at the supper and had said, "Lord, who is going to betray you?") When Peter saw him, he asked, "Lord, what about him?"

What About Him?

Peter must have heard someone walking behind him and turned to see that it was John, the author of this book. John identified himself by where he <u>leaned and</u> what he <u>asked</u> at the Passover dinner, rather than by name. Now that his job and destiny were settled, curious Peter wanted to know what would happen to John.

☞ **GO TO:**

John 13:23–25 (leaned and asked)

> **John 21:22–23** Jesus answered, "If I want him to remain alive until I return, what is that to you? You must follow me." Because of this, the rumor spread among the brothers that this disciple would not die. But Jesus did not say that he would not die; he only said, "If I want him to remain alive until I return, what is that to you?"

None Of Your Business

Jesus told Peter to mind his own business. He needed to stay focused on Jesus, not on other people. Jesus' question started a rumor that John wouldn't die; he would live until Jesus returned to earth. That rumor was one reason John added this chapter to the book. Jesus didn't say John wouldn't die. It was none of Peter's business if John lived or died. He was responsible for following Jesus regardless of what happened to the other disciples.

What Others are Saying:

apostolic: by the apostles, Jesus' early followers

Yeshua: Jesus

W. E. Vine: In John's record concerning Peter and the Lord's reply to his question regarding himself we cannot but note the continued and special intimacy between these two disciples, an intimacy which would be seen in the earliest **apostolic** testimony. Noticeable also are the Lord's combined foreknowledge of, and authority over, the future lives of His servants.[9]

David H. Stern: Yeshua rules out curiosity about matters that do not concern us or help us live a holy life, although he does not rule out scientific inquiry into how the world works. Likewise he excludes unhealthy, jealous competition concerned with comparing our lives, tasks, gifts, accomplishments, interests and calling with those of others. In both matters Yeshua's central point is: You, follow me![10]

Jesus talked with Peter about his disciple's love for him. To drive home the point of wanting to use Peter in spite of his failure to stand up for Jesus during his trials, Jesus asked Peter three times if he loved him. As a result, Peter proclaimed his love and Jesus gave him the ministry of caring for his "sheep" (followers).

Conversations with Christ

> **John 21:24–25** This is the disciple who testifies to these things and who wrote them down. We know that his testimony is true.
>
> Jesus did many other things as well. If every one of them were written down, I suppose that even the whole world would not have room for the books that would be written.

The End

Greek, Roman, and Jewish legal documents ended with a testimony by witnesses. As John concluded this Gospel, he added his endorsement that what he wrote was true since he had been an eyewitness to the events. *"We know that his testimony is true"* may have been added by someone who was a contemporary of John. It was similar to a seal of approval. Since John was writing for the second generation of believers who didn't know Jesus personally and hadn't seen any of his miracles, this statement would have been important in judging the accuracy of his words.

But what John recorded in this one book was only a fraction of what Jesus did and said in three years. He had already written that he <u>selected miracles</u> that supported his purpose for writing. By the time John penned this book, there were three other **Gospels** in existence, each containing events the other writers omitted. We can read all the words Jesus spoke that are recorded in the four Gospels in about three hours. There is no question that Jesus said and did much more—so much that many more books could have been written.

John's book has ended, but Jesus' work continues today. If you want to find out what happened in the early years after his resurrection, read the Book of Acts.

☞ **GO TO:**

John 20:30–31 (selected miracles)

Gospels: *Matthew, Mark, Luke*

John Calvin: Christ's **majesty**, because it is infinite, swallowed up (so to speak) both human understanding and heaven and earth as it demonstrated a miraculous display of its own splendor in those deeds. If the evangelist, looking at Christ's brightness, exclaims in astonishment that even the whole world does not have room for a complete narrative, who can be surprised?[11]

What Others are Saying:

majesty: greatness

Study Questions

1. What did Peter lead the disciples to do while they were waiting for Jesus?
2. How did John recognize the man on shore as Jesus?

3. How did Jesus meet Peter's needs before talking with him about a serious subject?
4. Why did Jesus ask Peter the same question about loving him three times?
5. What ministry did Jesus assign Peter to do?
6. When Peter wanted to know what would happen to John, what did Jesus answer?

CHAPTER WRAP-UP

- Seven disciples met together. When Peter decided to go fishing, they went with him but didn't catch anything. (John 21:1–3)

- When the disciples followed Jesus' instructions, they caught a net full of fish. (John 21:4–11)

- Jesus invited his disciples to join him for breakfast on the beach. (John 21:12–14)

- Jesus restored Peter to service and assigned him the ministry of caring for believers. (John 21:15–19)

- When Peter wanted to know what would happen to John, Jesus told him it was none of his business. Then Jesus predicted Peter's death. (John 21:20–23)

- John concluded this book with a statement about its truthfulness since he was an eyewitness of the events. (John 21:24–25)

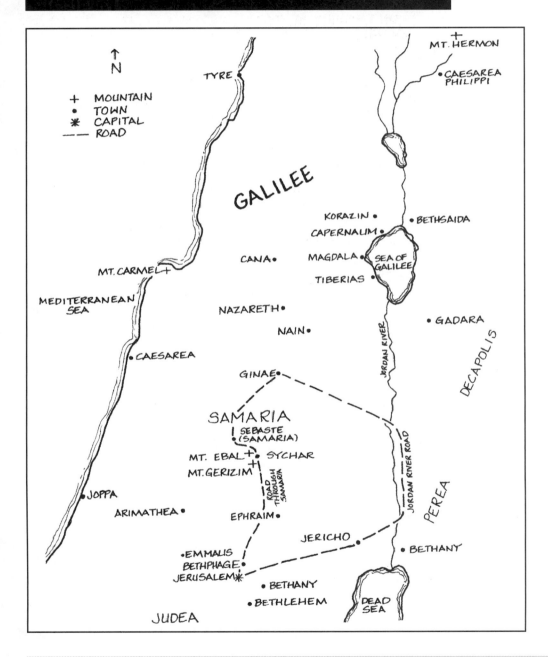

APPENDIX B—THE ANSWERS

JOHN 1: JESUS THE WORD

1. John described Jesus as the Word, as God, as the one who made all things. John also called Jesus life, the light of men, and the true light. (John 1:1–9)
2. John the Baptist was a witness to the light, but he wasn't the light. The passage also demonstrates John's willingness to let his own disciples follow Jesus, the one whom they were announcing. His whole point was to bring others to belief in the true light. (John 1:6–9, 35–39)
3. All who trust Jesus as a sacrifice for their sin become children of God—receiving him, believing on his name, reaching out and accepting the supernatural gift from God. (John 1:10–13)
4. Everything John the Baptist said pointed to Jesus. John testified of him, spoke of how Jesus surpassed him. He said, "I am not the Christ," and prepared the way for Jesus. (John 1:15–23, 29–31)
5. John and Andrew followed Jesus immediately. Then Andrew looked for Simon to tell him about Jesus. Philip answered Jesus by finding Nathanael and bringing him to Jesus. Their immediate response and contagious attitude demonstrated their belief in Jesus. (John 1:35–46)

JOHN 2: JESUS THE AUTHORITY

1. By telling Jesus that they had run out of wine, Mary demonstrated her understanding of his authority. She knew he wasn't only her son but was also the Son of God. By telling the servants to *do whatever he tells you,* she further pointed out her faith in Jesus. (John 2:3–5)
2. Jesus responded first by distancing himself as her son and helping her transition from seeing him as her child to seeing him as the Messiah. (John 1:3–5)
3. Jesus changed the water into wine so his disciples as well as Mary would believe. The servants, too, also knew what he had done. (John 2:11)
4. Jesus drove all the animals and vendors out of the Temple with a whip, scattering money and overturn-

ing tables. He knew how much God longed to be with his people, and he was furious that the money changers kept the people from worshiping the God who loved them so much. (John 2:13–17)
5. Jesus answered them with the statement *"Destroy this temple, and I will raise it again in three days."* The Jews didn't understand and thought he was talking about the literal temple building. They missed the point entirely. (John 2:18–22)
6. The people loved the miracles and professed to believe in Jesus as a result. However, Jesus didn't put much stock in their commitment. (John 2:23–25)

JOHN 3: JESUS THE CHOICE GIVER

1. Nicodemus had lived all his life knowing and teaching God's Word and keeping the rules. But now miracles were happening (though not in his life), and he needed to get some straight answers. Unfortunately, he got sidetracked with his literalism. (John 3:1–8)
2. We are born physically alive but spiritually dead. "Born again" means facing that death—the sin in our hearts—and repenting and letting God through Jesus Christ make us alive again. (John 3:3–8)
3. The new birth is supernatural and unseen, like the wind, but you see the impact of both. Birth helps us visualize the "new life" of the Spirit, and the snake pole shows the choice we have—to look to Jesus and live. (John 3:3–15)
4. He loved us so much that he didn't want us to die. We are his beloved creation! So he sent Jesus, his only Son, on a rescue mission. There was no other way. (John 3:16–18)
5. John joyfully cleared the path for Jesus. He happily saw his ministry and mission as decreasing. He fully acknowledged that Jesus was above all. (John 3:27–33)

JOHN 4: JESUS THE GIVER OF SPIRITUAL LIFE

1. Jewish people avoided Samaria, even though it meant a detour of many miles, because they loathed the

Samaritans. For Jesus not only to go through Samaria but also to stop there was unheard of. Jews and Samaritans had been enemies for seven hundred years. (John 4:4–6)

2. "Living water" symbolizes eternal life, the soul-satisfying experience of life through Jesus. (John 4:10–15)

3. The woman didn't get it at first, but she wanted not to be thirsty: "Sir, let me have this so I don't have to come back here!" She was miserable enough with her life to want something to change. (John 14:13–15)

4. Jesus was saying, in essence, "Open your eyes! There are people all around who need my love!" He used food as a way to broaden their understanding of ministry and God's love. (John 4:31–38)

5. The Samaritan woman went out and told the townspeople (people who despised her, rejected her, avoided her): "Come! Come! See the man!" Many of them believed. (John 4:27–42)

6. The official's faith was evidenced in his long walk. Jesus warned him about only believing because of miracles, then he healed the son long-distance. (John 4:48–53)

7. Jesus has power over distance. We don't have to see the miracle—or even the Son of God—to receive his healing love. (John 4:50–53)

JOHN 5: JESUS THE HEALER

1. They hoped a miracle might occur at those waters, and so they gathered there day after day. They were desperate for anything that might work. (John 5:1–3)

2. Dependency is a difficult lifestyle to break, especially after thirty-eight years. Jesus rightly challenged the man: How badly do you want to be healed? (John 5:6–8)

3. The Scriptures don't indicate how Jesus healed him, but it's clear from the man's obedience to Jesus' command that the healing was instantaneous. (John 5:6–8)

4. The Jewish leaders were upset about any healing they didn't perform. They were bent on punishing rule breakers, and this man had been healed on the Sabbath, when work was prohibited. (John 5:10–13)

5. He wanted the man to not only be healed physically but to be healed spiritually as well. Perhaps, too, he wanted to be sure that God received the glory for the healing. Jesus also knew that, when he sought out

the man in the Temple, the man would both identify him and report him to the Jews and persecution would begin. (John 5:14–18)

6. He called God "My Father," implying a close and familiar connection, and he identified himself as the Son of God. He also said, essentially, that because God was always working, Jesus was always working, making himself the same as God. (John 5:14–18)

7. God, Moses, and John all testify about Jesus. (John 5:31–40, 45–47)

8. His final statement about Moses, whom the Jews revered, closed the case. The Jews knew very well that Moses testified about Jesus. (John 5:45–47)

JOHN 6: JESUS THE MIRACLE WORKER

1. The people were hungry for the miraculous. They followed him because they'd seen him do such dramatic miracles. (John 6:1–4)

2. Even though he was tired from the crowds and constant ministry, Jesus was gracious. He asked his disciples, "How can we buy food for these people?" (John 6:5–9)

3. This miracle made it clear that Jesus was more than your average lay preacher. The people believed after this that he was the Prophet they'd been waiting for. (John 6:14–15)

4. The people loved this miracle. They were so captivated by it that they wanted to make him king by force. (John 6:14–15)

5. When the disciples got halfway across the sea, a storm blew up quickly and violently. The frightened disciples rowed for several miles in the wind and waves. Then they saw Jesus walking across the water to them. He got in the boat, and immediately the boat reached shore. (John 6:16–21)

6. Jesus' walking on the water and bringing the boat ashore instantly proved he was the Lord—indeed, the Creator—of the wind and waves. He was not held back by material or natural things. (John 6:19–21)

7. Jesus let them know he saw through their flattery. They wanted the food he could provide. They wanted the miracles, not the life he was offering. (John 6:26–27) Furthermore, he clarified exactly what he offered: a deep soul satisfaction of their hunger and thirst. (John 6:35–40)

8. The people kept obsessing about the physical food, taking everything literally. As soon as Jesus said, *"I am the bread that came down from heaven,"* they got caught up in the logistics. "Isn't this Joseph's son?

He can't be from heaven" (John 6:41–42). Even the disciples griped about it (John 6:60–65). Many of those professing to be his followers left after this teaching (John 6:67–71). To follow Jesus would require more faith than these people wanted to invest. It's much easier to just have miracle food appear on your plate daily (John 6:67–71).

JOHN 7: JESUS THE DIVIDER

1. Jesus' brothers wanted him to make a grand entrance at the feast to prove that he was indeed the Messiah. "If you're real, then show yourself," they seemed to be saying. They, too, believed in the miracles but not in the man, the Son of God. (John 7:1–5)

2. Some people said Jesus was a good man; others said he was a deceiver (John 7:10–13). Some said he was demon-possessed (John 7:20–24). Many figured Jesus couldn't be the Messiah because they knew his parents, and they had decided the Messiah would just show up without a background (John 7:25–27).

3. The religious leaders saw Jesus as a lawbreaker (John 7:16–19). The people liked all the miracles but were not certain he was the Messiah, and the Jewish leaders were such tyrants that the people were afraid to take sides in public (John 7:10–13).

4. Jesus challenged people to check him out. He said that if you want to do God's will, you'll find out if his teaching comes from God or not. The true test is this: Whom do you honor with your teaching? Jesus didn't gain honor for himself through his teaching but gave honor to God. (John 7:16–19)

5. The Feast opened with the proclamation from Zechariah that living water would flow out from Jerusalem. When Jesus announced that he could quench their thirst and that living waters could flow out of them if they believed in him, he basically was saying, "I'm the one you've been waiting for! I'm the Messiah, the Christ, the fulfillment of the prophecy." (John 7:37–39)

6. The fact that Nicodemus stood up for Jesus indicates that his earlier conversation with Christ had taken root. As one of the Pharisees, Nicodemus knew the law and probably wanted to give Jesus a fair hearing. (John 7:50–53)

JOHN 8: JESUS THE FREEDOM GIVER

1. The religious leaders wanted to trap Jesus. The law demanded stoning for the sin of adultery. If Jesus condemned her to stoning, his teachings of mercy would be thrown in his face. If he let her go, the Jews would accuse him of disobeying God's Word. (John 8:3–8)

2. The leaders' attitude toward the woman was one of condemnation, but Jesus said, "I don't condemn you." He saw her as a child of God with sins as serious as everyone else's. He showed his love for her by forgiving her. (John 8:6–11)

3. Jesus meant that he was God. The use of "I am" made it clear, and the Jewish people understood both that statement and the use of the word "light." Light stood for God's holiness. (John 8:12)

4. Jesus knew that something was proved by two witnesses, so he used himself and his Father. (John 8:13–18)

5. Knowing the truth sets us free. (John 8:31–32)

6. Because children follow their fathers. If the Jews were in fact Abraham's children, then they would be doing the things Abraham did, not trying to kill Jesus (John 8:39–41). Besides that, Abraham rejoiced at the thought of the coming Messiah (John 8:54–56).

7. Jesus said their father was the devil, a murderer and a liar. They proved that relationship because they wanted to kill Jesus. (John 8:42–44)

8. At Jesus' last words, "I am," when he again equated himself with God, the Jews picked up rocks to stone him. Making oneself equal to God was blasphemy, deserving of death. (John 8:57–59)

JOHN 9: JESUS THE SIGHT GIVER

1. The disciples wanted to figure out who was to blame for the man's blindness. Was it because he sinned or because his parents sinned? (John 9:1–2)

2. The man's blindness was more about displaying God's glory than about the man's problem or even his sin. His life could become a place where God's work was displayed. (John 9:3–5)

3. He made mud out of dirt and saliva, packed it on the man's eyes, and told him to go and wash in the Pool of Siloam. (John 9:6–7)

4. The people were upset, disturbed, and critical of the healer. Their questioning of the man showed no joy or thankfulness, only prodding about Jesus. The fact that Jesus had healed on the Sabbath again became an issue. (John 9:8–12)

5. The man just told the facts: He put mud on my eyes; I washed; now I see. (John 9:13–15)

6. Jesus had freed the man from a lifetime of blindness. He credited the healing to God and told the Pharisees, *"He is a prophet."* (John 9:16–17). Later, the man ar-

gued that someone with sin couldn't have done such a miracle, so Jesus had to be from God. (John 9:30–34).

7. Jesus knew the man had stood up for him and was being persecuted by the Pharisees. He wanted to solidify the man's experience with fact. So he introduced himself as the Son of Man, giving the former blind man a chance to believe and worship him. (John 9:35–38)

8. When Jesus said he was the Son of Man, the former blind man instantly responded, *"Lord, I believe,"* and worshiped Jesus. (John 9:35–38)

9. Because the Pharisees claimed they could see, Jesus told them they were guilty. The truly blind, who acknowledge they have no sight, are given spiritual sight by believing in Jesus. The Pharisees, with their self-righteousness, couldn't acknowledge any spiritual lack and thus condemned themselves to blindness. (John 9:39–41)

JOHN 10: JESUS THE GOOD SHEPHERD

1. The sheep Jesus is talking about are all who belong to him, who listen to his voice. (John 10:4–6)

2. The shepherd is Jesus. (John 10:11)

3. The thieves and robbers are all the religious leaders who came before Jesus, pretending to lead the people. (John 10:7–8)

4. A good shepherd would literally die to keep his sheep safe. Jesus, good from the inside out, would ultimately lay down his life for his sheep. (John 10:11)

5. Jesus is a gate, in that anyone who enters into relationship with God through him will be saved. (John 10:9–10)

6. People follow Jesus, the Good Shepherd, because they know his voice, recognize the love in his voice, and know he wants only good for them. (John 10:14–16)

7. The Jewish leaders wanted to know if Jesus were truly the Christ. *"Tell us plainly."* (John 10:22–24)

8. Jesus answered by saying he'd already told them, and they wouldn't believe. They didn't recognize his voice because they weren't his sheep. (John 10:25–26)

9. Jesus' response did not go over well with the leaders. They picked up stones to stone him with, not because of the miracles, but because he claimed to be God. (John 10:31–39)

JOHN 11: JESUS THE RESURRECTION AND THE LIFE

1. Jesus wanted, again, to be sure that God got the glory in the Lazarus situation. (John 11:3–4)

2. Martha told Jesus that Lazarus wouldn't have died if he'd gotten there sooner. But her faith seemed intact because she added, *"I know that God will give you whatever you ask."* (John 11:21–22)

3. Jesus is the one who has power over both life and death. His statement, "I am," again made him equal with God, the Life-giver. He gives eternal life and raises us from spiritual death. (John 11:25–27)

4. Jesus was deeply moved at Mary's grief. Troubled, he wept over Lazarus's death. Jesus mourned with Mary. (John 11:33–35)

5. He prayed, gave God glory and thanks, and called Lazarus to come out of the tomb. (John 11:41–44)

6. Once again, Jesus' miracles produced a divided camp. Some of the people believed in him and put their faith in him. Others, however, went tattling to the Pharisees. Those religious leaders felt terribly threatened and called a meeting of the Sanhedrin, which would sentence Jesus to die. (John 11:45–53)

JOHN 12: JESUS THE KING WHO WILL DIE

1. Mary took a container of expensive perfume and poured it on Jesus' feet, then wiped them with her hair because her heart overflowed with love for him (John 12:3). This was an act of worship and also a means of preparing Jesus' body for burial (John 12:7–8).

2. Judas had a different response than Jesus, who accepted her love gift. Judas, who kept the money bag, jealously asked, "Shouldn't we have sold this and [wink, wink] given the money to the poor?" John makes it clear that Judas dipped into the reserves when he wanted money. (John 12:4–6)

3. The crowd rushed out to greet Jesus with palm branches and loud praises, shouting *"Hosanna! Blessed is he who comes in the name of the Lord. Blessed is the King of Israel!"* They wanted to make him their literal, political, reigning king. (John 12:12–13)

4. Jesus rode into the city on a donkey to fulfill the prophecy that the king would come on a donkey as a servant. The people expected him to ride in on a huge horse or in a chariot, as befitted an earthly king. (John 12:14–15)

5. If we want to gain our lives, we must give them over to God's care, trusting him with all that we are and have. When we let go of our own lives and focus on God's priorities, God takes over and grants us eternal life. (John 12:23–26)

6. The Jews didn't expect a king who would die; they

knew that the Messiah would live forever. So when Jesus said he would be lifted up (die), they didn't get it. (John 12:34)

JOHN 13: JESUS THE SERVANT

1. During the Passover dinner, Jesus took the role of a servant by washing the disciples' feet to demonstrate humility. (John 13:1–5)
2. When Peter protested about getting his feet washed, Jesus confronted him with the truth that he must be cleansed to be united with him. (John 13:6–10)
3. By washing the disciples' feet, Jesus taught that his followers need to receive cleansing from sin and that they must reflect his lifestyle of humble servanthood. (John 13:12–17)
4. Upon hearing that one of them would betray Jesus, the disciples were stunned and began to question which one of them would be the traitor. (John 13:22–25)
5. Jesus said that the mark of his followers would be the quality of their love for one another, which reflected his unconditional, humble, and sacrificial love. (John 13:34–35)
6. Jesus predicted that Peter would betray him by disowning him three times before the rooster crowed. (John 13:37–38)

JOHN 14: JESUS THE COMFORTER

1. After Jesus leaves the earth, he will prepare a place in heaven for his followers and then return to bring them to their eternal dwelling place with him. (John 14:1–4)
2. As he spoke with Thomas, Jesus described himself as *"the way and the truth and the life."* Jesus explained that anyone who has seen him has seen the Father. (John 14:5–7)
3. Jesus' followers will do greater works than he did by reflecting his power and greatness while being weak, sinful humans. Through the Holy Spirit, the number and extent of his workings in his followers will be greater than what he did alone on earth. (John 14:12–14)
4. We prove we love Jesus by obeying his commands and receiving his Holy Spirit to continually teach us his truths. (John 14:15–17)
5. Jesus said he would send his Holy Spirit when he went back to heaven. The Holy Spirit is our Counselor, Comforter, and the Spirit of truth. (John 14:16–17)
6. The kind of peace that Jesus gives his followers is directly and uniquely from him, confident of God's care and not dependent on situations. His peace in-

cludes wholeness and fulfillment because it is a fruit of a relationship with God through Jesus. (John 14:27)

JOHN 15: JESUS THE VINE

1. Jesus used an object familiar to the disciples—the vine—to describe his relationship with them. He called himself the *"true vine."* God the Father is the gardener, and believers are the branches. (John 15:1–2)
2. When we abide in Jesus, we produce the fruit of his character. As we become more and more like him, we realize our utter dependency on him. (John 15:4–6)
3. To be sure we are productive, God "prunes" us like a gardener who cuts back the vine. God's "pruning" removes anything that hinders his life from bearing fruit in our lives. (John 15:1–2)
4. Jesus calls his disciples friends because he entrusted his followers with everything he learned from his Father and also because he desires a loving, intimate bond with his followers. (John 15:14–15)
5. Jesus told his followers to expect the world's hatred, persecution, and rejection toward them after he was gone. (John 15:18–19)

JOHN 16: JESUS THE TEACHER

1. People who believe in Jesus can expect to be persecuted because those who reject Jesus may think that they are righteous in rejecting, harming, or even killing his followers. Jesus was not spared from persecution, so his followers will not be spared either. (John 16:1–3)
2. The Counselor will help believers and convict unbelievers in relation to sin, righteousness, and judgment. (John 16:8–11)
3. After Jesus returns to heaven, the Spirit of truth will help believers understand God's Word and know Jesus with an increasing passion. (John 16:12–15)
4. When Jesus taught that he was going away, his disciples questioned each other about what he meant because they did not understand. (John 16:16–18)
5. Asking in Jesus' name means requesting what Jesus desires in order to serve and honor God. This involves bringing God a yielded and moldable heart. (John 16:23–24)
6. Jesus' followers can be sure of having peace because Jesus promised them his peace and because he is victorious over everything that may attempt to cause a troubled heart. (John 16:33)

JOHN 17: JESUS THE PRAY-ER

1. As Jesus prayed, his main request for himself was that he would glorify the Father. (John 17:1–2)

2. Jesus defined eternal life as intimately knowing God and himself. He explained that through this relationship eternal life can be experienced on earth as well as in heaven after death. (John 17:3–5)

3. Jesus prayed for his disciples to be protected by the power of God's name and to be closely united with God. He also prayed that the disciples would be filled with his joy and be set apart for daily walking with God and fulfilling his purposes. (John 17:11–19)

4. Jesus asked the Father that future believers would be unified in love with a close bond similar to the oneness he and the Father shared. (John 17:20–23)

5. Jesus called God *"righteous Father"* to express that God is sinless and that his children must approach him with reverence through knowing Jesus. (John 17:25–26)

JOHN 18: JESUS THE PRISONER

1. Judas showed up with a group of priests and temple police to arrest Jesus. (John 18:2–3)

2. Jesus showed he was in control of his arrest when he identified himself with God's name, "I am." Jesus also revealed his divine authority when he healed Malchus's ear after Peter had cut it off. (John 18:4–6, 10–11)

3. When Peter was questioned about his association with Jesus, he denied being one of his disciples. (John 18:17–18)

4. Jesus told Annas to question the people he had taught in public. By doing so, Annas would then know more about Jesus' teachings, which were not secret. (John 18:19–21)

5. The religious leaders took Jesus to Pilate because, as the Roman governor, Pilate was the only one who could order the death sentence. (John 18:28–29)

6. When Pilate questioned Jesus privately, he learned that Jesus was a king. However, Pilate didn't understand that Jesus' kingdom was a spiritual one rather than a political one. (John 18:33–37)

7. When Pilate offered to release a prisoner, the Jewish people chose Barabbas, a criminal who had been arrested for murder and rebellion against the government. (John 18:38–40)

JOHN 19: JESUS THE CORPSE

1. The soldiers mocked Jesus by jamming a crown of thorns on his head, clothing him in a purple robe, and calling him *"king of the Jews."* (John 19:1–3)

2. They said Jesus claimed to be the Son of God and a king who opposed Caesar. (John 19:7, 12)

3. Pilate's power came from God, who chose to give that power to him. (John 19:11)

4. Pilate identified him in three languages as *"JESUS OF NAZARETH, THE KING OF THE JEWS."* (John 19:19)

5. Jesus entrusted his mother to John's care as though John were her real son. (John 19:26–27)

6. Joseph of Arimathea and Nicodemus, two secret disciples, handled Jesus' burial. They got permission from Pilate to take the body off the cross, then they wrapped it in spices and linen strips and buried it in Joseph's tomb. (John 19:38–42)

JOHN 20: JESUS THE RISEN LORD

1. Mary expected to see Jesus' dead body in the tomb. (John 20:1–2)

2. Peter and John saw strips of linen in the shape of a body as though Jesus was beamed out of them. (John 20:5–8)

3. Jesus told Mary to tell his disciples that he was alive and would return to his Father. (John 20:17)

4. Jesus appeared to his disciples without walking through the door, and he showed them his wounded hands and feet. (John 20:19–20)

5. Jesus breathed the Holy Spirit on them. (John 20:22)

6. Thomas had to see Jesus for himself. He also wanted to put his finger in the nail holes in Jesus' hands and put his hand in the wound in Jesus' side. (John 20:25, 27–28)

7. John wrote this book to encourage people to believe in Jesus. (John 20:31)

JOHN 21: JESUS THE COMMISSIONER

1. Peter led the other disciples to go fishing. (John 21:3)

2. John probably recognized the man as Jesus because the miracle of the fish was similar to one Jesus had performed before. (John 21:5–7)

3. Jesus fed Peter breakfast and gave him time to dry off and warm up by the fire. (John 21:9, 12–13)

4. Jesus asked Peter if he loved him three times because Peter had denied him three times. (John 18:17, 25, 27)

5. Jesus assigned Peter to feed and take care of his "sheep," the people who believed in him. (John 21:15–17)

6. Jesus told him to mind his own business and follow him. (John 21:22)

APPENDIX C—THE EXPERTS

Mark Bailey—Associate professor of Bible exposition, vice president of academia, and dean of faculty at Dallas Theological Seminary.

Louis Barbieri—Served as pastor and Bible professor at Moody Bible Institute and Dallas Theological Seminary.

William Barclay—Minister of Trinity Church, Renfrew, Scotland, professor of divinity and biblical criticism at the University of Glasgow, and author of numerous commentaries.

Karl Barth—Influential twentieth-century Swiss theologian and author or editor of many books.

Bruce B. Barton—Editor of the Life Application Bible Commentary series.

George R. Beasley-Murray—Principal of Spurgeon's College of London, professor of New Testament interpretation at Southern Baptist Theological Seminary, Louisville, Kentucky.

Henry Blackaby—Best-selling author and speaker, and special consultant to the presidents of the North American Mission Board and LifeWay Christian Resources of the Southern Baptist Convention.

Edwin A. Blum—Associate professor of historical theology at Dallas Theological Seminary.

James Montgomery Boice—Former pastor of the Tenth Presbyterian Church in Philadelphia and speaker on the "Bible Study Hour," and author of numerous commentaries.

Gerald L. Borchert—Professor of New Testament interpretation at Southern Baptist Theological Seminary, Louisville, Kentucky, and author of several books.

F. F. Bruce—Former Rylands professor of biblical criticism and exegesis at Manchester University, England, and author of numerous books and commentaries.

Victor Buksbazen—Former missionary, commentator, and author.

John Calvin—One of the Reformation's most influential Bible teachers and author of commentaries on most of the Bible books.

D. A. Carson—Professor of New Testament at Trinity Evangelical Divinity School, Deerfield, Illinois, and author of numerous books.

Tom Constable—Department chairman and senior professor of Bible exposition at Dallas Theological Seminary.

Roger L. Fredrikson—Retired pastor of First Baptist Church, Wichita, Kansas.

David E. Garland—Professor of New Testament at Southern Baptist Theological Seminary.

Norval Geldenhuys—Former minister in South Africa and director of publications of the Reformed Church of South Africa in Cape Town.

Mitch and Zhava Glaser—Mitch is minister-at-large for Jews for Jesus, San Francisco, California, and Zhava has served as a Jews for Jesus missionary.

Ed Glasscock—Vice president of academics and director of biblical studies at Southeastern Bible College, Birmingham, Alabama.

F. L. Godet—Swiss theologian in the 1800s, professor of New Testament in the University of Neuchâtel.

Louis Goldberg—Former pastor and professor of Jewish studies and Bible/theology at Moody Bible Institute, currently serving with Jews for Jesus.

Manford George Gutzke—Author of two dozen books in the *Plain Talk* Bible commentary series.

Everett F. Harrison—Professor emeritus of New Testament at Fuller Theological Seminary and collaborator on various theological works.

William Hendriksen—Pastor emeritus of the Creston Christian Reformed Church in Grand Rapids, Michigan, and former professor of New Testament literature at Calvin Seminary.

Matthew Henry—Seventeenth century biblical expositor, expelled from the Church of England in 1662; Puritan, Presbyterian pastor, author of multivolume Bible commentary still used today.

D. Edmond Hiebert—Former professor of Greek and New Testament at Mennonite Brethren Biblical Seminary, Fresno, California.

Herschel H. Hobbs—Past president of the Southern Baptist Convention, speaker on the "Baptist Hour" radio program, and former pastor.

R. Kent Hughes—Senior pastor of College Church, Wheaton, Illinois, and author of several books.

David Jeremiah—Pastor of Shadow Mountain Community Church in San Diego, California, and speaker on the "Turning Point" radio program.

Craig S. Keener—Professor of New Testament at Hood Theological Seminary, Salisbury, North Carolina, and author of several books.

Phillip Keller—Best-selling author who spent many years as a shepherd and agricultural researcher.

Homer A. Kent Jr.—Former president and professor of New Testament and Greek at Grace Theological Seminary, Winona Lake, Indiana, and author of several books and commentaries.

J. Carl Laney—Professor of biblical literature at Western Conservative Baptist Seminary, Portland, Oregon, and the author of numerous commentaries and other books.

C. S. Lewis—Former writer, scholar, and lecturer at Oxford and Cambridge universities.

Paul Little—Served with InterVarsity Christian Fellowship for twenty-five years and former associate professor of evangelism at Trinity Evangelical Divinity School, Deerfield, Illinois.

Anne Graham Lotz—Evangelist, author of several books, and founder of AnGel Ministries.

Max Lucado—Pastor of Oak Hills Church of Christ in Texas and best-selling author and speaker on the radio program "UpWords."

Martin Luther—Father of the German Reformation.

Erwin W. Lutzer—Senior pastor of Moody Church in Chicago, speaker, and author of numerous books.

John MacArthur Jr.—Pastor of Grace Community Church, Sun Valley, California, speaker on "Grace to You" radio program, and popular author and conference speaker.

Alexander MacLaren—One of Britain's most famous preachers in the late 1800s, known as the "prince of expository preachers."

Josh McDowell—Internationally known speaker, author, and traveling representative for Campus Crusade for Christ.

J. Vernon McGee—Former radio broadcaster for "Thru the Bible," as well as teacher, speaker, author of numerous books, and pastor.

Bruce Milne—Minister of First Baptist Church, Vancouver, British Columbia.

Leon Morris—Former president of Ridley College in Melbourne, Australia, and author of numerous books and commentaries.

Bill Myers—Award-winning writer/director for TV and film, youth worker, author of numerous books.

Ruth Myers—Staff member with the Navigators.

J. Dwight Pentecost—Professor of Bible exposition at Dallas Theological Seminary and author of several books, primarily dealing with prophecy.

Arthur W. Pink—Former conference speaker, pastor, and author of various books on Bible exposition.

Brenda Quinn—Staff editor for Serendipity House and editorial coordinator for MOPS International, Inc.

Lawrence O. (Larry) Richards—General editor for the *Biblically-Inept* series and author of more than 175 books, including Christian education, Bible, theology, and devotional works.

Sue Richards—Wife of Larry; retired English teacher and women's Bible study teacher in her church.

Fritz Ridenour—Youth editor for Gospel Light curriculum.

W. Graham Scroggie—Pastor of several churches in England and Scotland.

Charles H. Spurgeon—London's most popular preacher in the 1800s.

James M. Stalker—Scottish scholar, pastor, and professor of church history in the United Free Church College, Aberdeen.

David H. Stern—Messianic Jew living in Jerusalem, author of several books, former professor at Fuller Theological Seminary, and former officer of the Messianic Jewish Alliance of America.

R. V. G. Tasker—Former dean of faculty of theology, King's College, University of London, professor of New Testament exegesis, and author of several books.

Paul N. Tassell—Former national representative of the

General Association of Regular Baptist Churches and author of several books.

Hudson Taylor—Pioneer missionary to China and founder of the China Inland Mission.

Merrill C. Tenney—Professor emeritus of Bible and theology and former dean of the graduate school at Wheaton College.

David R. Veerman—Veteran youth worker and author and vice president of Livingstone Corporation in Naperville, Illinois.

W. E. Vine—One of the world's foremost Greek scholars and author of the best-selling expository dictionary of Bible words and numerous commentaries.

Charles U. Wagner—A prolific author with more than thirty years of pastoral experience and past president of Grand Rapids Baptist College and Seminary, Grand Rapids, Michigan.

Thomas Whitelaw—Former Scottish minister and biblical scholar.

Warren W. Wiersbe—Writer-in-residence at Cornerstone College in Grand Rapids, Michigan, distinguished professor of preaching at Grand Rapids Baptist Seminary, and author of numerous books.

Philip Yancey—Editor-at-large for *Christianity Today* and award-winning author of numerous books.

Note: To the best of our knowledge, all of the above information is accurate and up to date. In some cases we were unable to obtain biographical information.

—THE STARBURST EDITORS

ENDNOTES

Introduction
1. Merrill C. Tenney, *New Testament Survey* (Grand Rapids, MI: Wm. B. Eerdmans Publishing Co., 1961), 185.
2. Warren W. Wiersbe, *Be Alive* (Colorado Springs: ChariotVictor Books, 1986), 10.

John 1: Jesus the Word
1. Lawrence O. Richards, *Victor Bible Background Commentary* (Wheaton, IL: Victor Books, 1994), 212.
2. Manford George Gutzke, *Plain Talk on John* (Grand Rapids, MI: Zondervan Publishing House, 1968), 12–13.
3. J. Dwight Pentecost, *The Words and Works of Jesus Christ* (Grand Rapids, MI: Zondervan Publishing House, 1981), 30.
4. Leon Morris, *The Gospel According to John* (Grand Rapids, MI: Wm. B. Eerdmans Publishing Co., 1971), 90.
5. Ibid., 96.
6. Pentecost, *Words and Works of Jesus Christ*, 31.
7. Merrill C. Tenney, *John: The Gospel of Belief* (Grand Rapids, MI: Wm. B. Eerdmans Publishing Co., 1976), 70.
8. Edwin A. Blum, "John" in *The Bible Knowledge Commentary*, vol. 2: New Testament, eds. John F. Walvoord and Roy B. Zuck (Wheaton, IL: Victor Books, 1983), 273.
9. Wiersbe, *Be Alive*, 15.
10. Merrill C. Tenney, "John" in *Zondervan NIV Bible Commentary*, vol. 2: New Testament, eds. Kenneth L. Barker and John Kohlenberger III (Grand Rapids, MI: Zondervan Publishing House, 1994), 298–299.
11. James Montgomery Boice, *The Gospel of John*, vol. 1 (Grand Rapids, MI: Zondervan Publishing House, 1975), 127–128.
12. Wiersbe, *Be Alive*, 17–18.
13. William Barclay, *The Gospel of John*, vol. 1, rev. ed. (Philadelphia: Westminster Press, 1975), 87–88.
14. Morris, *Gospel According to John*, 170–171.

John 2: Jesus the Authority
1. Wiersbe, *Be Alive*, 24–25.
2. Craig S. Keener, *The IVP Bible Background Commentary: New Testament* (Downers Grove, IL: InterVarsity Press, 1993), 268.
3. D. Edmond Hiebert, *An Introduction to the New Testament*, vol. 1: The Gospels and Acts (Chicago: Moody Press, 1975), 227–228.
4. William Hendriksen, *The Gospel of John* (Grand Rapids, MI: Baker Book House, 1953), 122.
5. D. A. Carson, *The Gospel According to John* (Grand Rapids, MI: Wm. B. Eerdmans Publishing Co., 1991), 180–181.
6. Wiersbe, *Be Alive*, 32.

John 3: Jesus the Choice Giver
1. Gutzke, *Plain Talk on John*, 32.
2. Philip Yancey and Brenda Quinn, *Meet the Bible* (Grand Rapids, MI: Zondervan Publishing House, 2000), 420.
3. Keener, *IVP Bible Background Commentary: New Testament*, 270.
4. Roger L. Fredrikson, *The Communicator's Commentary: John* (Dallas: Word Publishing, 1985), 84.
5. Bill Myers, *Jesus: An Eyewitness Account* (Wheaton, IL: Victor Books, 1988), 26.
6. J. Edwin Hortell, "All the Greatest," quoted in Barton, *Life Application Bible Commentary: John*, 62.
7. Morris, *Gospel According to John*, 231.
8. Merrill C. Tenney, "The Gospel of John" in *The Expositor's Bible Commentary*, vol. 9, ed. Frank E. Gaebelein (Grand Rapids, MI: Zondervan Publishing House, 1981), 50.
9. Barclay, *The Gospel of John*, vol. 1, 141.
10. George R. Beasley-Murray, *Word Biblical Commentary: John* (Nashville: Thomas Nelson Publishers, 1999), 52–53.
11. R. V. G. Tasker, *The Gospel According to St. John* (Grand Rapids, MI: Wm. B. Eerdmans Publishing Co., 1960), 73.

John 4: Jesus the Giver of Spiritual Life
1. Tenney, *Zondervan NIV Bible Commentary*, vol. 2, 307.
2. Bruce Milne, *The Message of John* (Downers Grove, IL: InterVarsity Press, 1993), 83.
3. Yancey and Quinn, *Meet the Bible*, 424.
4. Herschel H. Hobbs, *An Exposition of the Four Gospels* (Grand Rapids, MI: Baker Book House, 1968), 100.
5. Paul N. Tassell, *That Ye Might Believe* (Schaumburg, IL: Regular Baptist Press, 1987), 40–41.
6. Anne Graham Lotz, *Just Give Me Jesus* (Nashville: Word Publishing, 2000), 110.
7. Max Lucado, ed., *The Inspirational Study Bible: The Gospel of John* (Nashville: Word Publishing, 1994), 7.
8. Keener, *IVP Bible Background Commentary: New Testament*, 274.
9. Henry Blackaby, *Experiencing the Word through the Gospels* (Nashville: Holman Bible Publishers, 1999), 222.
10. Wiersbe, *Be Alive*, 54.
11. Matthew Henry, *Matthew Henry's Commentary on the Whole Bible*, vol. 4: Matthew to John (McLean, VA: MacDonald Publishing Co., 1721), 915–916.
12. Erwin W. Lutzer, *Seven Convincing Miracles* (Chicago: Moody Press, 1999), 72.

John 5: Jesus the Healer

1. Lotz, *Just Give Me Jesus,* 117.
2. R. Kent Hughes, *Behold the Lamb* (Wheaton, IL: Victor Books, 1984), 94–95.
3. Homer A. Kent Jr., *Light in the Darkness* (Grand Rapids, MI: Baker Book House, 1974), 88.
4. Lawrence O. Richards, *The Bible Reader's Companion* (Wheaton, IL: Victor Books, 1991), 682.
5. Dana Gould, ed., *Shepherd's Notes: John* (Nashville: Broadman & Holman, 1998), 31.
6. Morris, *Gospel According to John,* 309.
7. Tasker, *Gospel According to St. John,* 87.
8. Fredrikson, *Communicator's Commentary: John,* 117.
9. Barclay, *Gospel of John,* vol. 1, 198.
10. Paul Little, *How to Give Away Your Faith* (Downers Grove, IL: InterVarsity Press, 1988), 131.
11. Tenney, *Zondervan NIV Bible Commentary,* vol. 2, 314.

John 6: Jesus the Miracle Worker

1. Lutzer, *Seven Convincing Miracles,* 109.
2. Ibid., 126.
3. Hobbs, *Exposition of the Four Gospels,* 129.
4. Hughes, *Behold the Lamb,* 125.
5. Wiersbe, *Be Alive,* 73–74.
6. Lawrence O. Richards, *The 365-Day Devotional Commentary* (Wheaton, IL: Victor Books, 1990), 773.
7. W. E. Vine, *Vine's Expository Commentary on John* (Nashville: Thomas Nelson Publishers, 1997), 106.
8. W. Graham Scroggie, *The Gospel of John* (London: Pickering and Inglis Ltd., 1976), 45.
9. Barton, *Life Application Bible Commentary: John,* 131.
10. Yancey and Quinn, *Meet the Bible,* 474–475.
11. Carson, *Gospel According to John,* 295.
12. Wiersbe, *Be Alive,* 80.
13. James Montgomery Boice, *The Gospel of John,* vol. 2 (Grand Rapids, MI: Zondervan Publishing House, 1976), 219.

John 7: Jesus the Divider

1. J. Vernon McGee, *John Chapters 1–10* (Nashville: Thomas Nelson Publishers, 1991), 119.
2. Arthur W. Pink, *Exposition of the Gospel of John* (Grand Rapids, MI: Zondervan Publishing House, 1945), 379.
3. John Calvin, *John* (Wheaton, IL: Crossway Books, 1994), 183–184.
4. J. Carl Laney, *Moody Gospel Commentary: John* (Chicago: Moody Press, 1991), 141.
5. F. F. Bruce, *The Gospel of John* (Grand Rapids, MI: Wm. B. Eerdmans Publishing Co., 1983), 177.
6. Mitch and Zhava Glaser, *The Fall Feasts of Israel* (Chicago: Moody Press, 1987), 179.
7. Tenney, *John,* 136.

John 8: Jesus the Freedom Giver

1. Wiersbe, *Be Alive,* 95.
2. Myers, *Jesus,* 63–64.
3. Keener, *IVP Bible Background Commentary: New Testament,* 284.
4. Everett F. Harrison, *John: The Gospel of Faith* (Chicago: Moody Press, 1962), 52.
5. David H. Stern, *Jewish New Testament Commentary* (Clarksville, MD: Jewish New Testament Publications, 1992), 181.
6. Gould, *Shepherd's Notes: John,* 44.
7. Ibid., 46.
8. Charles U. Wagner, *This Is Life,* Senior Instructor (Schaumburg, IL: Regular Baptist Press, 1981), 46.

9. Boice, *Gospel of John,* vol. 2, 365.
10. Beasley-Murray, *Word Biblical Commentary: John,* 139.
11. Henry, *Matthew Henry's Commentary on the Whole Bible,* 1008.

John 9: Jesus the Sight Giver

1. Fredrikson, *Communicator's Commentary: John,* 168.
2. Henry, *Matthew Henry's Commentary on the Whole Bible,* 1011.
3. Richards, *Bible Reader's Companion,* 686.
4. Lotz, *Just Give Me Jesus,* 188.
5. Harrison, *John,* 58–59.
6. Gerald L. Borchert, *The New American Commentary* (Nashville: Broadman & Holman, 1996), 321.
7. Tasker, *Gospel According to St. John,* 125.
8. Kent, *Light in the Darkness,* 137.
9. Hughes, *Behold the Lamb,* 164–165.
10. Lutzer, *Seven Convincing Miracles,* 152, 154.

John 10: Jesus the Good Shepherd

1. Phillip Keller, *A Shepherd Looks at the Good Shepherd and His Sheep* (Grand Rapids, MI: Zondervan Publishing House, 1978), 40.
2. Ibid., 169.
3. Gutzke, *Plain Talk on John,* 109.
4. Yancey and Quinn, *Meet the Bible,* 483.
5. Henry, *Matthew Henry's Commentary on the Whole Bible,* 1032.
6. William Barclay, *The Gospel of John,* vol. 2, rev. ed. (Philadelphia: Westminster Press, 1975), 63.
7. Louis Goldberg, *Our Jewish Friends* (Chicago: Moody Press, 1977), 59.
8. Victor Buksbazen, *The Gospel in the Feasts of Israel* (Fort Washington, PA: Christian Literature Crusade, 1954), 63.
9. David R. Veerman, ed., *Life Application Bible for Students* (Wheaton, IL: Tyndale House Publishers, 1992), 988.
10. Laney, *Moody Gospel Commentary: John,* 194.
11. Scroggie, *Gospel of John,* 74.
12. Hobbs, *Exposition of the Four Gospels,* 170.
13. Little, *How to Give Away Your Faith,* 114.

John 11: Jesus the Resurrection and the Life

1. James Montgomery Boice, *The Gospel of John,* vol. 3 (Grand Rapids, MI: Zondervan Publishing House, 1977), 186.
2. Milne, *Message of John,* 160.
3. Lutzer, *Seven Convincing Miracles,* 169.
4. Charles H. Spurgeon, *The Treasury of the Bible,* vol. 2 (Grand Rapids, MI: Zondervan Publishing House, 1962), 456.
5. Hudson Taylor, quoted in Milne, *Message of John,* 158.
6. Carson, *Gospel According to John,* 411.
7. Bruce, *Gospel of John,* 243.
8. Max Lucado, *Life Lessons with Max Lucado: Book of John* (Nashville: Word Publishing, 1996), 71.
9. Barton, *Life Application Bible Commentary: John,* 233.
10. Lotz, *Just Give Me Jesus,* 213.
11. Lucado, *Life Lessons with Max Lucado: Book of John,* 72.
12. Calvin, *John,* 281.
13. F. L. Godet, *Commentary on the Gospel of John* (Grand Rapids, MI: Zondervan Publishing House, 1893), 189.
14. Lutzer, *Seven Convincing Miracles,* 168.
15. Wagner, *This Is Life,* Senior Instructor, 61.
16. Alexander MacLaren, *Expositions of Holy Scripture: St. John,* vol. 10 (Grand Rapids, MI: Wm. B. Eerdmans Publishing Co., 1944), 108.

John 12: Jesus the King Who Will Die

1. Richards, *365-Day Devotional Commentary,* 790.
2. Boice, *Gospel of John,* vol. 3, 304.

3. Pink, *Exposition of the Gospel of John*, 244.

4. David E. Garland, *The NIV Application Commentary: Mark* (Grand Rapids, MI: Zondervan Publishing House, 1996), 428.

5. Norval Geldenhuys, *The New International Commentary on the New Testament: The Gospel of Luke* (Grand Rapids, MI: Wm. B. Eerdmans Publishing Co., 1983), 480.

6. Barclay, *Gospel of John*, vol. 2, 118.

7. Wiersbe, *Be Alive*, 152.

8. Myers, *Jesus*, 94.

9. Barton, *Life Application Bible Commentary: John*, 258.

10. R. Kent Hughes, *John: That You May Believe* (Wheaton, IL: Crossway Books, 1999), 309.

11. J. Vernon McGee, *John Chapters 11–21* (Nashville: Thomas Nelson Publishers, 1991), 52.

12. Harrison, *John*, 78.

13. Hendriksen, *Gospel of John*, 212.

14. Bruce, *Gospel of John*, 275.

John 13: Jesus the Servant

1. Yancey and Quinn, *Meet the Bible*, 512.

2. Fritz Ridenour, *Tell It Like It Is* (Glendale, CA: Regal Books, 1968), 138.

3. John MacArthur Jr., *The Legacy of Jesus* (Chicago: Moody Press, 1986), 13.

4. Laney, *Moody Gospel Commentary: John*, 240–241.

5. Pink, *Exposition of the Gospel of John*, 315.

6. Yancey and Quinn, *Meet the Bible*, 510.

7. Hughes, *John*, 316–317.

8. Hobbs, *Exposition of the Four Gospels*, 214.

9. Garland, *NIV Application Commentary: Mark*, 526.

10. MacArthur, *Legacy of Jesus*, 21.

11. Morris, *Gospel According to John*, 628.

12. Myers, *Jesus*, 99.

13. Larry and Sue Richards, *The Teen Study Bible* (Grand Rapids, MI: Zondervan Publishing House, 1993), 1452.

14. Warren W. Wiersbe, *Be Transformed* (Colorado Springs: Chariot Victor Books, 1986), 24.

15. Vine, *Vine's Expository Commentary on John*, 164.

John 14: Jesus the Comforter

1. James Montgomery Boice, *The Gospel of John*, vol. 4 (Grand Rapids, MI: Zondervan Publishing House, 1978), 95.

2. Karl Barth, quoted in Earl F. Palmer, *The Intimate Gospel* (Waco, TX: Word Books, 1978), 124.

3. Kent, *Light in the Darkness*, 173.

4. C. S. Lewis, *Mere Christianity* (New York: Macmillan Publishing Co., Inc., 1960), 56.

5. R. Kent Hughes, *Behold the Man* (Wheaton, IL: Victor Books, 1984), 60.

6. Lawrence O. Richards, *Expository Dictionary of Bible Words* (Grand Rapids, MI: Zondervan Publishing House, 1985), 484.

7. Blackaby, *Experiencing the Word through the Gospels*, 252.

8. Calvin, *John*, 344.

9. Richards, *365-Day Devotional Commentary*, 797.

10. R. Wade Paschal Jr., quoted in *The Bible for Everyday Life*, ed. George Carey (Grand Rapids, MI: Wm. B. Eerdmans Publishing Co., 1996), 211.

11. MacArthur, *Legacy of Jesus*, 88–91.

12. Ibid., 95.

John 15: Jesus the Vine

1. Tenney, *John*, 226.

2. Richards, *365-Day Devotional Commentary*, 798.

3. Hughes, *Behold the Man*, 69–70.

4. Wayne Jacobson, *In My Father's Vineyard*, adapted by Anne Christian Buchanan (Dallas: Word Publishing, 1997), 16.

5. Richards, *Victor Bible Background Commentary*, 255.

6. MacArthur, *Legacy of Jesus*, 113.

7. Blackaby, *Experiencing the Word through the Gospels*, 255.

8. Calvin, *John*, 356.

9. Tasker, *Gospel According to St. John*, 175.

10. Barclay, *Gospel of John*, vol. 2, 178.

11. Jacobson, *In My Father's Vineyard*, 20.

12. MacArthur, *Legacy of Jesus*, 135.

13. Hobbs, *Exposition of the Four Gospels*, 231–232.

John 16: Jesus the Teacher

1. Hendriksen, *Gospel of John*, 321.

2. Henry, *Matthew Henry's Commentary on the Whole Bible*, 1134.

3. Harrison, *John*, 96.

4. Stern, *Jewish New Testament Commentary*, 202.

5. D. A. Carson, *The Farewell Discourse and Final Prayer of Jesus* (Grand Rapids, MI: Baker Book House, 1980), 157–158.

6. Ibid., 160.

7. Yancey and Quinn, *Meet the Bible*, 516.

8. Larry and Sue Richards, *Teen Study Bible*, 1457.

9. Morris, *Gospel According to John*, 708.

10. Ruth Myers, *The Satisfied Heart* (Colorado Springs: WaterBrook Press, 1999), 48.

11. McGee, *John Chapters 11–21*, 117.

12. Vine, *Vine's Expository Commentary on John*, 188.

13. Gould, *Shepherd's Notes: John*, 76.

John 17: Jesus the Pray-er

1. Martin Luther, quoted in McGee, *John: Chapters 11–21*, 119.

2. Harrison, *John*, 99.

3. Pink, *Exposition of the Gospel of John*, 95.

4. Hughes, *John*, 395.

5. Vine, *Vine's Expository Commentary on John*, 191.

6. Tassell, *That Ye Might Believe*, 112.

7. Morris, *Gospel According to John*, 728.

8. Carson, *Farewell Discourse and Final Prayer of Jesus*, 191.

9. Wagner, *This Is Life*, 104.

10. Kent, *Light in the Darkness*, 192.

11. David Jeremiah, *Prayer: The Great Adventure* (Sisters, OR: Multnomah Publishers, Inc., 1997), 201.

John 18: Jesus the Prisoner

1. Hughes, *Behold the Man*, 126–127.

2. Blum, *Bible Knowledge Commentary*, 334.

3. McGee, *John: Chapters 11–21*, 136.

4. D. Edmond Hiebert, *Mark: The Portrait of a Servant* (Chicago: Moody Press, 1979), 365.

5. MacLaren, *Expositions of Holy Scripture: St. John*, vol. 11, 224.

6. Fleming H. Revell, *The Revell Bible Dictionary* (Grand Rapids, MI: Fleming H. Revell, 1990), 69.

7. Lawrence O. Richards, *The Teacher's Commentary* (Wheaton, IL: Victor Books, 1987), 751.

8. Thomas Whitelaw, *Commentary on John* (Grand Rapids, MI: Kregel Publications, 1993), 384.

9. *The Life and Times Historical Reference Bible* (Nashville: Thomas Nelson Publishers, 1997), 1440.

10. Tenney, *Expositor's Bible Commentary*, 179.

11. Louis Barbieri, *Moody Gospel Commentary: Mark* (Chicago: Moody Press, 1995), 346.

12. Garland, *NIV Application Commentary: Mark*, 579.

John 19: Jesus the Corpse

1. James M. Stalker, *The Trial and Death of Jesus Christ* (Grand Rapids, MI: Zondervan Publishing House, 1961), 59.
2. John MacArthur Jr., *The Murder of Jesus* (Nashville: Word Publishing, 2000), 184.
3. Gutzke, *Plain Talk on John,* 188.
4. J. W. Shepherd, *The Christ of the Gospels* (Grand Rapids, MI: Wm. B. Eerdmans Publishing Co., 1946), 480.
5. Goldberg, *Our Jewish Friends,* 127.
6. C. Marvin Pate, *Moody Gospel Commentary: Luke* (Chicago: Moody Press, 1995), 453.
7. MacArthur, *Murder of Jesus,* 216.
8. Blum, *Bible Knowledge Commentary: New Testament,* 340.
9. Yancey and Quinn, *Meet the Bible,* 525.
10. Mark Bailey and Tom Constable, *The New Testament Explorer* (Nashville: Word Publishing, 1999), 191.
11. Ed Glasscock, *Moody Gospel Commentary: Matthew* (Chicago: Moody Press, 1997), 543.

John 20: Jesus the Risen Lord

1. Milne, *Message of John,* 294.
2. Josh McDowell, *The New Evidence That Demands a Verdict* (Nashville: Thomas Nelson Publishers, 1999), 203–204.

3. Laney, *Moody Gospel Commentary: John,* 360.
4. Calvin, *John,* 444.
5. Tenney, *Zondervan NIV Bible Commentary,* 369.
6. Wiersbe, *Be Transformed,* 128.
7. Wagner, *This Is Life,* 124.
8. Vine, *Vine's Expository Commentary on John,* 208.
9. Richards, *365-Day Devotional Commentary,* 811.
10. Palmer, *Intimate Gospel,* 172.
11. Lutzer, *Seven Convincing Miracles,* 188–189.
12. Godet, *Commentary on the Gospel of John,* 436.

John 21: Jesus the Commissioner

1. Lotz, *Just Give Me Jesus,* 317, 319.
2. Richards, *365-Day Devotional Commentary,* 812.
3. Lucado, *Inspirational Study Bible: The Gospel of John,* 35.
4. Bailey and Constable, *New Testament Explorer*, 193.
5. Palmer, *Intimate Gospel,* 176.
6. Tenney, *John,* 290.
7. Yancey and Quinn, *Meet the Bible,* 532–533.
8. Lotz, *Just Give Me Jesus,* 330–331.
9. Vine, *Vine's Expository Commentary on John,* 213–214.
10. Stern, *Jewish New Testament Commentary*, 214.
11. Calvin, *John,* 472.

INDEX

Boldface numbers refer to defined (What?) terms in the sidebar.

on the Holy Spirit, 200
on knowing God, 55
Blasphemy, **64**, 141, 249, 250–251, 263–264
Blessings, **11**
Blind man, Jesus healing, 26, 92, 120–129, 138
Blindness, literal and spiritual, 127–129, 139
Blum, Edwin A.:
on death of Jesus, 273
on grace, 11
on Judas, 244
Body of Christ, 237
Boice, James Montgomery:
on glorifying God, 146
on heaven, 194
on Jesus, realness of, 85
on John the Baptist, 14
on Mary of Bethany, 164
on parable of tree and fruit, 113
Books of the Bible (*see* individual Books)
Borchert, Gerald L., on giving glory to God, 125
Born again, 8, 33, **35**–36
Nicodemus, 34–38
Bread:
Jesus giving Judas, 188
literal and spiritual, 79–85, 87
loaves and fishes miracle (feeding of the five thousand), xiii, 26, 73–77, 87
Unleavened, Feast of (*see* Passover)
Bread of life, Jesus as, xiii, 82–85, 87
Brothers, **26**
Bruce, F. F.:
on believers vs. unbelievers, 175
on Martha's faith, 150
on Sabbath law, 95
Buddhism, 289
Buksbazen, Victor, on Hanukkah, 139
Burial:
customs, first-century, 150, 154–155
of Jesus, 276–278

C

Caesar, 265–267
Caiaphas, 158, 242, 246–247, 257, 265
Calvin, John:
on Christ's love, 210
on Christ's majesty, 303
on the empty tomb, 283
on hatred for Jesus, 92–93
on Jesus at tomb of Lazarus, 154
on orphans, 201
Cana, Jesus returning to, 55–56 (*See also* Wedding at Cana)

Capernaum, 26–27, 55–58, 77–79, 84
Carnal, **92**
Carson, D. A.:
on cleansing the Temple, 29
on the cross, 222
on mourners for Lazarus, 150
on prayer for disciples, 235
on sacrifice of Jesus, 83
Cattle, 27
Cavil, **92**
Cephas, 16–17 (*See also* Peter)
Ceremonial washing, **23**–25, **41**
Certified, **43**
Chahin, Jesus, 59
Character:
Christlike, 152–153, 224
"fruit of the Spirit," 206
Charoset, 188
Chief priests (*see* Enemies of Jesus; Priests)
Childbirth, first-century, 223
Chooses, **93**
Christ, the, **52**, **95** (*See also* Jesus Christ; Messiah)
Christian communion, 27, 84, 180
Christianity, 37, 69, 97, 282, 289
religion vs., 137, 195–196, 282
(*See also* Belief; Believers; Faith)
Church of St. Anne, 61
Circumcised, **94**
Cleopas, 286
Commandment, last, 190
Commandments, Ten, 11, 200
Commission, **301**
Communion, Christian, 27, 84, 180
Condemn, **38**
Condemning, **106**
Constable, Tom (*see* Bailey, Mark, and Tom Constable)
Convicting ministry, Holy Spirit's, 219–221
Counselor, 199, 214, 219 (*See also* Holy Spirit)
Courage (*see* individual names)
Court of Women, 109
Creation, 3–5, 287
Cross, the, 222 (*See also* Crucifixion)
Crown of thorns, 261–263
Crucifixion, 170, 261, 274, 275
of Jesus, 263–264, 267–275
of Peter, 293, 300–301
Psalm describing, 268–269

D

Daily bread (*see* Bread)
Darkness, xiv, 5–6, 39, 171–172, 174
David, 99, 135, 186
describing crucifixion, 268–269
Death, 114–115, 145, 147, 161

as approaching, 120–121
authority of Jesus over, 137
as beginning of new life, 68
burial customs, 150, 154–155
eternal, 6, 97, 165
God as controlling, 6, 151
Satan and, 154
to self-interest, 168–169, 176
sin and, 109
spiritual, 80, 110
Death of Jesus, 267–276
preparing disciples for, 164, 217–228
Deceiver, **92**
Dedication, Feast of (*see* Feast of Dedication)
Defile, **25**
Delhi, India, 59
Demon-possession:
Jesus healing, 92
Jesus accused of, 94, 114–115, 138
Deuteronomy, Book of, 277
Devil (*see* Satan)
Didymus (*see* Thomas)
Disciples, **xiv**, **16**, **86**
arguing before Last Supper, 181
Capernaum as home of, 27
deserting Jesus, 85–86, 87
faith of, 198, 232
financial support of, 163
as fishermen, xiii, 245, 247, 294–298
as forgiven, 287
as friends of Jesus, 211–212
glory revealed to, 92
hatred for, 212–214, 217–218
heaven as destination for, 193–196
Jesus praying for, 232–239
John (author) as, xiii
larger group of, 286
loyalty of, 148–149
mission of, 236
as New Testament authors, 236
secret, 40, 276–277
true, 111
(*See also* Apostles; individual names, events, and topics)
Disciples of John the Baptist, 15–16, 40–41
Discourses, **xiii**
Docile, **21**
Donkey, Jesus as riding, 166–167
Doubt, 287–289
Dove(s):
Holy Spirit as, 15
in the Temple courts, 27
Dream, of Pilate's wife, 264
Dusseldorf, Germany, 59

John as intimate friend of, xiv
as key to personal relationship with
    God, 69
as king (See under King)
knowledge of, 231, 23
life and mission of, 225, 230, 254
as Messiah (see Messiah)
miracles of (see Miracles of Jesus)
misconceptions regarding, 21
as origin of life, 5–6
persecution of (see Persecution)
personal relationship with, 84–85
popularity of, 73, 96
public response to, differing, 89,
    92, 99–101, 138, 153
reasons for seeking, 80
rejected as Messiah, 8, 20, 64, 67–
    71, 113–114, 172–175, 213
resurrection of (see Resurrection of
    Jesus)
salvation as through (see Salvation)
Second Coming of, 201
as Son of God (see Son of God)
as Son of Man, 126–127, 171, 189
as the Word, 3–4, 8–9
world, as overcoming, 212–213,
    226–227, 230
    (See also Messiah; individual
        events, names, and topics)
Jesus as deity, 64, 214, 225–226, 290
claims of, 66–71, 93–94, 96–98,
    138–144
Lazarus as proof of, 165
seven sign miracles proving (see
    Seven signs)
testimony to, 68–69, 71, 108, 213,
    275–276
    (See also "I am"; Son of God)
Jewish feasts and holidays, 159 (See
    also individual feasts)
Jews, the (Jewish leaders), **63**, **84**, **92**
    (See also Enemies of Jesus)
Jews, the (people), xi
Abraham as forefather of, 111–113
Gentile converts as, 36
God's chosen people, 8–9, 111
Jacob as founder of nation, 46
Jesus as, 8, 47–48, 60
Jesus rejected by, 20, 67–71, 113–
    114, 172–175, 213
John as, xiii
languages of, 17
Old Testament as history of, xi
religious beliefs of, first-century, 8,
    63, 66, 84
Samaritans, feud with, 47, 51 (See
    also Samaritans)
Satan, as called children of, 113–
    114

John (author; "the disciple whom Jesus
    loved") xiii–xiv, 187, 167, 215
as eyewitness to Jesus' life, 9
faith of, 282
as fisherman, xiii, 247
James as brother of, xiv
Jesus as intimate friend of, xiv
as John the Baptist's disciple, 16
and Mary, mother of Jesus, xiv,
    270–271
New Testament books by, xiv
John (father of Andrew and Peter), 16
John Mark (see Mark)
John the Baptist, 6, 7, 10–16, 143
as forerunner of Jesus, 15–16, 20,
    40–43
Jesus mentioning testimony of, 68
John, Book of (Gospel), xi, 303
compared to other Gospels, xiii
epilogue, 293
purpose statement for, 289–290
seven signs in (see Seven signs)
summary of contents, xiv, 191
themes in, xiv, 6
timetable, 179–180
1, 2, 3 John, Books of (Epistles), xiv
Jordan River, 13, 41, 143
Joseph (earthly father of Jesus), 17–18,
    22–23, 26, 82
Joseph (of Arimathea), 40, 174, 247,
    276–277
Joseph (son of Jacob), 46
Joy, 98, 206, 209–210, 224, 234
Judah (clan of), 96
Judas Iscariot, 86, 183, 185–186, 208
betrayal of Jesus by, 180–181, 183,
    185–192, 243–245
divine purpose and, 233–234
greed of, 163
kiss of, 245
and movement to crown Jesus king,
    76
Judas (another disciple; not Judas
    Iscariot), 201
Judea, 12, 40–41, 45–46, 89–90, 147–
    148
Jesus tried in, 256
Judgment, 39, 43, 66–68, 110, 175
Holy Spirit and, 219–220
human vs. divine, 108
by Moses, 70
result of Christ's coming, 128

K

Kangaroo court, **241**
Keener, Craig S.:
on Jesus and the Samaritans, 55
on Jesus writing on the ground, 105
on Nicodemus, 36

on stone water jars, 24–25
Keller, Philip, on the shepherd's voice,
    132–133
Kent, Homer A., Jr.:
on disciples, mission of, 236
on Jesus as way to God, 196
on judgment, 128
on lame man, Jesus healing, 62
Kidron Valley, 205, 241–243
Kindness, 206
King(s), 254
    Jesus as thought to be, xiii,
        166–167
    movement to crown Jesus, 75–76
"King of the Jews," 261–269
    (See also Kingdom of Jesus;
        individual names)
Kingdom, **xiii**, **98**
Kingdom of Jesus, 251–254
Kiss, of Judas, 245

L

Lake, **77**
Lamb(s):
Peter as to feed, 298–299
sacrificial, 79, 243
    (See also Sheep)
Lamb of God, Jesus as, 14–16, 79, 243,
    275
Lame man, Jesus healing, 26, 60–64,
    90
Laney, J. Carl:
on the empty tomb, 282
on names, importance of, 140
on Peter and the foot-washing, 182
on willingness to do God's will, 94
Last Supper, painting of, 181, 187
Latin, 269
Law (legal system), 251–252
    Jesus' trial contrary to, 241, 248–
        249, 251, 256–257
    Nicodemus as raising questions of,
        100
Law (Old Testament law; Law of
    Moses), **11**, 51, 93
    Jesus' teaching and, 94–95, 101
Lazarus, 161, 164–165
    plot to kill, 164–165
    resurrection of, 26, 145–157, 160,
        164–165, 167
Lazarus in grave clothes, illustration of,
    156
Levites, **12**, 243–244
Lewis, C. S., on Jesus, 196
Life, 5–6
    authority of Jesus over, 137
    death as beginning of new, 68
    eternal (see Eternal life)
    God as source of, 65–66

Jesus as origin of, 5–6, 195–196
spiritual dimension of, 6, 110
Life and Times Historical Reference Bible, The, on kingdom, concept of, 253
Light, xiv, 5–6
God's love as, 40
Light of the World, Jesus as, 6–7, 82, 107, 120, 147–148, 171–172
Little, Paul, on Christianity and intelligence, 69
Livid, **27**
Living water, Jesus as source of, 97–98, 101, 273
Loaves and fishes (feeding of the five thousand), xiii, 26, 73–77, 87
Logos, 4
Lord:
Jesus as, 183–184
in Old and New Testaments, xvi
Lord's Prayer, the, 229
Lotz, Anne Graham:
on blind man, healing of, 121
on Peter, 294
on Peter's restoration, 300
on the Pool of Bethesda, 60
on suffering and Christlike character, 152–153
on worship, 51
Love, xiv, 190–191, 206
acts of (showing), 162, 163, 201
among believers, 6, 190, 210–212
false, 213
for God, 70
of God for Jesus, 65–66
God's, 38–40, 225, 238
Holy Spirit as bringing, 98
humility and, 181
of Jesus, 181, 191, 209–210
Jesus on, 199–201, 209–210
Jesus as valuing our, 164
"Love one another," 190
meanings of, 299
unconditional, 191
Loved, **38**
Loyalty, of Thomas, 149
Lucado, Max:
on death, God in face of, 151
on death and Satan, 154
on Jesus declaring Messianic identity, 52
on Peter and resurrected Jesus, 297
Luke, xiii, 92, 245
Luke, Book of (Gospel), xiii, 76, 186, 303 (*See also* Gospels)
Luther, Martin, on Jesus' prayer before arrest, 230
Lutzer, Erwin W.:
on blindness, literal and spiritual, 128

on a Buddhist's conversion, 289
on death and God's presence, 147
on faith, 57
on feeding the five thousand, 74–75
on movement to crown Jesus king, 76
on resurrection of Lazarus as seventh sign, 156

M

MacArthur, John, Jr.:
on Christ's love and humility, 181
on Jesus' obedience, 204
on Jesus' return to heaven, 203
on Jews rejecting Christ, 213
on Judas, 188
on mother of Jesus at crucifixion, 271
on Pontius Pilate, 265
on prayers of non-Christians, 209
Maccabees, Book of, 139
MacLaren, Alexander, on the Pharisees, 157
Made himself known, **11**
Maelstrom, **181**
Majesty, **303**
Malchus, 245
Malice, **93**
Manna, **76**, 80–81, 83–84
Mark, xiii, 92
Mark, Book of (Gospel), xiii, 76, 186, 303 (*See also* Gospels)
Martha, 146, 150–151, 161–162 (*See also* Resurrection of Lazarus)
Mary (mother of James), 280, 286
Mary (mother of Jesus), 82
at Capernaum, 26
at crucifixion, xiv, 270–271
at wedding at Cana, 21–25
Mary (wife of Clopas), 270–271
Mary Magdalene:
angels, meeting with, 283
at crucifixion, 271
resurrected Jesus and, 279–281, 283–285, 295
Mary of Bethany, 146, 161
anointing Jesus' feet, 162–164
(*See also* Resurrection of Lazarus)
Matthew, xiii, 92
Matthew, Book of (Gospel), xiii, 76, 186, 303 (*See also* Gospels)
Matzah, 188
McDowell, Josh, on the resurrection of Jesus, 281
McGee, J. Vernon:
on God's time, 91
on Jesus and temple guards, 244–245
on peace, 227

on rejection of Jesus, 173
McLaren, Alexander, on Gospels, whole story of, 246
Men, **75**
Menorah, 107, 139; illustration of, 108
Mercy, **104**
Messiah, **7, 52**
as from line of David, 99
attitudes regarding Jesus as, 89, 96–97, 99–100
expectations and misconceptions regarding, 15, 70, 95, 139, 171–172
Jesus declaring identity as, 51–52
Jewish eagerness for, 12
prophecy regarding birth of (*see* Prophecy)
refusing to do miracle to prove self as, 92
rejection of Jesus as, 8, 20, 64, 67–71, 113–114, 172–175, 213
Mexico, Tlacote, 59
Micah, prophecy in Book of, 96
Milne, Bruce:
on the empty tomb, 281
on gender prejudice, 47–48
on God's timetable, 147
Milquetoast, **21**
Miracles of Jesus—the seven signs (*see* Seven signs)
Miracles of Jesus, xii–**xiii**, 65, 92, 122, 142
ear of high priest's servant, healing, 245
fish, big catch after resurrection, 295–297
as proof of deity, 68–69, 197
public reaction to, 30, 34, 80–81, 96, 156–157
refusal to do to prove self Messiah, 92
on the Sabbath, 65, 71, 94–95, 123, 155
unbelief persisting despite, 172–174
unrecorded, 289–290
(*See also* Seven signs; individual miracles)
Money changers, Jesus confronting, 27–28
Morris, Leon:
on angels, 19
on God as father, 65
on Jesus as the Word, 8–9
on joy, God-given, 224
on Judas, 189
on Judas and divine purpose, 234
on salvation, 40
on witnessing, 7
Mosaic system, **11**

in Jesus, 82, 127 (*See also* Faith)
Truth, 11, 39, 235–236, 255
    of God, 92, 111
    Holy Spirit as, 199
    Holy Spirit showing believers, 221
    Jesus as, 82, 195–196, 213
    knowing and living it, 111, 121
    meaning of, 255
    Pilate's perception of, 254–255
    Spirit of, 213
    spiritual and literal interpretation
      of, 84
    unbelief and, 114
Twelve, the (*see* Apostles)

U
Unbelief, xiv
Unbelievers, 43, 173–174
    despite miracles, 172–174
    end-time judgment of, 68
    first-century Jews as, 140
    hating Christians, 212–214, 217–
      218
    Holy Spirit and, 220–221
    Jesus' brothers as, 90
    Jewish leaders as, 114
    Judas as, 183
    persecution by (*see* Persecution)
    prayers of, 209
    and spiritual death, 110
    witnessing to, 220
Upper-room discourse, 179–204

V
Veerman, David R., on spiritual
    blindness, 139
Veneer, **135**
Verb, **227**
Vicarious, **83**
Vilified, **203**
Vine, Jesus as the true, 82, 205–209
Vine, W. E.:
    on God's seal of approval placed on
      Jesus, 79

on Jesus encouraging disciples, 227
on Jesus, life's work of, 231
on John and Peter, 302
on Peter, 191
on resurrected Jesus, marks on, 286
Vineyards, 206

W
Wagner, Charles U.:
    on Abraham, 111–112
    on Jesus' prayer for disciples, 235
    on peace, Jesus' greeting of, 286
    on the Pharisees, 157
Walking on water, 26, 77–78, 87
Water:
    literal and spiritual, 48–49, 53, 97–
      98
    living, Jesus as offering, 97–98, 101
    second birth and, 35
Water Gate, 98
Water turned to wine, 21–25, 26, 31
Way, the truth, and the life, Jesus as,
    82, 195–196
Wedding at Cana, 21–25, 26, 31
Wedding practices, first-century
    Jewish, 42
Weeping, Jesus as, 153, 180
Well, Jacob's, illustration of, 46
Well, woman at (*see* Samaritan
    woman)
Whips, Roman, 262–263; illustration
    of, 262
Whitelaw, Thomas, on Jesus before
    Pilate, 252
Wiersbe, Warren W.:
    on four Gospels, comparison, xiii
    on grace, 11
    on Jesus and his mother, 23
    on the Lamb of God, 14
    on love, 191
    on Mary Magdalene and resur-
      rected Jesus, 285
    on public response to Jesus'
      ministry, 56

on Sea of Galilee storm, 77
on surrender to God, 169
on truth, literal and spiritual, 84
on unsaved believers, 30
on woman caught in adultery, 104
Wine, Jesus turning water to (wedding
    at Cana), 21–25, 26, 31
With, **4**
Witness, Christian, 7, 220
Witnesses, to deity of Jesus (*see*
    Testimony)
Witnesses, false, 256–257
Woman's Seed, **230**
Women, first-century, 47–48, 162, 281
    (*See also* individual events,
      names)
Women, Court of, 109
Word, Jesus as, 3–4, 8–9
Works, faith vs., 79
World, **8**, 38
World, Jesus as overcoming, 212–213,
    226–227, 230
Worship, 51, 207
Wrath, **43**

X, Y
Yancey, Philip:
    on crowd as doubting Jesus, 82
    on death of Jesus, 273
    on Jesus as good shepherd and gate,
      135
    on the Last Supper, 181
    on Nicodemus, 35
    on pain and joy, 223
Yeshua, **106**, **220**, **302**
You people, **36**

Z
Zeal, **27**
Zebedee; wife of Zebedee (parents of
    John and James), xiv, 294, 270–
    271
Zechariah, 275
Zechariah, Book of, 98

Books by Starburst Publishers®

(Partial listing—full list available on request)

The **God's Word for the Biblically-Inept™** series is already a best-seller with over 100,000 books sold! Designed to make reading the Bible easy, educational, and fun! This series of verse-by-verse Bible studies, topical studies, and overviews mixes scholarly information from experts with helpful icons, illustrations, sidebars, and time lines. It's the Bible made easy!

John—God's Word for the Biblically-Inept™
Lin Johnson

From village fisherman to beloved apostle, John was an eyewitness to the teachings and miracles of Christ. Now, readers can join in an easy-to-understand, verse-by-verse journey through the fourth and most unique of all the Gospels. Witness the wonder of Jesus, a man who turned water into wine, healed the blind, walked on water, and raised Lazarus from the dead.
(trade paper)   ISBN 1892016435 $16.95

The Bible—God's Word for the Biblically-Inept™
Larry Richards

An excellent book to start learning the entire Bible. Get the basics or the in-depth information you are seeking with this user-friendly overview. From Creation to Christ to the Millennium, learning the Bible has never been easier.
(trade paper)   ISBN 0914984551 $16.95

Daniel—God's Word for the Biblically-Inept™
Daymond R. Duck

Daniel is a book of prophecy and the key to understanding the mysteries of the Tribulation and end-time events. This verse-by-verse commentary combines humor and scholarship to get at the essentials of Scripture. Perfect for those who want to know the truth about the Antichrist.
(trade paper)   ISBN 0914984489 $16.95

Genesis—God's Word for the Biblically-Inept™
Joyce L. Gibson

Genesis is written to make understanding and learning the Word of God simple and fun! Like the other books in this series, the author breaks the Bible down into bite-sized pieces making it easy to understand and incorporate into your life. Readers will learn about Creation, Adam and Eve, the Flood, Abraham and Isaac, and more.
(trade paper)   ISBN 1892016125 $16.95

Health & Nutrition—God's Word for the Biblically-Inept™
Kathleen O'Bannon Baldinger

The Bible is full of God's rules for good health! Baldinger reveals scientific evidence that proves the diet and health principles outlined in the Bible are the best for total health. Learn about the Bible diet, the food pyramid, and fruits and vegetables from the Bible! Experts include Pamela Smith, Julian Whitaker, Kenneth Cooper, and T. D. Jakes.
(trade paper)   ISBN 0914984055 $16.95

Life of Christ, Volume 1—God's Word for the Biblically-Inept™
Robert C. Girard

Girard takes the reader on an easy-to-understand journey through the Gospels of Matthew, Mark, Luke, and John, tracing the story of Jesus from his virgin birth to his revolutionary ministry. Learn about Jesus' baptism, the Sermon on the Mount, and his miracles and parables.
(trade paper)   ISBN 1892016230 $16.95

Life of Christ, Volume 2—God's Word for the Biblically-Inept™
Robert C. Girard

Life of Christ, Volume 2, begins with events recorded in Matthew 16. Read about Jesus' transfiguration, his miracles and parables, triumphal ride through Jerusalem, capture in the Garden of Gethsemane, and his trial, crucifixion, resurrection, and ascension. Find out how to be great in the kingdom of God, what Jesus meant when he called himself the light of the world, and what makes up real worship.
(trade paper)   ISBN 1892016397 $16.95

Men of the Bible—God's Word for the Biblically-Inept™
D. Larry Miller

Benefit from the life experiences of the powerful men of the Bible! Learn how the inspirational struggles of men such as Moses, Daniel, Paul, and David parallel the struggles of men today. It will inspire and build Christian character for any reader.
(trade paper)   ISBN 1892016079 $16.95

Prophecies of the Bible—God's Word for the Biblically-Inept™
Daymond R. Duck

God has a plan for this crazy planet, and now understanding it is easier than ever! Best-selling author and end-time prophecy expert Daymond R. Duck explains the complicated prophecies of the Bible in plain English. Duck shows you all there is to know about the end of the age, the New World Order, the Second Coming, and the coming world government. Find out what prophecies have already been fulfilled and what's in store for the future!
(trade paper)   ISBN 1892016222 $16.95

Revelation—God's Word for the Biblically-Inept™
Daymond R. Duck

End-time Bible prophecy expert Daymond R. Duck leads us verse by verse through one of the Bible's most confusing books. Follow the experts as they forge their way through the captivating prophecies of Revelation!
(trade paper)   ISBN 0914984985 $16.95

Romans—God's Word for the Biblically-Inept™
Gib Martin

The best-selling *God's Word for the Biblically-Inept™* series continues to grow! Learn about the apostle Paul, living a righteous life, and more with help from graphics, icons, and chapter summaries.
(trade paper)   ISBN 1892016273 $16.95

Women of the Bible—God's Word for the Biblically-Inept™
Kathy Collard Miller

Finally, a Bible perspective just for women! Gain valuable insight from the successes and struggles of such women as Eve, Esther, Mary, Sarah, and Rebekah. Interesting icons like "Get Close to God," "Build Your Spirit," and "Grow Your Marriage" will make it easy to incorporate God's Word into your daily life.
(trade paper)   ISBN 0914984063 $16.95

The **What's in the Bible for . . .™** series focuses on making the Bible applicable to everyday life. Whether you're a teenager or senior citizen, this series has the book for you! Each title is equipped with the same reader-friendly icons, call-outs, tables, illustrations, questions, and chapter summaries that are used in the *God's Word for the Biblically-Inept™* series. It's another easy way to access God's Word!

What's in the Bible for . . .™ Women
Georgia Curtis Ling

What does the Bible have to say to women? Women of all ages will find biblical insight on topics that are meaningful to them in four sections: Wisdom for the Journey; Family Ties; Bread, Breadwinners, and Bread Makers; and Fellowship and Community Involvement. This book uses illustrations, bullet points, chapter summaries, and icons to make understanding God's Word easier than ever!
(trade paper)   ISBN 1892016109 $16.95

What's in the Bible for . . .™ Mothers
Judy Bodmer

Is home schooling a good idea? Is it okay to work? At what age should I start treating my children like responsible adults? What is the most important thing I can teach my children? If you are asking these questions and need help answering them, *What's in the Bible for . . .™ Mothers* is especially for you! Simple and user-friendly, this motherhood manual offers hope and instruction for today's mothers by jumping into the lives of mothers in the Bible (e.g., Naomi, Elizabeth, and Mary) and by exploring biblical principles that are essential to being a nurturing mother.
(trade paper)   ISBN 1892016265 $16.95

What's in the Bible for . . .™ Teens
Mark Littleton and Jeanette Gardner Littleton

This is a book that teens will love! *What's in the Bible for . . .™ Teens* contains topical Bible themes that parallel the challenges and pressures of today's adolescents. Learn about Bible prophecy, God's plan for relationships, and peer pressure in a conversational and fun tone. Helpful and eye-catching "WWJD?" icons, illustrations, and sidebars included. (Available Fall 2000.)
(trade paper)   ISBN 1892016052 $16.95

What's in the Bible for . . .™ Couples
Larry and Kathy Miller

Restore love, unity, and commitment with internationally acclaimed relationship experts Larry and Kathy Miller as they explore God's Word on such topics as dating, sex, money, and trauma. Don't miss the "Take It from Them" feature, which offers wisdom from couples who have lived and learned, and the "Couples of the Bible" feature that spotlights the experiences of such couples as Adam and Eve, Abraham and Sarah, and Joseph and Mary.
(trade paper)   ISBN 1892016028 $16.95

(see page 334 for purchasing information)

• **Learn more at www.biblicallyinept.com** •

Bible Seeds: A Simple Study-Devotional for Growing in God's Word
From the creators of the *God's Word for the Biblically-Inept™* series

Growing your faith is like tending a garden—just plant the seed of God's Word in your heart, tend it with prayer, and watch it blossom. At the heart of this unique study for women is a Bible verse or "seed" that is combined with an inspirational lesson, a word study, application tips, thought provoking questions with room to write, a prayer starter, and a final thought.
(trade paper)   ISBN 1892016443 $13.99

God Things Come in Small Packages: Celebrating the Little Things in Life
Susan Duke, LeAnn Weiss, Caron Loveless, and Judith Carden

Enjoy touching reminders of God's simple yet generous gifts to brighten our days and gladden our hearts! Treasures like a sunset over a vast sparkling ocean, a child's trust, or the crystalline dew on a spider's web come to life in this elegant compilation. Such occasions should be celebrated as if gift wrapped from God; they're his hallmarks! Personalized Scripture is artfully

combined with compelling stories and reflections.
(cloth)   ISBN 1892016281 $12.95

God Things Come in Small Packages for Moms: Rejoicing in the Simple Pleasures of Motherhood
Susan Duke, LeAnn Weiss, Caron Loveless, and Judith Carden

The "small" treasures God plants in a mom's day shine in this delightful book. Savor priceless stories, which encourage us to value treasures like a shapeless, ceramic bowl presented with a toothy grin; a child's hand clinging to yours on a crowded bus; or a handful of wildflowers presented on a hectic day. Each story combines personalized Scripture with heartwarming vignettes and inspiring reflections.
(cloth)   ISBN 189201629X $12.95

God Things Come in Small Packages for Friends: Exploring the Freedom of Friendship
LeAnn Weiss, Susan Duke, and Judy Carden

A heartwarming combination of true stories, paraphrased Scripture, and reflections that celebrate the simple yet cherished blessings shared between true friends. This series combines the beauty of gift books with the depth of devotionals. Includes reflective meditation, narrative vignettes detailing powerful moments of revelation, and encouraging scripture passages presented as letters to a friend.
(cloth)   ISBN 1892016346 $12.95

God Things Come in Small Packages for Women: Celebrating the Unique Gifts of Women
LeAnn Weiss, Susan Duke, and Judy Carden

Women will experience God's love like never before through wonderfully paraphrased Scripture, true stories, and reflections, which celebrate the unique character of women. Includes reflective meditation, narrative vignettes detailing powerful moments of revelation, and encouraging scripture passages presented as letters from God.
(cloth)   ISBN 1892016354 $12.95

The Weekly Feeder: A Revolutionary Shopping, Cooking, and Meal-Planning System
Cori Kirkpatrick

A revolutionary meal-planning system, here is a way to make preparing home-cooked dinners more convenient than ever. At the beginning of each week, simply choose one of the eight preplanned menus, tear out the corresponding grocery list, do your shopping, and whip up each fantastic meal in less than 45 minutes! The author's household management tips, equipment checklists, and nutrition information make this system a must for any busy family. Included with every recipe is a personal anecdote from the author emphasizing the importance of good food, a healthy family, and a well-balanced life.
(trade paper)   ISBN 1892016095 $16.95

God Stories: They're So Amazing, Only God Could Make Them Happen
Donna I. Douglas

Famous individuals share their personal, true-life experiences with God in this beautiful new book! Find out how God has touched the lives of top recording artists, professional athletes, and other newsmakers like Jessi Colter, Deana Carter, Ben Vereen, Stephanie Zimbalist, Cindy Morgan, Sheila E., Joe Jacoby, Cheryl Landon, Brett Butler, Clifton Taulbert, Babbie Mason, Michael Medved, Sandi Patty, Charlie Daniels, and more! Their stories are intimate, poignant, and sure to inspire and motivate you as you listen for God's message in your own life!
(cloth)   ISBN 1892016117 $18.95

God's Little Rule Book: Simple Rules to Bring Joy & Happiness to Your Life
Starburst Publishers

Let this little book of God's rules be your personal guide to a more joyful life. Brimming with easily applicable rules, this book is sure to inspire and motivate you! Each rule includes corresponding Scripture and a practical tip that will help to incorporate God's rules into everyday life. Simple enough to fit into a busy schedule, yet powerful enough to be life changing!
(trade paper)   ISBN 1892016168 $6.95

Life's Little Rule Book: Simple Rules to Bring Joy & Happiness to Your Life
Starburst Publishers

Let this little book inspire you to live a happier life! The pages are filled with timeless rules such as, "Learn to cook, you'll always be in demand!" and "Help something grow." Each rule is combined with a reflective quote and a simple suggestion to help the reader incorporate the rule into everyday life.
(trade paper)   ISBN 1892016176 $6.95

God's Abundance
Edited by Kathy Collard Miller

Over 100,000 sold! This day-by-day inspirational is a collection of thoughts by leading Christian writers such as Patsy Clairmont, Jill Briscoe, Liz Curtis Higgs, and Naomi Rhode. *God's Abundance* is based on God's Word for a simpler, yet more abundant life. Learn to make all aspects of your life—personal, business, financial, relationships, even housework a "spiritual abundance of simplicity."
(cloth)   ISBN 0914984977 $19.95

Promises of God's Abundance
Edited by Kathy Collard Miller

Subtitled: *For a More Meaningful Life.* The Bible is filled with God's promises for an abundant life. *Promises of God's Abundance* is written in the same way as the best-selling *God's Abundance.* It will help you discover these promises and show you how simple obedience is the key to an abundant life. Scripture, questions for growth, and a simple thought for the day will guide you to a more meaningful life.

(trade paper)   ISBN 0914984098 $9.95

Treasures of a Woman's Heart: A Daybook of Stories and Inspiration

Edited by Lynn D. Morrissey

Join the best-selling editor of *Seasons of a Woman's Heart* in this touching sequel where she unlocks the treasures of women and glorifies God with Scripture, reflections, and a compilation of stories. Explore heartfelt living with vignettes by Kay Arthur, Elisabeth Elliot, Emilie Barnes, Claire Cloninger, and more.

(cloth)   ISBN 1892016257 $18.95

Seasons of a Woman's Heart: A Daybook of Stories and Inspiration

Edited by Lynn D. Morrissey

A woman's heart is complex. This daybook of stories, quotes, Scriptures, and daily reflections will inspire and refresh. Christian women share their heartfelt thoughts on seasons of faith, growth, guidance, nurturing, and victory. Includes Christian writers Kay Arthur, Emilie Barnes, Luci Swindoll, Jill Briscoe, and Florence Littauer.

(cloth)   ISBN 1892016036 $18.95

Stories of God's Abundance for a More Joyful Life

Compiled by Kathy Collard Miller

Like its successful predecessor, *God's Abundance*, this book is filled with beautiful, inspirational, real-life stories. Those telling their stories of God share Scriptures and insights that readers can apply to their daily lives. Renew your faith in life's small miracles and challenge yourself to allow God to lead the way as you find the source of abundant living for all your relationships.

(trade paper)   ISBN 1892016060 $12.95

Why Fret That God Stuff?

Edited by Kathy Collard Miller

Subtitled: *Stories of Encouragement to Help You Let Go and Let God Take Control of All Things in Your Life.* Occasionally, we all become overwhelmed by the everyday challenges of our lives: hectic schedules, our loved ones' needs, unexpected expenses, a sagging devotional life. *Why Fret That God Stuff* is the perfect beginning to finding joy and peace for the real world!

(trade paper)   ISBN 0914984500 $12.95

Purchasing Information

www.starburstpublishers.com

Books are available from your favorite bookstore, either from current stock or special order. To assist bookstores in locating your selection, be sure to give title, author, and ISBN. If unable to purchase from a bookstore, you may order direct from STARBURST PUBLISHERS. When ordering please enclose full payment plus shipping and handling as follows:

Post Office (4th class)
$4.00 with a purchase of up to $20.00
$5.00 ($20.01–$50.00)
8% of purchase price for purchases of $50.01 and up

United Parcel Service (UPS)
$5.00 (up to $20.00)
$7.00 ($20.01–$50.00)
12% ($50.01 and up)

Canada
$5.00 (up to $35.00)
15% ($35.01 and up)

Overseas
$5.00 (up to $25.00)
20% ($25.01 and up)

Payment in U.S. funds only. Please allow two to four weeks minimum for delivery by USPS (longer for overseas and Canada). Allow two to seven working days for delivery by UPS. Make checks payable to and mail to:

Starburst Publishers® • P.O. Box 4123 • Lancaster, PA 17604

Credit card orders may be placed by calling 1-800-441-1456, Mon–Fri, 8:30 A.M. to 5:30 P.M. Eastern Standard Time. Prices are subject to change without notice. Catalogs are available for a 9 x 12 self-addressed envelope with four first-class stamps.